HOW MAOISM
DESTROYED COMMUNISM

HOW MAOISM DESTROYED COMMUNISM

by Gerhard Schnehen

Analyses, Documents, Texts, and Reports on Mao Zedong, his 'ideas', and Maoism in Practice

With texts by Wang Shiwei, Wang Ming, Dai Qing, Li Zhisui, Jung Chang, Le Duan, Ouk Villa, William B. Bland, A. Shelokhevzev, Pjotr P. Vladimirov, and Henry Kissinger

Algora Publishing
New York

Library of Congress Cataloging-in-Publication Data

Names: Schnehen, Gerhard, 1949- editor.
Title: How Maoism destroyed Communism / analyses, documents, texts, and
    reports on Mao Zedong, Mao's 'ideas,' and Maoism in practice Gerhard
    Schnehen, ed.
Description: New York : Algora Publishing, 2023. | Includes bibliographical
    references. | Summary: "Many people still think that Maoism and Marxism are more
or less the same concept, "Communism" — or the failure of Communism. The texts and
    analyses presented here show that Mao essentially destroyed Communism, and the
totalitarianism came from Mao himself, along with the disrespect for human rights"—
Provided by publisher.
Identifiers: LCCN 2022050419 (print) | LCCN 2022050420 (ebook) | ISBN
    9781628944914 (trade paperback) | ISBN 9781628944921 (hardcover) | ISBN
    9781628944938 (pdf)
Subjects: LCSH: Mao, Zedong, 1893-1976—Influence. | Mao, Zedong,
    1893-1976—Political and social views. | Communism—China—History. |
    Communism—Southeast Asia—History.
Classification: LCC HX418.5 .H678 2023 (print) | LCC HX418.5 (ebook) |
    DDC 335.43/45—dc23/eng/20221123
LC record available at https://lccn.loc.gov/2022050419
LC ebook record available at https://lccn.loc.gov/2022050420
16525

Printed in the United States

In memory of William B. Bland, the excellent British analyst of the People's Republic of China's social development who gave me many valuable insights into what really happened in China in the second half of the 20th century.

Author's note:

All quoted material from foreign languages, mostly German, have been translated into English by the author. I assume full responsibility for possible errors or inaccuracies. For a better understanding of book titles cited, I have, in some cases, added translations.

TABLE OF CONTENTS

Ten Questions To Start With

1. In general Mao Zedong is considered to be a 'Marxist.' If this was true, then why did he purge the Marxists Gao Gang and Rao Shushi from the Communist Party and put them behind bars? Gao had taken part in the liberation of China before the proclamation of the People's Republic in 1949 and was a widely renowned Communist.

2. 'Mao Zedong Thought' is usually described by Maoists as a further development of Marxism-Leninism. If this was really so, then why did Mao Zedong propagate building socialism by prioritizing agriculture and light industry over heavy industry? According to Marxist Political Economy, in the first stages of socialism heavy industry must be prioritized to equip agriculture with modern and labor-saving machinery.

3. In the late 1950s Mao Zedong, without asking his own Party, introduced the Peoples' Communes. At the same time, the Chinese peasants were forced to smelt iron in tiny home-made backyard furnaces. Later he recommended shooting sparrows to protect the grain harvest. Would a normal person, or even a reasonable leader, order the people to do such things?

4. Mao Zedong launched the Great Leap Forward in 1958, causing nationwide famine. Millions of people died from exhaustion and hunger. His moderate critic, Defense Minister Peng Dehuai, himself a Maoist by conviction, was punished for having criticized him and lost all his party posts. Why wasn't Mao himself, who was chiefly responsible for the catastrophe, not punished and expelled from the Communist Party?

5. In 1966 Mao Zedong supported the 'Red Guards'. He tied a red armband around his arm to show his solidarity with them. These 'Red Guards' torched libraries and books like the German Nazis did, smashed Buddhist statutes, dese-

crated cemeteries, plundered museums, and demolished old statues and scriptures, thus destroying large parts of the Chinese cultural and intellectual heritage. Mao Zedong did not rein them in but let it happen. Lenin had said that the cultural heritage must be respected and preserved by all Communists, as such people are no Anarchists but highly cultured people.

6. Mao Zedong tolerated an excessive personality cult around his person, especially during the Cultural Revolution. His supporters, among them Lin Biao, then Chinese Defense Minister, whipped it up in a way never known before. In the First International (mid 19th century), the International Workers Association, of which Karl Marx was a leading member, he rejected in harsh terms endeavors to glorify him. He did not tolerate a personality cult around his person. If Mao was a real Marxist, then why did he tolerate the cult?

7. After President Richard Nixon's and Secretary of State Henry Kissinger's visit to Beijing in 1972, Mao Zedong supported the US foreign policy worldwide and considered himself an ally of the United States. He recognized the military bases of the US in Asia, in Europe and elsewhere and stopped sending weapons to the Vietnamese people fighting the imperialists. He even gave a substantial loan to the fascist Pinochet regime in Latin America; he also recognized the fascist regime in Spain, the Franco regime. Marxists are anti-imperialists and wholeheartedly support national liberation movements. Why did Mao Zedong act in this way if he was a 'Marxist'?

8. Let's look into Mao Zedong's past: He was never arrested by Chinese reaction in his whole lifetime. Stalin was arrested six times by the czarist police and spent years in prison and labor camps. In the Special Area in Yenan in the 1940s, Mao Zedong and his people were given weapons and supplies by the US army. Freedom fighters such as Salvador Allende of Chile (ousted and murdered by the CIA in 1973) and Patrice Lumumba of the independent Congo (ousted and murdered by the CIA in 1960) were not given weapons but were killed. Why did the US support Mao Zedong if he was a freedom fighter, a 'servant of his people' and also a Marxist?

9. If Mao Zedong was really a Marxist, how could he tell Foreign Minister Henry Kissinger in the early seventies that he thought of himself as 'a successor of the Chinese emperors'? Marxists despise emperors, kings, queens, and feudal lords as they live at the expense of the working people, enslaving and exploiting them.

10. In the 1960s Mao Zedong told the Indian Prime Minister Nehru that he did not fear the A-bomb because if such a bomb was dropped over China and killed 300 million people, there would still be another 300 million to survive [something no other nation could claim]. The A-bomb was a 'paper tiger' in his view. Marxists are friends of the people; they fight for their rights and freedoms, they fight for nuclear free zones. They want peace and do everything possible to preserve it. If Mao Zedong was a Marxist, why did he say such a thing?

Preface

First, I should note that I am not writing this book for entrenched Maoists or other leftist extremists. They are hardly likely to read this anyway and would call it "bourgeois" or "reactionary" without even looking at it, simply resorting to labeling or name calling. I have had uncountable written exchanges with such people over the past years and to absolutely no avail. One cannot have a rational discussion with them, because a closed, indoctrinated mind is not a thinking mind. Only those who might find some of their ideas intriguing but who have not been fully indoctrinated yet, can still be reached.

Many people still think that Maoism and Marxism constitute more or less the same ideological concept or, at least, have a lot in common. Allegedly, they both stand for "Communism" — or the failure of Communism, and are both some sort of totalitarian system with no respect for human rights and basic individual freedoms.

Here I'm trying to disprove these assumptions which, to my mind, are wrong. Originally, especially in the last century, Marxism was the banner of liberation, also of national liberation and freedom from colonialism — an ideological tool or a practical philosophy to liberate the poor and the toilers from exploitation, alienation, and suppression by the rich and powerful to enable them to create a new and freer society and a new state — the state of the working people. Especially in the first half of the last century, millions of people rallied behind the red flag in their struggle against capitalism, fascism, militarism, and tyranny. Marxism was looked upon as the number one tool for liberation, for achieving basic human rights, equally, brotherhood, and freedom — the successor of the French enlightenment and the French Revolution of 1789.

Nobody can deny that in was the socialist Soviet Union that defeated German fascism by rallying a whole nation behind the red flag which was also the banner of Soviet patriotism. Soviet Communism overcame the fascist Nazi aggressors almost on its own for which Russia is hated to this day by the Western elites.

Today the situation has become completely different. People who have woken up in their millions take to the street demanding freedom, nationhood, and self-determination no longer carry the red flag with them. They carry their own little placards, and national and local flags can also be seen quite often.

How can this be explained? Why don't people no longer turn to Marxism as a liberation ideology? Has Marxism lost its credibility or its authority or both? It seems so. But how to explain this? Why has Marxism lost its attraction for so many freedom-loving people who nowadays take to the streets all over the world, demanding an end to mass vaccinations, an end to the stealing of basic human rights by the authorities in times of Corona for example?

My hypothesis is this: I belief that Maoism and Mao Zedong but also the fall of the Soviet Union cleverly engineered by people like Gorbachev and others have largely contributed to the destruction of Marxism over a long period of time. They have perverted Marxism and changed it into a totalitarian system of slavery, mass supervision and state control serving the interests not of the working people anymore but of rich elites and oligarchs based largely in the West. Not just in China but also In the Soviet Union and the former socialist countries of Eastern Europe Marxism and Marxism-Leninism were used to justify unjust systems only serving rich elites to the delight of anti-Communist crusaders all over the world.

How this came about in Asia in particular in the last century can be seen in this book. Especially sad for me was what happened to the Chinese people in the late 1950s and 1960s but also in Cambodia (Kampuchea) in the mid and late seventies. Millions of people died at the hands of pseudo-Communists and adventurists who carry a name: Mao Zedong and his pupil Pol Pot. The international Western ruling elites, the CIA and other Western secret services and their media jumped with joy at the occasion, at these two examples to show the world that Communism is tantamount to tyranny, genocide and mass murder and that it cannot work. Only capitalism and so-called "market economies" can, and only they would guarantee basic freedoms from oppression, from the tyranny of an all-powerful state machine.

Today we experience the following all over the world: Public Private Partnerships have been established all over the world, especially in the Western world, allowing greedy billionaire oligarchs like Bill Gates or Rockefeller to control not just the United States but countless other states all over the world. They have hijacked the states and have turned them into mere tools and ATMs for their permanent enrichment, thus robbing the taxpayers' money on a daily basis and destroying the middle classes at the same time.

The once greatest and coherent system of liberation, Marxism, is no longer there to stop them and to expose their dealings. On the contrary: it seems that Marxists have almost entirely disappeared from the scene, sometimes even becoming tools and useful idiots of Western globalists and their mass media. But to overcome big money, big tech, big pharma, big chemical, big media, big data or big oil, Blackrock and Vanguard, and to overcome the small ruling elite in whose hands more and more capital and riches are being concentrated, a set of proven ideas are needed to give a clear orientation for the new struggles for freedom and liberation. Can this be achieved by the Fourth Political Theory (Alexander Dugin, Russia), or by a new version of "liberal democracy" (Robert Kennedy jr.) or even by conservatism?

These tools for liberation may work in the short run to stop the predatory class of globalists trying to impose their Great Reset (Klaus Schwab and the World Economic Forum) from carrying out their depopulation project and to control seven billion people by introducing the Green Passport. But is this enough to topple the globalists and to dispossess them, to dispossess the Rockefellers and Gates, the Bezos and the Warren Buffets and all the other oligarchs who are getting richer and richer by the day on the backs of the majority of the world population? Only Marxism, genuine Marxism, that is, shows the way: social revolution and the establishment of socialism. Only by a more or less violent social revolution can the class rule of the oligarchs be overcome, as they won't disappear of their own free will.

History teaches us that there is no other option. The job can't be done by just exposing the rich and their corporations on social media, by peacefully marching in the streets, or by winning certain law suits against Monsanto or Pfizer, by limiting their powers here and there; it can only be achieved by mobilizing huge amounts of people being guided by a set of valid and tested ideas, empowering them to take over the reins of the state machine and to turn it into a tool of popular democracy, exclusively serving the interests of the ordinary working people, the poor and dispossessed. And a powerful and disciplined organization is certainly also needed to achieve this goal.

A social revolution needs a lot of organizing and a headquarters. By rallying here and there and by going home afterwards peacefully nothing can be achieved. The rulers of the world, led by the US oligarchs and their NGOs and protected by the Deep State, will still be there and will not listen to the protesters because they simply do NOT care. A genuine revolution is needed to oust them for good, to send them packing or to arrest them'.

But how to present the new rulers from misusing their new-won power again, as has been done under the rule of socialism? If we were to make a fresh attempt toward socialism/Communism, a classless society, the only viable alternative to the tyranny of big private corporations, we would have to make sure that the abuse of power is avoided once and for all and that the mistakes made in the past are carefully avoided and not repeated.

Maybe Lenin's old recipe of democratic centralism could again become an option to make sure that democratic structures within an organization leading the struggle for freedom cannot be subverted and turned into suppression by a power-hungry leader who is only interested in his glory. Maybe we have to find other, more efficient ways described by the term of decentralization.

Mao Zedong was certainly one of those political leaders who contributed to a very great extent to the demise of Marxism, not just in China. We are now in a position to trace back his attempts to subvert Marxism by his own private ideas and to turn the Chinese Communist Party into his own private realm, engineering a process of slow degeneration with devastating consequences.

Peter Vladimirov, the Soviet TASS correspondent, watched him in Yenan/ North China in the Special Area of the Communist Party of China in the early forties, when Mao was seizing and consolidating his power at the top of the Party and became the self-proclaimed "chairman." It made him deeply sad watching the process of degeneration of a once proud socialist party being turned into a fan club of applauding sycophants and brainwashed disciples of the "great" leader, also leading a questionable life-style in Yenan.

On September 23, 1943, he wrote in his diary:

> In the CCP democratic centralism is replaced by suppression of anyone who disagrees with "Chairman Mao" and degenerates into the slavery by conviction ridiculed by Marx.[1]

Thus the Communist Party was destroyed by a group of nationalists and chauvinists, who did not even know Marxism properly, who abused Marxism for their own petty-bourgeois purposes, leading to a Chinese state where the ordinary Chinese peasant or working man are completely excluded from power. The private Public Partnership (PPP), which nowadays is put into practice nearly everywhere, was created by none other than Mao Zedong and his speech writers, not creating a socialist state but a corporate state, a partnership between big corporations and billionaires on the one hand and a pseudo-Communist elite on the other — a reactionary model now eagerly copied in the West.

The following selection of analyses, documents, and text excerpts may give some insight into how this happened.

---

[1] Peter Vladimirov, *The Vladimirov Diaries, Yenan, China: 1942-1945*, p. 155., New York, 1975

1. The 'Great Leap Forward,' Or: What Practical Value Do Mao Zedong's Ideas Have?

(G. Schnehen)

For Marxists, concrete social practice is the number one criterion of truth, revealing whether ideas, thoughts, assumptions or concepts are true or not — or just merely constitute speculation, illusions, misconceptions, mirages or fixed ideas of no social and practical value. Lenin noted, "In his practice or in technology, man makes the test for the correctness of his perceptions, thus arriving at the objective truth."[1]

Stefan Engel once said that Mao Zedong's ideas are "universal truths." He was the chairman of the Maoist Marxist-Leninist Party of Germany, so he should have known what he was talking about. But look at China in 1958–1961: did Mao's ideas work in social practice or did they fail? Engel wrote:

> [T]hey (the ultra leftists — ed.) cannot deny the universal truth of Mao Zedong Thought, as it can only be discovered under the peculiarities of specific social conditions.[2]

To begin with: Are there such "universal truths" at all, from a Marxist point of view? The philosopher Friedrich Engels once said:

> He who hunts for definite truths, for genuine unchangeable truths, will bring home little except platitudes and commonplaces of the worst kind.[3]

And Friedrich Engels' teacher, the German philosopher G. W. F. Hegel, used to scorn people who go on about "universal truths" and sure remedies. He called them dogmatists:

---

[1] W. I. Lenin, *Aus dem philosophischen Nachlass*, Berlin, 1943, p. 121; from Lenin's philosophical legacy.
[2] Stefan Engel, *Mao Tse-tung Thought and the Doctrine of the Mode of Thinking*, Essen, 1993, p. 4.
[3] Friedrich Engels, *Anti-Dühring. Herrn Eugen Dührings Umwälzung der Wissenschaft*, Beijing, 1972, p. 114.

> Dogmatism in the way of thinking, in knowledge and in the study of philosophy is nothing but the opinion that the truth can be found in a single sentence that is a fixed result or is intuitively known.[1]

According to Lenin, who is copiously quoted and referred to by Maoists, the truth must prove itself in social practice. Does the truth, or even the "universal truth" of Mao Zedong's "ideas" prove itself in concrete social practice? If so, then we could rightfully assume that there is at least some truth in Mao Zedong Thought or that his "ideas" come close to the truth. What do we mean by "practice"? Do we mean technology? Are practice and technology identical terms? Béla Fogarasi in his book *Dialectical Logic:*

> It means that practice is a much wider term than technology. Practice also includes all forms of social action.[2]

Correct insights prove their worth in social practice, thus serving social progress; wrong ideas, however, which do not correctly reflect reality, are useless and harmful for social progress. And what is more: they can even contribute to bringing about disastrous developments and catastrophic social regression lasting for a long time. So there is a close connection between theory (ideas) and practice (social practice).

Lenin pointed out the relationship between theory and practice. Fogarasi:

> Lenin emphatically emphasized the close relationship and the union between theory and practice.[3]

But even before Lenin Friedrich Engels knew that there is a close connection between theory and practice. Engels on practice as a criterion of truth:

> The very moment we use these qualities, depending on what we see in them, to our own advantage, we subject our sensory perceptions to an infallible test for their correctness or incorrectness. If these perceptions were wrong, then our judgment about the usability of such a thing must be wrong too and our endeavors to make use of it come to nothing.[4]

Engels, who (like his friend Marx) was in love with Anglicisms, sized it up by used the common saying: "The proof of the pudding is in the eating."

Back to Mao Zedong's "ideas" or Mao Zedong Thought, as supporters of Mao call them: Have they proved their worth? Do we have evidence that these ideas have proved to be suitable for social progress? Did they prove their worth under the concrete circumstances of Chinese social and economic reality so that ordinary Chinese people and also people all over the world could benefit from them? Were their living standards improved as a consequence? In short: Did they pass the test of time or did they fail the exam of social practice?

[1] G. W. F. Hegel, *Recht, Staat, Geschichte*, edited by Friedrich Bülow, Stuttgart, 1970, p. 144.
[2] Béla Fogarasi, *Dialektische Logik*, Offenbach, 1997, p. 380; dialectical logic.
[3] Ibid.
[4] Ibid., p. 383, citing Friedrich Engels, *Die Entwicklung des Sozialismus von der Utopie zur Wissenschaft*, Berlin 1953, pp. 90f; the development of socialism from utopia to science.

To these "ideas" of Mao also belongs the theory that by simply mobilizing the masses and their revolutionary work enthusiasm, simply by means of a policy of "great leaps" or by "great leaps forward," it was possible to give the social development of a given country a mighty impulse within a very short period of time.

Mao Zedong in his "notes" on the publication of a Soviet textbook on Political Economy:

> On page 392 it says that "machine and tractor stations were an important tool for the socialist transformation of agriculture." Frequently, the role of machines for socialist development is emphasized in the textbook. But what can be achieved if we do not raise the awareness of the peasants and if we do not change the thinking of the people, if we only rely on machines?[1]

This, by the way, is not quite correct. Mao Zedong simplifies or has not read the textbook thoroughly enough. The Soviet textbook does stress the necessity of raising the awareness of the working people. The book is not just talking about machines:

> The building of socialism is inextricably linked with a cultural revolution. In the countries of people's democracy the broadest masses of the working people are given culture and knowledge.[2]

Obviously, Mao Zedong prefers a different path from the one pursued in the Soviet Union under Stalin. He is of the opinion that there agriculture had been "neglected":

> During Stalin's times the planning of agriculture was neglected because heavy industry was given priority and special attention.[3]

Further below, we will see how agriculture in China during the Great Leap Forward was neglected when peasants were forced to do steel mining in backyard furnaces. If agriculture was "neglected" in the Soviet Union during Stalin's times, when he was General Secretary of the Soviet Communist Party, how comes that following the collectivization of agriculture in the USSR in the early thirties the country was never again struck by a famine? How does he explain that even during the Great Patriotic War when the Soviet Union had temporarily lost control over almost half of its agricultural production in its Western part due to the Nazi occupation, the Red Army and the urban areas were reliably supplied with food during the entire war? And despite the monstrous devastation caused by the Nazi Wehrmacht, the whole nation was in no danger of starving even at

---

[1] Helmut Martin, ed., *Mao Tse-tung. Das machen wir anders als Moskau! Kritik an der sowjetischen Politökonomie*, Hamburg, 1975, p. 32; Mao Zedong: Things we do differently from Moscow. Critique of the Soviet political economy.

[2] *Politische Ökonomie. Lehrbuch*, Berlin, 1955, p. 663; official Soviet textbook on Political Economy from 1955.

[3] Helmut Martin, ed., ibid., p. 51, citing Mao Zedong.

that time, if under Stalin "agriculture was neglected"? The Belgian Ludo Martens, himself a Maoist, writes in his book on Stalin:

> The overwhelming majority of peasants has shown how strongly they were connected with the new agricultural system. Despite the German occupation and the destructive attempts of the Nazi authorities in the occupied territories, the collective system was maintained.[1]

Mao Zedong either did not know the Soviet agricultural system well or he did know it but had different ideas on bringing "socialism" to China. Even though the Soviet system was highly successful in the thirties, he rejected it and chose a different path for his own country by "not neglecting planning of agriculture." So it seems that he was a great fan of planning and also a great supporter of agriculture.

Let's assume for a moment he really intended to build a better socialist agriculture in China when he was in power than was done in the Soviet Union under Stalin. Then we must ask what he actually did to realize these plans, to implement his own ideas.

The key to doing it his own way was his idea of coordinated promotion of agriculture and industry. what exactly does he mean by that. Helmut Martin quoting Mao:

> If one wants to achieve a rapid development of heavy industry, then you need general activism, a general happy mood, and if you want to achieve that, you need the coordinated promotion of industry and agriculture, of light and heavy industry.[2]

So he is in favor of developing industry and agriculture at the same time, in tandem as it were, and both should develop very fast, in leaps and bounds, also to overtake imperialist countries such as Great Britain and the United States within a short period of time. But how to do that in practice? How was this ambitious project, or should we say "idea," implemented in practice?

To give agriculture a big productive boost, Mao Zedong, without having even asked his own politburo, first of all arbitrarily introduced a system of "People's Communes" all over the Chinese countryside — rural communes where practically everything was collectivized, even private dwellings, land, trees and kitchen utensils. The program was legalized retroactively by the Party at the Conference of Peitaho in August 1958 where Mao and his followers got their way.

The expert on Communist China, Roderick MacFarquahar wrote:

Mao Zedong jumped the gun, pressing for the formation of communes without prior formal endorsement even by the Politburo.[3]

---

[1] Ludo Martens, *Stalin anders betrachtet*, Frankfurt/Main, 2014, pp. 113f.
[2] Helmut Martin, ed., ibid., pp. 51f.
[3] Roderick MacFarquahar, *The Origins of the Cultural Revolution*, Oxford, 1983, p. 77, quoted by William B. Bland, *Class Struggles in China*, London, 1997, p. 96.

Edwin P-w. Leung wrote that in August 1958 Mao Zedong himself "established the first People's Commune in Hopei province."[1]

Eating was to take place in big dining halls and cooking was done by specific staff. Under the new system, peasants and their families were required to also perform non-agricultural tasks. They could be drafted for mining, road building, construction work, for digging canals, or for steel production. Geoffrey Hudson provides more interesting details on that:

> Under the commune system, peasants may either be required to perform non-agricultural tasks during the slack periods of the agricultural year, or they may be drafted for mining, construction and industrial work in their localities more or less permanently...Since the establishment of the communes the total of work required of the peasants has been enormously increased without any corresponding increase in their real incomes; indeed, in many cases their living standards have declined.[2]

It is hard to imagine how Mao Zedong wanted to increase work enthusiasm after having robbed the Chinese peasants of their private plots, after the disruption of family life, a drop in wages and the requirement to work extra hours to also boost steel production.

And here we have Mao's idea of "coordinated promotion of agriculture and industry": Since the majority of the Chinese population lived in the countryside, Mao thought that their labor could also be used to give steel production a similar big boost.

Between August and October 1958 (after the Peitaho Conference) the whole of China was busy with steel production, mostly using little backyard furnaces. To develop heavy industry first of all to lay the foundations of a sound industrial basis for all sectors of the economy and to wait with agricultural communization, as had been done in Stalin's Soviet Union and had also been tried during China's first five-year plan (1953–1957, with the help of many Soviet experts), was no longer considered necessary.

A special target for steel production was set to catch up with Great Britain within 15 years and to make China great again:

> All China was plunged into an all-out steel drive in the effort to reach the new national target of 10.7 million tons...By mid-September, over 20 million people were engaged in producing iron and steel; at the height of the steel drive the figure rose to 90 million...The 1.07 million ton target was achieved by mid-December (1958—Ed.).[3]

---

[1] Edwin P-w. Leung, *Historical Dictionary of Revolutionary China: 1939-1976,* New York, 1992, p. 414, quoted by W. B. Bland, ibid., p. 97.

[2] Geoffrey Hudson, *The Chinese Communes: A Documentary Review and Analysis of the "Great Leap Forward,"* London, 1960, p. 10, cited by W. B. Bland, ibid.

[3] Roderick MacFarquahar (1983), ibid., pp. 113f, 116, in: W. B. Bland, ibid., p. 101.

These furnaces made of bricks could be seen everywhere, even in the back-yards of government offices. The slogan for the whole country was: "The entire nation making steel."

Even though the year 1958 experienced a bumper harvest, soon a big crisis loomed on the horizon, mainly because of the diversion of rural labor to backyard steel-making. MacFarquahar writes:

> In the fields, bumper harvests of grain, cotton, and other crops awaited collection. A massive tragedy was in the making...Even with shock work, many areas failed to gather in all the harvest.[1]

Mao's steel production, 1958-1961, using backyard furnaces

So Mao Zedong's "idea" to have not just one Great Leap Forward — the one in agriculture — but simultaneously another one in steel production, without professionally developing the Chinese steel industry as such — soon turned to disaster. In consequence:

> Acreage sown to grain declined by 6 million hectares in 1958, and a further 11.6 million hectares in 1959, a total reduction of 13% over the two years.[2]

Grain rations now had to be reduced drastically, as shown by the following table.

---

[1] Ibid., pp. 116, 120, in: W. B. Bland, ibid.
[2] Ibid., p. 126.

Grain rations in the late 1950s–early 1960 in Mao's China:

Year	1957	1958	1959	1960
Kg per capita	203.0	198.0	185.5	163.5[1]

Especially in the countryside, people started to die from exhaustion and hunger. Even kitchen utensils, pots and pans, had to be used for backyard steel production, so there were no utensils left to cook or fry food. Many started to flee the most stricken areas, just as they had done in periods of hunger during the times of feudalism when famines were nothing out of the ordinary.

The urban population was not much better off. In her biography of Mao Zedong, the Chinese historian Jung Chang writes that the meat ration "declined annually from 5.1 kg per person in 1957 to an all-time low of just over 1.5 kg in 1960."[1]

She quotes Han Suyin, who was a supporter of Mao Zedong, as saying that housewives in towns and cities were only getting a maximum 1,200 calories a day in 1960, adding that according to her information even slave-laborers at Auschwitz concentration camp got between 1,300 and 1,700 calories a day:

> They worked about eleven hours a day, and most who did not find extra food died within several months.[2]

She also quotes a study made in Anhui province which recorded 63 cases of cannibalism in the spring of 1960 alone.[3]

The mortality rate surged in Mao Zedong's China in those years when his "ideas" were being put into practice:

> The mortality rate doubled from 1.08% in 1957 to 2.54% in 1960. In that year the population actually declined by 4.5%. Anywhere from 16.4 to 29.5 million extra people died during the leap, because of the leap.[4]

The historian MacFarquahar notes that by the end of the year 1960 over half of the cultivated crops had been devastated, and one year later, China was forced to import food from capitalist countries such as Canada and Australia.

How did Mao Zedong react to the food crisis? His personal physician, Dr. Li Zhisui writes that when he got the news that something had gone wrong, he started contacting his relatives living in Shaoshan where he was born. Dr. Li accompanied him, and for the first time learned something about the disaster:

> Only the women and children were at home. The men were away working on the backyard steel furnaces or water conservancy projects. Mao did not have to delve far to learn that life was hard for the families

---

[1] Jung Chang, Jon Halliday, *Mao – The Unkown Story*, London, 2007, p. 533.
[2] Ibid.
[3] Ibid.
[4] Roderick MacFarquahar (1983), ibid., p. 330, in: W. B. Bland, ibid., p. 102.

of Shaoshan. With the construction of the backyard steel furnaces, every-one's pots and pans had been confiscated and thrown into the furnace to make steel — and nothing had been returned. Everyone was eating in the public mess halls. The families had no cooking equipment. Even if they still had had pots and pans, their earthen hearths had been destroyed so the mud could be used as fertilizer. Mao took a swim in the newly constructed Shaoshan reservoir that afternoon...[1]

What was the situation like in the Soviet Union under Stalin where, according to Mao Zedong, agriculture had been "neglected"? Stalin in a speech to the best combine harvester drivers on 1 December 1935:

The mortality rate is lower, the birth rate higher, and the absolute increase in population is incomparably larger. This is a good thing, of course, and we welcome it. The absolute population growth now amounts to approximately three million per year, which means that now we have got an annual increase in population as big as the whole of Finland.[2]

In his report to the 18th Congress of the All-Union Communist Party given on 10 March, 1939, Stalin presented the following statistics on grain production in the USSR between 1913 and 1938:

Gross Production of Grain and Industrial Crops in the USSR in million metric hundredweights:

	1913	1934	1935	1937	1938
Grain	801	894	901	1,202.9	949.9
Cotton	7.4	11.8	17.2	25.8	26.9
Flax	3.3	5.3	5.5	5.7	5.46
Sugar beet	109.0	113.6	162.1	218.6	166.8
Oil fruit	21.5	36.9	42.7	51.1	46.6

The Soviet Union had experienced a steady growth in grain production, but even more so in industrial production in those years. The vast majority of grain production was from Soviet cooperatives, either from farms in state owner-ship or from collective farms in collective ownership. But Soviet farms were of a completely different type than the ones created by Mao Zedong in 1958. The so-called *artel* was used as the model for the entire country: peasants were allowed private plots and also a certain amount of cattle and were not forced to eat in huge dining halls either, and what is maybe most important: they were not drafted to non-agricultural labor. Machine and Tractor Stations were used to supply the cooperatives with the most modern machinery and also with tractor

---

[1] Dr. Li Zhisui, *The Private Life of Chairman Mao*, New York, 1994, p. 303.
[2] J. W. Stalin, *Werke (Works)*, Vol. 14, Dortmund, 1976, p. 51.

and combine harvester drivers and other experts, advising leaders of cooperatives how to do bookkeeping or how to manage farms most efficiently. Each cooperative had its drama or parachuting club and was provided with libraries and reading rooms. Many urban people then moved to the countryside as life on a Soviet cooperative had been made attractive.

Under Soviet leader Nikita Khrushchev (1953-64), however, the disease of false policies and certain "ideas," the scourge of voluntarism, chauvinism, and grandiose schemes was also imported to Russia, and after his multiple "reforms" and fancy projects in agriculture, the USSR, too, had to import grain from capitalist countries like Canada or Australian in the early 1960s, especially in 1963.

How did Mao Zedong's second "Great Leap Forward," the one in steel production fare?

Soon the decreed target of 10.7 million tons of steel had to be lowered, and the quality of the steel was not always that good.

Roderick MacFarquahar:

> Of the 10.7 million tons produced, only 9 million were of good quality; the following autumn the figure would be reduced further to 8 million tons.[1]

Wu Yuan-li in his book on the economy of Communist China has this to say:

> High material cost and low quality of product gave rise to a negative contribution from the native iron-smelting sector to the GNP (Gross National Product — Ed.) during the period of the "Great Leap Forward"... Many of the "native" iron and steel furnaces were either abandoned or replaced by furnaces of improved design.[2]

What about the "work enthusiasm" Mao Zedong had praised so highly to achieve a mighty boost in China's wealth and development to enable the country to catch up with Great Britain and the United States in the not too distant future? Was there any left in view of the fact that people had lost much of their property, had to work extra shifts in the people's communes, were drafted to mining, had to cope with a militarized life-style and were on the brink of starving from exhaustion and hunger even by October 1958?

Let's listen to Jürgen Domes:

> Opposition of the peasantry to the new collectives...had not been particularly strong at the start of the campaign, but it increased rapidly and soon began to turn into open resistance.

> From mid-October 1958 this open resistance took on, in many regions, the character of a general though entirely uncoordinated movement. The peasants refused to march to their work in the fields in military formation and they secretly continued cooking food at home despite orders from

---

[1] Roderick MacFarquahar (1983), ibid., p. 128, in: W. B. Bland, ibid., p. 102.
[2] Wu Yuan-li, *The Steel Industry in Communist China*, New York, 1975, p. 236, in: W. B. Bland, ibid., p. 103.

the cadres to the contrary. Parents took their children out of the nurseries and kindergartens in large numbers, and elderly people left their "houses of happiness" and returned to their families, often over great distances. Grain was not delivered to the state granaries because the labor units in the villages divided it among their members...During November and December 1958...these activities escalated into local rebellions which began to pose a serious threat to the structures of political and economic control.[1]

Work enthusiasm had turned into passive resistance and even open revolt in some places. Mao inquired about the backyard steel furnaces in his home province of Shaoshan, where things were still comparably good: Again he heard nothing but complaints.[2]

Did Mao Zedong change his mind? Did he come back to reality or did he stick to his schemes which had little to do with reality? At an enlarged Politburo meeting which took place in Lushan soon after the delegation was back in Beijing he still praised the "achievements" of the Great Leap. Dr. Li, who was present:

> Mao praised the achievements of the Great Leap Forward, alluded to the problems, and said he hoped that the participants would appreciate the energy and creativity of the Chinese people. Mao's confidence in the Great Leap Forward remained unshaken...He knew that in many places there was no rice to eat...When I met Mao that night, he said the meeting would continue for about two weeks, and he was relaxed and in good spirits. He wanted to go sightseeing. Lushan was a vast mountain range, famous for its scenic spots.[3]

What happened to Defense Secretary Peng Teh-huai, who had criticized Mao Zedong at the Lushan Conference and who did not like his "idea" of having peasants work at backyard furnaces at all? He himself came from a peasant background. In July 1959, shortly before the plenum of the Communist Party, Peng wrote a "Letter of Opinion" to Mao which was then copied and distributed to all the participants of the gathering by Mao himself, even though the letter was private. In it Peng, himself a staunch Maoist, listed the disasters stemming from the Great Leap Forward and the establishment of People's Communes, and what is more, he held Mao Zedong personally responsible for the mess caused. In the letter he says:

> Some small and indigenous blast furnaces which were not necessary were built, with the consequences that some resources (material and financial) and manpower were wasted. This is, of course, a relatively big loss... The habit of exaggeration spread to various areas and departments, and some unbelievable miracles were also reported in the press. This has surely

---

[1] Jürgen Domes, *Peng Teh-huai, The Man and the Image*, London, 1985, p. 81.
[2] Dr. Li Zhisui, ibid., p. 307.
[3] Ibid., p. 310.

done tremendous harm to the prestige of the Party...Petty-bourgeois fanaticism makes us liable to commit "left" mistakes.[1]

From then on the former Defense Minister of China was called an "anti-party element".

Mao had to make some phony self-criticism, also citing Karl Marx. Accused of petty-bourgeois fanaticism, he tried to get help from the German philosopher by saying:

> Marx also committed many errors. He hoped every day for the advent of the European revolution, but it did not come...Wasn't this bourgeois fanaticism?...We have blown some communist wind, and enabled the people of the entire nation to learn a lesson.[2]

Mao lost his position as Chairman of China but remained Chairman of the Party. For his courageous criticism Peng Teh-huai was stripped of all his state positions. A Plenum resolution criticized his "clique" for their "anti-Party activity".[3] Under a compromise agreement the policy of the Great Leap Forward was tacitly ended. Mao Zedong, however, escaped unharmed, even though tens of millions of people had died. The newspapers did not publicize the debate and the criticism, but said that production figures had to be adapted to reality. They were adjusted downwards.

Dr. Li Zhisui, Mao's personal physician, participated in the meetings and later gave his impressions:

> The latest party decision left me befuddled and anxious. To place the problem with Peng Dehuai in the category of "class struggle," to see him as an "anti-party element" and "right opportunist," was to put him in a category almost as bad as the Guomindang. I knew Peng was not an enemy of the party. I knew him to be a good and honest man.[4]

Mao Zedong had rediscovered the "two-line struggle," a theory he first developed in Yenan in the early forties when he was facing severe criticism by Communist Wang Ming, his fiercest critic at that time. Those who did not accept his line then were called "dogmatists" or "Moscowites." Now his critic number one was Peng who could not be called a "dogmatist" because he was just talking common sense, was only in favor of reversing a wrong course and of adapting the official policy to reality. People were dying in the millions, so something had to be done urgently. Now Mao Zedong turned out to be the "dogmatist" who wanted to stick to his militarized communes. So other ideological weapons had to be used to defame Peng, and they were found easily and, yet again, couched

---

[1] Donald S. Zagoria, *The Case of Peng Teh-huai*, Hong Kong, 1968, pp. 9, 11, in: W. B. Bland, ibid., p. 106.

[2] Ibid., p. 42, in: W. B. Bland, ibid.

[3] W. B. Bland, ibid., p. 109.

[4] Dr. Zhisui, ibid., p. 321.

in Marxist-Leninist terms, using stereotypes like "right opportunist," "counter-revolutionary" or "anti-party element," etc.

By the way: Soviet Premier Nikita Khrushchev — who came under fire in the summer of 1957 by other members of the Soviet politburo, whose First Secretary he was at the time, and who was deposed by majority vote in the summer of 1957 but was soon after reinstated by the Central Committee of the party with the help of the Soviet Army — also made use of such terms as soon as he had been reinstated. Molotov, Kaganovich, Malenkov and some other fierce critics who had tried to vote him out of office were then also called the "anti-party group." And we could also quote the example of Walter Ulbricht, the leader of the Socialist Unity Party of East Germany who, in a power struggle within the German politburo, called his opponents Herrnstadt and Zaisser an "anti-party group," only because they had tried to vote Ulbricht out of office after the events of June 17, 1953 in the German Democratic Republic, when the East German workers organized a nationwide rebellion and also numerous strikes which could only be suppressed with the help of the Soviet military. Ulbricht survived and then took his revenge, bombarding his critics with similar Marxist verbiage.

So this tool of slandering critics by using "Marxist" terms was very widespread in the Communist world and had been made use of long before Mao Zedong's rise to power. It was not one of his own "ideas," but he adopted it for his own purposes from his Soviet counterparts, and by doing so, could win over other people who were sympathizers of Marxism. Posing as a wise Marxist-Leninist was still necessary because Marxism enjoyed high esteem among ordinary party members at the time. He knew that ideology was a powerful weapon in his struggle against his opponents and rivals. So he developed the theory of the "two-line struggle" to show that having to fight others is normal business. But to cover up the pettiness of witch-hunting his opponents he then used the Marxist theory of class struggle and twisted things this way: My position is under threat by certain critics, so my position is the proletarian position and theirs is the counter-revolutionary bourgeois one. Therefore, the struggle in the party is nothing but class struggle, and I am going to win it, because I am on the right side of history. I'm on the proletarian side, the others, my critics, are bourgeois and counterrevolutionaries! Whenever he got under threat, he turned to mass campaigns and then labeled his critics this way, especially during the so-called Great Proletarian Cultural Revolution as we shall see later in greater detail.

Conclusions

The great human tragedy of the Chinese famine in the years 1958–1961 was the direct result of the policy of the "Great Leap Forward" with which Mao Zedong tried to overtake Great Britain within a short period of time with regard to steel production and to make China great again without taking into account the dire consequences of this adventurous policy. He refused to learn from the Soviet Union and from the experiences made there. The Soviet example proved that socialism can be built successfully by prioritizing heavy industry over light industry and agriculture. The Soviet Union became so strong, also economically, that it was in a position to defeat the fascist coalition during WWII almost on its own. Instead, Mao Zedong followed his own grandiose chauvinistic schemes (on behalf of Marxism-Leninism), which were not based in reality at all, and the ordinary Chinese workers and peasants finally had to pay a very high price for Mao's figments of imagination. Millions of Chinese peasants — but also many urban people — died during the years of the "Great Leap Forward." Asked by the Soviet ambassador, Liu Shao-chi, then President of China, admitted in the early 1960s that probably 30 million people had died from hunger and starvation in the country. This figure is probably far too moderate as one can imagine. So we cannot escape the conclusion that Mao Zedong's "ideas' cannot be called "universal truths" as the leader of the Maoist MLPD, Stefan Engel, is trying to tell us. Friedrich Engels was right when he said that "the proof of the pudding is in the eating." The test for true perceptions and correct theories and hypotheses is concrete human social practice. This practice has passed judgment on Mao Zedong "ideas." They have been proven unworkable. They were not based in reality but constituted willful thinking and they will fail again if fanatical people try to put them into practice again.

In Pol Pot's Kampuchea roughly the same policy was pursued by the Maoist Khmer Rouge who were supported by Mao Zedong financially and militarily in 1975. The price the Khmer people had to pay was equally high: about one million people died from exhaustion, hunger, ethnic cleansing, persecution of minorities, and political repression in the years 1975–1979. Social practice has refuted these Maoist ideas lock, stock and barrel. To uphold them even today will automatically lead to new defeats, will be of no service for the working class and can only further discredit Marxism in the eyes of the general public. The ruling classes have used and still use the failure of Maoism to smear Marxism and communism, putting Maoism and communism in one basket. They keep insisting that socialism or communism cannot work (look at what happened in China under Mao!) and that modern finance capitalism and the Western political system has no alternative. Sadly, Marxism was dealt a heavy blow this way and whether the theory will ever recover from these blows is far from certain.

2. Dr. Li Zhisui Discusses Mao Zedong's 'Great Leap Forward' [1]

Introduction by G. Schnehen

From 1954 until Mao Zedong's death twenty-two years later, Dr. Li Zhisui was Mao's personal physician, which put him in almost daily contact with him and his inner circle.[2] He discussed political and private matters with him and recorded many of the conversations he had with him. Dr. Li Zhisui knew that Mao Zedong's decision to initiate the Great Leap Forward was made even without having consulted his fellow members of the politburo of the Communist Party of China. It resulted in the worst famine in Chinese recorded history, claiming the lives of tens of millions of Chinese. Even after having been confronted with people in his native province of Shaoshang and their complaints, he stubbornly adhered to the decision. Peng Dehuai, the former Chinese Defense Minister, who criticized him, putting the blame squarely on him during the Lushan Conference (August 1959), was called a "right opportunist" and an "anti-Party element" and was stripped of all his state positions on Mao Zedong's initiative. When the "Cultural Revolution" was launched by Mao Zedong and his circle in 1966,

---

[1] Excerpts from Dr. Li Zhisui's book, *The Private Life Of Chairman Mao*. New York, 1994
[2] In his book on China (*Socialism with Chinese Characteristics*, London 2020, p. 79), the Maoist Harpal Brar, enraged about Dr. Li's book, makes some remarks about the memoirs:

"When Li Zhisui, claiming to be *"Mao's personal physician"* published his abominably scandalous *The Private Life of Chairman Mao*, in which he portrays Mao as a sexual pervert, Chinese academics and professionals living in the United States expressed their feelings on the execrable piece of writing in an open letter...." In the book Dr. Li is seen standing next to Mao Zedong on various private and official occasions. We see him even swimming with Mao.

Peng was arrested and labeled a "counterrevolutionary" like so many other of his critics. He died in prison eight years later. All those who supported Peng's criticism were put in the same category and also lost their high positions in the party. A campaign followed to show the Chinese people the danger posed by the "rightists," "right opportunists," "anti-Party elements," etc.

Up to that point in time, Dr. Li had been in awe of his patient, but from then on he judged him differently and took his inner distance.[1] He also gives some information about Mao Zedong's questionable private life during the crisis years.

Excerpts from Dr. Li Zhisui

pp. 303-331:

Mao began contacting his relatives to learn firsthand how the Great Leap Forward had affected them. Only the women and children were at home. The men were away working on the backyard steel furnaces or water conservancy projects. Mao did not have to delve far to learn that life was hard for the families in Shaoshan. With the construction of the backyard steel furnaces, everyone's pots and pans had been confiscated and thrown into the furnace to make steel — and nothing had been returned. Everyone was eating in public mess halls. The families had no cooking equipment. Even if they still had had pots and pans, their earthen hearths had been destroyed so that the mud could be used as fertilizer.

When Mao took a swim in the newly constructed Shaoshan reservoir that afternoon, he talked to the local folk about the project. Everyone criticized it. The reservoir had been poorly built, one old peasant pointed out...

Mao asked about the backyard steel furnaces. Again he heard nothing but complaints. Indigenous raw materials were scarce. They used locally mined low-quality coal to fuel the furnaces, but there was not enough coal and no iron ore at all. The only way to comply with the directive to build the furnaces was to confiscate the peasants' pots and pans, and shovels for iron ore and their doors and furniture for fuel. But the furnaces were producing iron nuggets that no one knew what to do with. Now with no pots or pans, people couldn't even boil drinking water at home, let alone cook...

Thus it was that I, and certainly Mao, began to be aware that the economic situation in the country had deteriorated. Mao's return to Shaoshan awakened him to reality, shaking him into a growing awareness that trouble was brewing. When he returned to Wuhan, his previous ebullience had evaporated. But there was still not doubt in his mind that the programs themselves were basically sound, and they simply needed

---

[1] Chatto & Windus, London, 1994.

further adjustment. Mao still did not want to do anything to dampen the enthusiasm of the masses. The problem was how to bring the cadres back to reality without crushing their spirit or spreading gloom to the people. It was a question of propaganda — how to mobilize cadres and peasants alike to the right level of realistic enthusiasm. Mao decided to call a propaganda meeting to discuss the issues...

The situation in Mao's native Shaoshan was good compared with the rest of China. A horrible famine was sweeping the country. The province of Anhui, where party secretary Zeng Xisheng had first shown Mao the backyard steel furnaces, had been badly hit, and so had Henan, where we had gone in August 1958 to see the new people's communes. People in some of the more remote and sparsely populated places, like Gansu, were starving. Peasants were starving in Sichuan, too — the nation's most populous province, larger than most countries and known as China's rice bowl. During the meetings in Chengdu, Sichuan, in March 1958, Mao had pushed his plan to overtake Great Britain in fifteen years. In many provinces, tens of thousands were fleeing, just as Chinese peasants always had done in face of famine.

I never witnessed the terrible famine myself. Group One (Mao Zedong's inner circle to which Dr. Li also belonged — Ed.) was protected from the awful realities. I learned about the famine on the way to Lushan (where the conference on the Great Leap Forward was to take place — Ed.), sailing down the magnificent Yangtze River with Mao, his staff, and several provincial leaders. Tian Jiaying was on board, and his memories of his six-month inspection tour of Henan and Sichuan were still fresh. I was standing on deck with him, Lin Ke, and Wang Jingxian, who had been put in charge of Mao's security after Wang Dongxing was sent away. Tian Jiaying described the famine in Sichuan. The government's efforts to alleviate the crisis had been inadequate. The overly optimistic target for steel production in 1959 had been cut from 20 million tons to 13 million. But 60 million able-bodied peasants, strong and healthy men who ought to have been at work in the fields, were still working on the backyard steel furnaces. The dislocation of labor was disastrous. The fields were not being farmed. The problem was getting worse.

Tian Jiaying was distressed not only because so many people were starving but because so many in authority were lying. Falsehoods are flying and getting more absurd with every passing day, he said. But the people speaking falsehoods are being praised; the ones who tell the truth are being criticized.

The conversation turned first obliquely and then more directly to Mao. Mao was a great philosopher, a great soldier, and a great politician, but he was a terrible economist. He had a penchant for grandiose schemes. He had lost touch with the people, forgotten the work style that he himself had promoted — seeking truth from facts, humility, attention to details. This was the source of the country's economic problems.

Wang Jingxian began telling us about Mao's many girlfriends. The Chairman's private life, Wang said, was shockingly indecent.

I was incredulous. I had known the economic situation was bad, but not that famine had swept the country and that millions were starving. I was surprised at the criticisms against Mao. My friend Tian Jiaying was ordinarily cautious, but the forthrightness with which he was speaking was dangerous, even among so close and sympathetic a group...

But while the critics talked among themselves, as we did on the boat down the Yangtze, conversation with the people making the preposterous claims was almost impossible. Those who insisted on the truth, and were thus willing to offend Mao, were rare indeed. Most trimmed their sails to the wind...

Mao's confidence in the Great Leap Forward remained unshaken, and I do not know how much of the real situation Mao knew when he spoke to then. His visit to Shaoshan had given him a clear sense that there were problems. He certainly knew that something had gone awry and that there were major shortages of food. He knew that in many places there was no rice to eat, and he was willing to discuss those problems and to solve them. But I do not think when he spoke on July 2, 1959, he knew how bad the disaster had become, and he believed the Party was doing everything it could to manage the situation. The purpose of the "fairy meeting" was to discuss both how to solve the problems and how to retain the enthusiasm of the masses. But his solution was simply for people to work harder still.

My notes record him as saying that "some people have asked, 'if our production is so high, why is our food supply so tight? Why can't female comrades buy hairpins? Why can't people get soap or matches? Well, if we cannot clearly explain the situation, let's not explain it. Let's just stick it out and carry on our work with even greater determination and energy. We will have more supplies next year. Then we will explain everything. In short, the situation in general is excellent. There are many problems, but our future is bright."

Following the meeting, the party leaders broke into small groups, divided geographically — north, northeast, east, central-south, and south-west — to discuss problems in their own regional areas.

When I met with Mao that night, he said the meetings would continue for about two weeks, and he was relaxed and in good spirits. He wanted to go sightseeing. Lushan was a vast mountain range, famous for its scenic spots — caves and temples and magnificent lookout points. Mao wanted to see them all.

Dr. Wang Shousong, the director of Jiangxi Hospital and a graduate of a Japanese medical school, had set up a clinic for the meeting participants and their entourage, staffing it with four young and energetic nurses from the nearby Lushan sanatorium. The Jiangxi provincial leadership arranged for evening entertainment, and performances by the Jiangxi provincial music and dance troupe were followed by the dances Mao so enjoyed. The young nurses joined the dancing parties, and within days, Mao was rotating between a young nurse and a member of the cultural troupe. The Chairman was becoming bolder about his dalliances. Security surrounding Mao's building was tight and the Chairman's privacy was still closely protected, but Mao himself did little to hide the fact that he was entertaining young women in his room.

The meetings were going so smoothly and Mao was having such a good time that he phoned Jiang Qing (his wife — Ed.) in Beidahe and told her not to come to Lushan. He would join his wife when the meeting was over...

On July 10, eight days into the Lushan meetings, Mao convened a meeting of the regional leaders. Again he spoke. He emphasized that only through unity and shared ideology could the party solve its problems. The general line, he argued, referring to the policy of the Great Leap Forward and catching up with Great Britain in fifteen years, was completely correct. The achievements of the past year were great. There had been failures, to be sure, but those failures were relatively minor. "Doesn't each person have ten fingers?" he asked. "We can count nine of those fingers as achievements, only one as a failure."

He warned against idealism of those who thought China was on the verge of entering communism. At the present stage of development, he said, the people's communes must be considered merely rural cooperatives — advanced cooperatives, to be sure, but not communist organizations. If people look at communes this way then there should be no serious problems at all. People — cadres and ordinary folk alike — have had unrealistically high expectations of the people's communes. Now expectations had to be lowered. In waging revolution, we have to pay a certain "tuition" for the experience. The nation had lost some 2 billion *renminbi* in the endeavor to build steel furnaces, but people everywhere in the country had learned a new skill — how to make steel. The money lost is really just tuition for learning a new skill.

Mao did not wait to hear the comments after his speech, and I left with him as soon as it was over. But Tian Jiaying told me later that everyone felt silent after the Chairman left. His speech had served as a warning to criticize no more.

Peng Dehuai, though, continued the debate. He did so discretely in a private, handwritten letter that he delivered to Mao on July 14. It was a long letter, and while I did not know at first what it said, I knew that Mao was unhappy. He did not sleep the night after receiving it...

Mao told the party leaders that rightists outside the party had already criticized the Great Leap Forward and that now some people within the Communist Party were criticizing it, too, saying that the Great Leap Forward had done more harm than good. Peng Dehui was one such person, as evidenced in his letter to Mao.

Mao said he was going to have Peng's letter distributed to the participants in the Lushan meetings so they could evaluate its contents themselves. He said, ominously, that if the party were to split in two, he would organize a new one — among the peasants. If the army were to split apart, he would organize another army.

The standing committee then began discussing the contents of Peng's letter. Mao had already impressed upon them how serious the issue was. His colleagues' remarks were guarded...

Mao's opening speech to the Central Committee set the tone for the meetings that followed. By calling upon the participants to criticize the divisive activities of the "anti-Party group," (meaning the critics of the Great Leap Forward — Ed.), Mao had turned Peng into an enemy, and no amount of talk or exchange of opinions could save him. For the next week, from August 3 to 10, the Central Committee broke up into small working groups, charged with criticizing both Peng's letter and those who supported him. The meaning of the incident was being transformed, blown out of proportion. There was in fact nothing anti-Party or anti-Mao about Peng's letter. But under Mao's direction, the letter was coming to be seen as part of a conspiracy. Peng and the men who had shared his views were being called upon to explain to the Central Committee how they had "plotted together both before and during the meeting." I began to understand better some of Mao's exaggerations and distortions in his conversations with me. "History" as Mao told it often diverged from the truth...

He spoke at another session on August 11. "Peng Dehuai and his supporters do not have the ideological preparation necessary for the proletarian socialist revolution," he said. "They are bourgeois democrats who made their way into our Party by pretending to be followers of Marxism. Chen Boda, Hu Qiaomu, and Tian Jiaying are our Party's scholars. We still need them. As for Li Rui, he is not in the same category. He is not a Party scholar." With these words, Tian Jiaying, Chen Boda, and Hu Qiaomu were saved. Li Rui was condemned to the anti-Party group...

In a Party document that circulated at the final meeting on August 16, Mao wrote that a great struggle had occurred at the Lushan conference. "It is a class struggle," Mao said, "a continuation of the life-and-death struggle between the two great classes — the bourgeoisie and the proletariat — and has been going on for the last years of socialist revolution." With these words, Peng Dehuai and his supporters were condemned to the ranks of the bourgeoisie.

The Lushan conference approved the document condemning Peng as an anti-Party element and defending the general line of the Great Leap Forward. The Party would launch yet another nationwide campaign against rightists, this time against Party members and cadres who shared Peng Dehuai's critical views of the Great Leap Forward and were deemed, by virtue of their realism, to be suffering from a new malady the Party dubbed "right opportunism"...

The next day, December 26, was Mao's birthday. His entire staff went to pay their respects. Mao had recovered completely, and his spirits were high. He thanked me for the treatment I had given, and we had a photograph taken together.

Eight tables of ten people each were set for the banquet that night, and the entire provincial leadership of Zhejiang participated. First Party secretary Jiang Hua and head of provincial public security Wang Fang represented all the guests and went to wish Mao a happy birthday.

Mao's warning against overindulgence was ignored. The feast that night was as extravagant as any I have ever had, consisting of the finest, most expensive delicacies Chinese cuisine can offer. We had real bird's-nest soup with baby doves, one of the rarest of Chinese dishes, and shark's fin soup cooked in a special clay pot, also rare and expensive. Nothing could top those two delicacies, but the other food was only slightly less delectable. The wine was superb as well, and Ye Zilong succeeded without effort in getting Wang Fang drunk.

Midway through our extravagant meal, Wang Jingxian turned to me.

"It's shameful for us to be consuming such a feast," he whispered. "So many people are starving to death."

I agreed. Outside, beyond the protective walls of Group One, beyond the special privileges of the country's leaders, the peasants of China were starving. The harvest of 1959 had been worse than the one the year before. The deaths were now in the millions, and before the famine was over tens of millions would die...

Mao (right) and Peng Dehui at the Lushan conference, 1959

3. Dr. Li Zhisui Discusses Mao Zedong's Views on History[1]

What fascinated Mao most and absorbed much of his time was Chinese history. 'We have to learn from the past to serve the present,' he often said. He had read the twenty-four dynastic histories — the series of official chronicles compiled by each new dynasty for the one it had just defeated and covering the years from 221 BC to 1644 AD — numerous times.[2]

But Mao's view of history was radically different from that of most Chinese. Morality had no place in Mao's politics. I was shocked to learn not only that Mao identified with China's emperors but that his greatest admiration was reserved for the most ruthless and cruel of our country's tyrants. He was willing to use the most brutal and tyrannical means to reach his goals.

One of the emperors Mao admired most was the Shang dynasty tyrant Emperor Zhou, who had reigned during the eleventh century BC. The Chinese people have always regarded Emperor Zhou with revulsion, horrified by his cruelty. The lives of his subjects meant nothing to Emperor Zhou, and he was in the habit of displaying the mutilated bodies of his victims as a warning to potential rebels. And his pool was filled with wine.

Zhou's excesses were nothing compared to his contributions, Mao argued; Emperor Zhou had greatly expanded China's territory, bringing the southeastern coastal area under his control and unifying many divergent tribes under a single rule. He had killed some loyal and able ministers, to be sure — the famous Bigan was the most notable example — but Bigan was killed because he had counseled against further expansion. Yes,

---

[1] From Li Zhisui's book, *The Private Life of Chairman Mao*
[2] pp. 122ff:

Emperor Zhou lived luxuriously. Of course he had thousands of concubines, but what emperor had not?

Qin Shihuangdi, Mao Zedong's favorite emperor

Another of Mao's favorites was Qin Shihuangdi (c 259–210 BC), the founding emperor of the Qin dynasty and of imperial China, which lasted for nearly two thousand years. This was the man credited with building the Great Wall, the emperor with whom he was most often compared. Qin Shihuangdi, like Emperor Zhou, expanded China's territory and consolidated a multitude of small 'kingdoms' into a single state. He had introduced unified measures and weights. He had constructed roads. But the Chinese people hated him because he had executed the Confucian scholars and burned the classic books. But Qin Shihuangdi killed the scholars, Mao argued, only because they got in the way of his efforts to unify China and build the Chinese empire. And he only killed 260 Confusion scholars. Where was the great tragedy in that? One ought not, in looking at Qin Shihuangdi, exaggerate the trivial and ignore the great.

Not only were Mao's views of history astonishing, they revealed a great deal about him. He used the stories of China's past both to understand and to manipulate the present and see himself in terms of his own contributions to the country's ongoing history. I am convinced that the intrigues in China's ancient imperial courts were a far more powerful influence on his thoughts than Marxism-Leninism...

Mao had grandiose ideas of his own place in history. He never had any doubt about his own role. He was the greatest leader, the greatest emperor of them all — the man who had unified the country and would then transform it, the man who was restoring China to its original greatness. Mao never used the work *modernization* with me. He was not a modern man. Instead, he talked about making the country rich and turning it to its original glory. A rebel and iconoclast, he would dare to transform China and make it great. He would build his own Great Walls. His own greatness and China's were intertwined. All of China was Mao's to experiment with as he wished. Mao *was* China, and he was suspicious of anyone who might challenge his place or whose vision differed from his. He was ruthless in disposing of his enemies. The life of his subjects was cheap.

I did not immediately understand, because it was so hard to accept, how willing Mao was to sacrifice his own citizens in order to achieve his goals. I had known as early as October 1954, from a meeting with India's prime minister Jawaharlal Nehru, that Mao considered the atom bomb a "paper tiger" and that he was willing that China lose millions of people in order to emerge victorious against the so-called imperialists. "The atom bomb is nothing to be afraid of," Mao told Nehru. "China has a lot of people. They cannot be bombed out of existence. If someone else can drop an atomic bomb, I can too. The death of ten or twenty million people is nothing to be afraid of." Nehru was shocked.

In 1957, in a speech in Moscow, Mao said he was willing to lose 300 million people. Even if China lost half its population, Mao said, the country would suffer no great loss. "We could produce more people."

It was not until the Great Leap Forward, when millions of Chinese began dying during the famine, that I became aware of how much Mao resembled the ruthless emperors he so admired. Mao knew that people were dying by the millions. He did not care...

4. Mao's Theory of the Three Worlds — Justification for an Alliance with the U.S.?

From: *Mao Zedong on Diplomacy*, Compiled by the Chinese Ministry of Foreign Affairs

1. The document[1] [verbatim record]

Chairman Mao (hereinafter referred to as Mao): "We hope that the Third World will unite. The Third World has a large population!"

President Kenneth David Kaunda (hereinafter referred to as Kaunda): "That's right."

Mao: "Who belongs to the Third World?"

Kaunda: "I think it ought to be the world of exploiters and imperialists."

Mao: "And the Second World?"

Kaunda: "Those who have become revisionists."

Mao: "I hold that the US and the Soviet Union belong to the First World. The middle elements, such as Japan, Europe, Australia, and Canada, belong to the Second World. We are the Third World."

---

[1] From: *Mao Zedong on Diplomacy*, compiled by the Ministry of Foreign Affairs of the People's Republic of China and the Party Literature Research Center under the Central Committee of the Communist Party of China, first edition 1998 by Foreign Language Press, Beijing, p. 454, also at: michaelharrison.org.uk/wp-content/uploads/2017/02/Mao-Zedong-On-Diplomacy-1998.pdf.

Kaunda: "I agree with your analysis, Mr. Chairman."

Mao: "The US and the Soviet Union have a lot of atomic bombs, and they are richer. Europe, Japan, Australia, and Canada, of the Second World, do not possess so many atomic bombs and as the Second World are not so rich, but richer than the Third World. What do you think of this explanation?"

Kaunda: "Mr. Chairman, your analysis is very pertinent and correct."

Mao: "We can discuss it."

Kaunda: "I think we can reach agreement without discussion, because I believe this analysis is already very pertinent."

Mao: "The Third World is very populous."

Kaunda: "Precisely so."

Mao: "All Asian countries, except for Japan, belong to the Third World. All of Africa and also the Latin American countries belong to the Third World."

2. A Marxist Analysis? (G. Schnehen)

Mao Zedong and his followers have always pretended and are still pretending to be "Marxists" or "Marxist-Leninists." The "ideas" of the "Chairman" have been and are still praised as a "continuation of Marxism-Leninism" or even as the "highest stage of Marxism," the pinnacle of Marxism and "universal truths" as well. But real Marxists know full well that the true divisions in today's and yesterday's world have never been divisions between rich and poor countries, between a "first," "second" or "third" world, but between a super-rich upper class and its administrative apparatus on the one hand and the working classes, the toilers, the suppressed and downtrodden on the other and that the first, the rich elites, live at the expense of the second exploiting their labor and reaping the fruits of it. So how can someone, who calls himself a Marxist, say that the true divisions are between a so-called "first," "second" and "third" world and not the divisions among different social classes within a given country?

As this "theory" is so blatantly anti-Marxist, Maoists have tried hard to attribute it to someone else. Allegedly, the "right-revisionist" Deng Xiaoping, Mao's successor, had developed it, and Mao Zedong was of course not its brainchild.[1] But whether this is true or false is not important at all. Mao Zedong is using the "theory" when talking to the Zambian president as we have seen in the document and strongly defends it. Kaunda, who seems to be unwilling to discuss the "theory," at one point says: "YOUR analysis is very pertinent and correct." Mao

---

[1] See: Harpal Brar, *Socialism with Chinese Characteristics*, London 2020, p. 62, note: 63: "As far as we know the Three Worlds' Theory was Deng's" (Deng Xiaoping, ed.).

Zedong did not contradict him. So we can rightfully assume that this was his theory or maybe a theory developed by someone else which he found very "pertinent" and then adopted it. Since Mao was the philosopher in the Chinese party and not the more down-to-earth Deng Xiaoping, we have reason to believe that Mao himself developed this "idea" and that it is part and parcel of "Mao Zedong Thought".

Falsifiers of Marxism or Marxism-Leninism have a long tradition of telling us that their new "theories" or "ideas" are a "further development of Marxism." In reality they have said goodbye to Marxism under the pretext of developing it further.

What does a division of the world in three regions — the first, the second, and the third — lead to in practice? practice always is the litmus test whether a theory is valid or invalid, whether it makes sense or whether it is nonsense. It led to an unholy alliance between Maoist China and reactionary Third World regimes that were utterly corrupt.

This theory which was presented to the United Nations by Deng Xiaoping in 1974, Mao Zedong's envoy there at the time, provided the theoretical rationale for a fundamental policy change which had already set in some years before. Whereas in the 1960s the leaders of the People's Republic of China still supported the anti-imperialist struggles of some countries such as Vietnam or Laos, after Nixon and Kissinger's visit to Beijing in 1972 China's foreign policy changed dramatically. Vietnam was no longer supported with weapons to defend itself against the US aggression; from now on the murderous Pol Pot regime that killed almost one million people between 1975 and 1979 was supported with finances and weapons; the fascist Chilean military junta under Augusto Pinochet which came to power on 9/11 of 1973 through a bloody putsch organized by the CIA (Kissinger later admitted he was involved), was also supported as Wang Ming, the former politburo member of the Communist Party of China tells us in his reminiscences:

> Mao expressed his support and sympathy for the coup in Chile; he expelled the Chilean ambassador of the Unidad Popular from Beijing and instead welcomed the arrival and the inauguration of the ambassador of the fascist junta in Beijing. He openly sided with the fascist dictatorship...[1]

A junta that murdered thousands of Chileans after the coup and incarcerated resistance fighters in concentration camps, among them the football arena of Santiago de Chile, was given Chinese weapons and financing by the "Marxist-Leninist" Mao Zedong! After the successful coup, the junta generals did not just ban Salvador Allende's Socialist Party but also Luis Corvalán's Communist Party

---

[1] Wang Ming, *50 Jahre KP Chinas und der Verrat Mao Zedongs*, Berlin, 1981, p. 269 (50 years of CP of China and Mao Zedong's treason).

as well as other democratic parties which had supported Salvador Allende's Unidad Popular and its progressive and anti-imperialist policies.

Now the Chinese leadership was also in favor of the North Atlantic Treaty Organization (NATO) and recognized it, but furthermore it also now supported other military alliances under the leadership of the US.

Mao Zedong now was in favor of a strong American–Japanese alliance and voiced support for all US military bases in South-East Asia; he established diplomatic relations with the fascist government in Madrid under General Franco; he was now in favor of having a normal relationship with the reactionary Shah of Iran, and the right-wing Marcos regime ruling the Philippines with an iron fist — as the Philippines surely belonged to the Third World, just like Chile or Iran which now needed Chinese support. The utterly corrupt Mobuto regime of Zaire was supported and Mobuto, who considered himself the king of the country, was invited to Beijing. The UNITÁ, the CIA sponsored pro-imperialist "movement" to rein in the anti-imperialist movements in Angola, Guinea-Bissau and Mozambique, was given military support. Chinese pilots were sent in to help the CIA puppet Jonas Zavimbi in his fight against the anti-imperialists in Angola. Socialist Albania under Enver Hoxha, a long-time ally of the Chinese government, was now no longer considered a friend, and all Chinese advisors were hastily withdrawn from the Socialist country, leaving many important projects in Albania unfinished. Enver Hoxha tells us in his memoirs:

5. The Cultural Revolution — Great Proletarian Revolution or Putsch?

The book *Class Struggles in China — A Marxist-Leninist Analysis of Mao Zedong*, by William B. Bland,[1] provides a chronicle of the "Cultural Revolution" (1966–1969) without passing judgment on events or individuals. The British Marxist then draws his own conclusion — nicely separating facts from opinion and leaving the reader to reach conclusions of his own. This approach is exemplary — reason enough for me to present his chronicle here.

1. William B. Bland

The Initiation of the "Cultural Revolution" (April 1966)

Premier Chou En-lai...called for a fierce and protracted struggle to wipe out 'bourgeois ideology' in the academic, educational and journalistic fields, in art, literature and all other fields of culture.[2]

In the same month, April 1966, the newspaper *Liberation Army Daily*, the most important press organ under the control of the comprador bourgeoisie grouping of the Party [Bland refers to Mao Zedong's inner circle — Ed.] published an editorial which declared: "There exists in our literary and art circles an anti-Party, anti-socialist black line running counter to Mao Zedong's thinking...We must...take an active part in the great socialist revolution on the cultural front, thoroughly eradicate this black line...We must not mind being blamed for 'brandishing the stick.'"[3]

---

[1] London, 1997. Chapter 15: The Cultural Revolution
[2] *Keesing's Contemporary Archives*, Vol. 15, p. 21,577.
[3] *Beijing Review*, Vol. 9, No. 18, 29 April 1966, pp. 6 and 9, quoted by W. B. Bland, ibid., p. 132.

In May 1966, Yao Wen-yuan, belonging to Mao Zedong's inner circle, published a violent attack on three journals published by the Beijing branch of the CP of China, denouncing them as "...instruments for opposing the Party and socialism."[1]

In June 1966, the *People's Daily*, now controlled by the comprador bour-geoisie grouping of the Party (Mao's followers GS), published a violent attack on the Party leadership at Beijing University:

Beijing University...is a key point of the 'Three Family Village' sinister gang, a stubborn bastion used by them to oppose the Party and socialism. The people of the whole country will rise up, oppose and knock down all those who oppose Chairman Mao...The whole nation will smash their sinister gang, sinister organization and sinister discipline to pieces.[2]

On the following day, it was announced that: "the Central Committee of the Communist Party of China had decided to reorganize the Beijing Party Committee as well as the Party Committee of Beijing University and that a new Beijing First Secretary in place of Peng Chen had been appointed.[3]

The 'Red Guards' (May 1966–January 1967)

The first stage of the Cultural Revolution was led by the students.[4] From May 1966, young people were recruited into a para-military fascist type organization called 'Red Guards':

The People's Liberation Army and People's Militia trained groups of teenagers in schools and universities to form Red Guard units which were designed...to promote the teachings of the Chairman.[5]

The 'Red Guards' were designed to function as a shock force against the polit-ical representatives of the national bourgeoisie (Mao Zedong's adversaries in the Politburo of the Communist Party of China — Ed.): "The Red Guards are the shock force of the great proletarian cultural revolution."[6]

Significantly, their allegiance was declared to be not to the Communist Party but to Mao Zedong personally: "The Red Guards say and they say it well: 'Chairman Mao is our red commander and we are the young, red soldiers of Chairman Mao... They carry with them copies of 'Quotations from Chairman Mao'."[7]

The dictum was accepted that "a genuine revolutionary" was one who accepts 'Mao Zedong Thought' without question:

---

[1] Ibid., No. 22, 27 May 1966, p. 5.

[2] Ibid., No. 37, 9 Sept. 1966, pp. 21 and 22.

[3] *Keesing's Contemporary Archives*, Vol. 15, p. 21,577.

[4] David Milton, Nancy Milton & Franz Schurman (Eds.): *People's China: Social Experimentation, Politics, Entry onto the World Scene: 1966 through to 1972*, New York, 1974, p. 230, quoted by W. B. Bland, ibid., p. 133.

[5] Clare Hollingworth, *Mao and the Men against him*, London, 1985, quoted by W. B. Bland, ibid.

[6] *Beijing Review*, Vol. 9, No. 39, 23 Sept. 1966, p. 15, quoted by W. B. Bland, ibid.

[7] Ibid.

The attitude towards Mao Zedong Thought, whether to accept or to reject it, to support or to oppose it, to love it warmly or be hostile to it — this is the touchstone to test and the watershed between true revolution and sham revolution, between revolution and counterrevolution.[1]

In June 1966, "Universities and schools were closed indefinitely to enable [the students] to participate in the Cultural Revolution.[2]

In July, "great prominence was given in the Chinese press...to a report that Mr. Mao had swum nine miles in the Yangtze River in 65 minutes, apparently in order to dispel rumors that he was in poor health."[3]

In August 1966, at a mass rally of Red Guards in Beijing, Mao "signified his approval of the movement by donning the red armband which they wore."[4]

Between August and December 1966, "eight such giant rallies of a million or more Red Guards were held in the great Tienanmen Square in Beijing."[5]

In August 1966, it was announced, "that the entire printing industry would be mobilized to print 35 million copies of the 'Selected Works of Mao Zedong' by the end of 1967."[6]

In November 1966, Deng Xiaoping was dismissed as General Secretary of the Communist Party. In December 1966, "Peng Chen was dragged from his bed and arrested by Red Guards and was displayed before a rally of 100,000 Red Guards in a Beijing stadium."[7]

Lo Jui-ching was also arrested by the Red Guards ; he had been secretly removed as Chief of Staff in November 1965, accused of "opposing the thorough establishment by our army of the absolute authority of the great thought of Mao Zedong."[8] Similarly, Lu Ting-yi, former head of the propaganda department and Minister of Culture, was removed from his posts in July 1966.[9]

The 11th Plenum of the 8th Central Committee of the Communist Party, August 1966

The Plenum was held in August 1966 and guarded by the troops of Lin Biao. Mao resorted to the extraordinary measure of packing the galleries with youthful supporters and convoking only about half of the total membership of the Central Committee.[10]

---

[1] Ibid., Vol. 9, No. 24, 10 June 1966, p. 7.
[2] *Keesing's Contemporary Archives*, Vol. 15, p. 21,986.
[3] Ibid., Vol. 15, p. 21, 579.
[4] Ibid., Vol. 15, p. 21,986.
[5] David Milton et al, Eds., ibid., p. 268, quoted by W. B. Bland, ibid., p. 134.
[6] *Keesing's Contemporary Archives*, Vol. 15, p. 21,579.
[7] Ibid., Vol. 16, p. 21,987.
[8] *Beijing Review*, Vol. 19, No. 46, 10 November 1967, p. 19, quoted by W. B. Bland, ibid., p. 135.
[9] *Keesing's Contemporary Archives*, Vol. 15, p. 21, 578.
[10] Lowell Dittmer, *Liu Shao-chi and the Chinese Cultural Revolution. The Politics of Mass Criticism*, Berkeley/USA, 1974, p. 95, quoted by W. B. Bland, ibid., p. 135.

At the Plenum presided over by Comrade Mao Zedong those present were confronted with a big character poster written by himself, reading "bombard the headquarters!"[1]

The poster was immediately understood by all delegates as an attack on Liu Shaoqi, Deng Xiaoping, and other prominent leaders of the powerful party apparatus. The Plenum demoted Liu and elevated Lin Biao, the Minister of Defense, to the post of Deputy Chairman of the Chinese Communist Party. Lin was officially proclaimed as 'Chairman Mao's closest comrade-in-arms and successor'.[2]

It gave formal approval both to the Cultural Revolution and to 'Mao Zedong Thought' and stressed that the series of directives by Comrade Mao Zedong concerning the great proletarian cultural revolution were the guide to action in the present cultural revolution of the country.[3]

It reiterated that "our objective is to struggle against and crush those persons in authority who are taking the capitalist road."[4]

It gave instructions to "trust the masses, rely on them, and respect their initiative, cast out fear, don't be afraid of disorder."[5]

In particular, the Plenum emphasized that the "intensive study of Comrade Mao Zedong's works by the whole Party and the whole nation is an important event of historic significance. Comrade Mao Zedong is the greatest Marxist-Leninist of our era. Comrade Mao Zedong...developed Marxism-Leninism with genius...and has raised Marxism-Leninism to a new stage. Mao Zedong's Thought is Marxism-Leninism of the era in which imperialism is heading for total collapse and socialism is advancing to world-wide victory. It is the guiding principle for all the work of our Party and country."[6]

The 'Revolutionary Rebels' (November–December 1966)

To counter the offensive of the 'Red Guards,' Liu Shaoqi organized "...a large number of work teams — perhaps four hundred teams with more than 10,000 members in all — and dispatched them to universities and high schools and to bureaucratic agencies...to reestablish Party leadership over

---

[1] David Milton et al, ibid., p. 268, in: W. B. Bland, ibid., p. 136.

[2] Ibid.

[3] *CCP Documents of the Great Proletarian Cultural Revolution, 1966-1967*, Hong Kong, 1968, p. 65, quoted by W. B. Bland, ibid., p. 136.

[4] Ibid., p. 42, decision of the Central Committee of the Communist Party concerning the Great Proletarian Cultural Revolution, August 1966, quoted by W. B. Bland, ibid.

[5] Ibid., p. 45, quoted by ibid.

[6] Ibid., p. 69, communique of the 11th Plenum of the 8th Central Committee of CPC, quoted by W. B. Bland, ibid., p. 137.

the student movement...The work teams were able to restore a modicum of normality to many universities."[1]

On the other hand, "...in the long run, the student movement became unmanageable because of factional quarrels."[2] Thus the representatives of the national bourgeoisie (Liu Shaoqi's people — Ed.) were "able to repulse the first attack by Red Guards in August and September (1966 — Ed.) by mobilizing workers...in their defense".[3]

As a result of the failure of the Red Guards to fulfill the role allotted to them, it was announced in November 1966 that free transport, food, and accommodation would no longer be provided for them when coming to Beijing and that Red Guards from the provinces had to leave the city within three days.[4]

The political representatives of the comprador bourgeoisie (Mao Zedong's inner circle — Ed.) responded to the failure of the campaign of the 'Red Guards' in November 1966 by seeking to supplement them with adult workers — called 'Revolutionary Rebels'. They were organized in industrial and mining establishments.

The 'Revolutionary Rebels' "...consisting of adult workers, replaced the Red Guards from this time on as the main agents of the Cultural Revolution...The Revolutionary Rebels, however, did not form a single movement organized on a national scale...Scores of Maoist organizations bearing a wide variety of names sprang up throughout the country, often operating independently and even in rivalry. In Shanghai, for example, there were at least 31 Revolutionary Rebel and Red Guard organizations...In many cities and provinces the Revolutionary Rebels were opposed by equally militant anti-Maoist organizations."[5]

In other words, under the direction of the political representatives of the national bourgeoisie (Liu Shaoqis group within the CPC — Ed.) armed organizations were formed to resist the Revolutionary Rebels.[6] The 'Revolutionary Rebels' also demanded "...higher wages, lower working hours, better housing, improved medical care and other benefits."[7]

In many areas, the 'Revolutionary Rebels' pursued their demands with strikes, which reached particular intensity in Shanghai: "Widespread

---

[1] Harry Harding, *China's Second Revolution. Reform after Mao*, Washington D.C., 1987, p. 136, see: Bland, ibid.

[2] David Milton et al, ibid., p. 229, quoted by W. B. Bland, ibid.

[3] Richard Baum, ed., *China in Ferment. Perspectives on the Cultural Revolution*, Engelwood Cliffs/USA, 1971, p. 122, article by Philip Bridgham, *Maoist Cultural Revolution in 1967*, quoted by W. B. Bland, ibid.

[4] *Keesing's Contemporary Archives*, Vol. 16, p. 21, 986.

[5] Ibid., Vol. 15, pp. 21,988f.

[6] Ibid., p. 21,985.

[7] Stanley Karnow, *Mao and China: From Revolution to Revolution*, London, 1973, p. 265, cited by W. B. Bland, ibid., p. 138.

strikes in support of demands for wage increases began in Shanghai at the end of December (1966 — Ed.)...The port was brought to a standstill."[1]

The port officials, fearful of being branded as 'revisionist,' promised to satisfy every demand.[2] As a result, they were then told they had been hood-winked into following the 'evil road of economism'. The struggle...raged even more fiercely through December.[3]

The 'Revolutionary Committees' (January 1967–September 1968)

During the early months of the Cultural Revolution, the Army had "... remained neutral in the struggle."[4]

But by January 1967, the Cultural Revolution had brought the country to a state of anarchy and "only one institution had the capacity to fill the power vacuum — the Army."[5]

Resistance to involving the Army in the Cultural Revolution "was apparently led by...officers like Marshal Ho Lung."[6] In May 1967, Red Guards arraigned Ho Lung...before a kangaroo court, and "he disappeared from public view."[7]

In January 1967, the policy of army non-involvement was changed "in the light of the general stalemate that had occurred throughout the fall, and the collapse of authority that had begun to appear around the turn of the year."[8]

The People's Liberation Army (PLA) was then ordered to intervene in the Cultural Revolution on the side of the 'revolutionary leftists': "All past directives concerning the army's non-involvement in the great cultural revolution...are null and void. Active support must be rendered to the broad masses of revolutionary leftists in their struggle to seize power...Counter-revolutionaries and counter-revolutionary organizations who oppose the proletarian revolutionary leftists must be resolutely suppressed."[9]

It was decided that "the former provincial and municipal administra-tions must be replaced by Revolutionary Committees, based on a 'triple

---

[1] *Keesing's Contemporary Archives*, Vol. 15, p. 21,989.

[2] Stanley Karnow, ibid., cited by W. B. Bland, ibid., pp. 138f.

[3] Joan Robinson, *The Cultural Revolution in China*, Harmondsworth, 1969, p. 57, cited by W. B. Bland, ibid., p. 139.

[4] *Keesing's Contemporary Archives*, ibid., p. 21,989.

[5] Stanley Karnow, ibid., p. 275, cited by W. B. Bland, ibid., p. 139.

[6] Ibid., p. 279, cited by W. B. Bland, ibid.

[7] Stanley Karnow, ibid., p. 282, Bland, ibid.

[8] Roderick MacFarquahar & John K. Fairbank, eds., *The Cambridge History of China*, Vol. 15, *The People's Republic*, part 2, p. 161, citing Harry Harding, *The Chinese State in a Crisis*, cited W. B. Bland, ibid.

[9] In: *CCP Documents of the Great Proletarian Cultural Revolution, 1966-67*, ibid., p. 196, in: W. B. Bland, ibid., p. 140.

alliance' with Revolutionary Rebels and Army representatives."[1] And also with old party cadres who had passed the test of the Cultural Revolution.[2] So 'Revolutionary Committees' "were set up between November 1967 and May 1968 in 16 provinces."[3]

In August and September 1968, 'Revolutionary Committees' were established...in the five remaining provinces."[4] The People's Liberation Army played by far the dominant role in the 'Revolutionary Committees': "The triple alliance policy in practice gave the Army control of the 'Revolutionary Committees.'"[5]

Maoist politicians played only a subsidiary role.[6] In most provinces "the chairman of the committee was the local political commissar or military commander."[7]

In January 1968, "the public sale of Red Guard literature was forbidden... on the grounds that certain of them fomented 'sectarianism'.[8]

July saw "the last campaign of the historic Beijing Red Guards. Massive worker and army teams were sent in to direct and lead the universities. The mass movement was over."[9]

Mao himself "repudiated the Red Guards."[10]

In October 1968, the Central Committee of the Communist Party of China ordered that "all schools and universities...should reopen immediately.[11]

The Rebuilding of the Party (September–August 1971)

During this time the Communist Party had disintegrated: "Except in the Army, the CP of China had virtually disintegrated during the Cultural Revolution...The Reorganization of the Communist Party...began in September 1968, local branches being established first."[12]

And the "pattern of military predominance was dutifully applied to the Party Committees germinating in the provinces."[13] At the provincial level "Party

---

[1] *Keesing's Contemporary Archives*, ibid., p. 21,992.
[2] David Milton et al, ibid., p. 354.
[3] *Keesing's Contemporary Archives*, ibid., p. 22,945.
[4] Ibid.
[5] Ibid., p. 21,993.
[6] Ibid., p. 22,945.
[7] Ibid., p. 22,949.
[8] Ibid.
[9] David Milton et al, ibid., p. 354, in: Bland, ibid., p. 141.
[10] Stanley Karnow, ibid., p. 441, in: Bland, ibid.
[11] *Keesing's Contemporary Archives*, p. 22,949.
[12] Ibid., Vol. 18, p. 24,698.
[13] Stanley Karnow, ibid., p. 462, Bland, ibid.

authority gradually slipped into the hands of the local PLA (People's Liberation Army) leaders;"[1] while "the Red Guards ended up with derisory treatment."[2] In almost all provinces, "the post of First Party Secretary was assumed by the Chairman of the Provincial Revolutionary Committee, who in most cases was an army officer or political commissar, whilst the majority of the assistant secretaries were also officers or political commissars."[3]

The last of the new Party Committees "were finally established in late August 1971."[4]

The 12th Plenum of the 8th Central Committee, October 1968

Like the 11th Plenum in August 1966 the Plenum was a "rump session...Only 54 full members of the Central Committee attended the meeting, representing a bare quorum of the surviving members of the body. Furthermore, like its predecessor the 12th Plenum was packed with people who were not Central Committee members...The extra participants were members of the Cultural Revolution Group, representatives of the provincial revolutionary committees, and principal responsible comrades of the Chinese People's Liberation Army."[5]

The Plenum "announced that Liu Shaoqi was being dismissed from all his government and Party positions, and was being expelled from the Party 'once and for all'."[6] He was called a "renegade, traitor and scab hiding in the Party, a lackey of imperialism and modern revisionism, and a Kuomintang reactionary."[7]

However, at the Plenum "the Cultural Revolution Group's proposal that Deng Xiaoping...be expelled from the Party altogether along with Liu Shaoqi, was rejected."[8]

The 9th National Congress of the CPC (April 1969)

The 9th National Congress of the CPC was held in April 1969, "the first such conference to be held in more than a decade."[9] It was held in "conditions of strict secrecy, no journalists or foreign observers being admitted."[10] And "no foreign parties were invited to send delegations."[11]

---

[1] Steve S. K. Chin, ed., *The Gang of Four: First Essays after the Fall*, Hong Kong, 1977, p. 124, quoting Liao Kuang-sheng: *Factional Politics after the Cultural Revolution*, W. B. Bland, ibid.
[2] Stanley Karnow, ibid., p. 458, in: Bland, ibid., p. 142.
[3] *Keesing's Contemporary Archives*, ibid.
[4] Stanley Karnow, ibid., p. 463, in: Bland, ibid., p. 142.
[5] Harry Harding, ibid., pp. 193f, in: Bland, ibid.
[6] Ibid., p. 194, in: ibid.
[7] Ibid., p. 194f, Resolution of the 12th Plenum of the 8th CC, CPC, October 1968, in: Bland, ibid.
[8] Ibid., p. 195, in: Bland, ibid., pp. 142f.
[9] Stanley Karnow, ibid., p. 454, in: Bland, ibid., p. 143.
[10] *Keesing's Contemporary Archives*, Vol. 17, p. 23,377.
[11] Ibid., p. 23,379, in: Bland, ibid.

Delegates to the Congress were "appointed by the central authorities after negotiation with the provinces."[1] Reporting on the Cultural Revolution, Lin Biao declared that it had achieved a "great victory,"[2] although admitting that "we cannot speak of final victory."[3] As has been said, the PLA "emerged as the single most powerful institution in China at the 9th Congress."[4]

The Congress adopted a new Party Constitution, replacing that of 1956. It declared:

> The Communist Party of China takes Marxism-Leninism and Mao Zedong Thought as the theoretical basis guiding its thinking. Mao Zedong Thought is Marxism-Leninism of the era in which imperialism is heading for total collapse and socialism is advancing to world-wide victory....[5]

> Comrade Lin Biao is Comrade Mao Zedong's close comrade-in-arms and successor.[6]

> A new Central Committee was elected, to which "only 54 out of the 167 members of the previous Central Committee were re-elected."[7] It was overwhelmingly "weighted in favor of army officers and party cadres who had survived the Cultural Revolution."[8]

> At its first plenum the new central committee elected a Politburo and its standing committee with Mao as chairman, Lin Biao as deputy chairman, Chen Po-ta, Chou En-lai and Kang Sheng.[9]

> New members of the Politburo "included Yeh Chun (Lin Piao's wife — Ed.), Chiang Ching (Mao's wife — Ed.), Chu Teh, Chiang-chiao, Yao Wen-yuan."[10]

Bland's Conclusion

With the 9th Congress of the CPC in April 1969, the "Great Proletarian Cultural Revolution" effectively, although not officially, came to an end. It left the comprador bourgeoisie grouping within the party, headed by Mao Zedong, in the dominant position and the national bourgeoisie grouping, headed by Liu Shaoqi, in a greatly — although not fatally — weakened position.

---

[1] Harry Harding, ibid., p. 193, in: Bland, ibid.
[2] Stanley Karnow, ibid., p. 405, citing Lin Piao's report on the Cultural Revolution, in: Bland, ibid.
[3] *Keesing's Contemporary Archives*, ibid., p. 23,377.
[4] Frederick C. Teiwes & Warren Sun, *The Tragedy of Lin Piao. Riding the Tiger during the Cultural Revolution, 1966-1971*, London, 1976, in: Bland, ibid.
[5] *Keesing's Contemporary Archives*, ibid., p. 23,378.
[6] Ibid., citing the new constitution adopted.
[7] Harry Harding, ibid., p. 197, in: Bland, ibid., p. 144.
[8] Stanley Karnow, ibid., p. 458.
[9] *Keesing's Contemporary Archives*, ibid.
[10] Ibid.

2. Excerpts from Jung Chang's book "Wild Swans — Three Daughters of China"[1]

Introduction by G. Schnehen

Mrs. Chang is a Chinese eyewitness of events that shaped China's evolution. She was born in Yibin, Sichuan Province, China in 1952. She spent more than 25 years in her home country where she experienced the Great Leap Forward and the great famine, as a child, and later Mao Zedong's Cultural Revolution as a young girl. Her parents were Communists, occupying leading positions within the Communist Party. Both parents were persecuted and humiliated by Mao Zedong and his followers. Her father had to burn his own books after a group of Red Guards stormed their house. In 1969 he was sent to a re-education camp where he had to stay for three years. Later Jung Chang became an electrician, a steelworker, and at times also a 'barefoot doctor'. She left China for Britain in 1978 and there obtained a Ph.D. in linguistics from the University of York in 1982. Together with her husband, Jon Halliday, she also wrote *Mao — The Unknown Story*, a biography of Mao Zedong.

Jung Chang, former "Red Guard"

Large parts of her report are confirmed by Dr. Li Zhisui's reminiscences, by Mao Zedong's long-time personal physician, but are condemned by Richard Corell in his book on the Cultural Revolution.[2]

Chapter 15: "Destroy First, and Construction Will Look after Itself." The Cultural Revolution begins (1965–1966)[3]

---

[1] New York, 2003. Chapters 15–19 on the Cultural Revolution.
[2] Richard Corell, *Die Große Proletarische Kulturrevolution*, Frankfurt/Main, 2009, p. 178; The Great Proletarian Cultural Revolution. There he writes: "whereas more recent anti-Mao literature, including the memoirs of his personal physician, Li Zhisui, and the thoroughly mendacious and spiteful biography of the Chinese-British renegade couple Chang/Halliday..."
[3] Jung Chang, *Wild Swans*, ibid., pp. 345-356.

At the beginning of the 1960s, in spite of all the disasters Mao had caused, he was still China's supreme leader, idolized by the population. But because the pragmatists were actually running the country, there was relative literary and artistic freedom. A host of plays, operas, films, and novels emerged after long hibernation. None attacked the Party openly, and contemporary themes were rare. At this time Mao was on the defensive, and he turned more and more to his wife, Jiang Qing, who had been an actress in the 1930s. They decided that historical themes were being used to convey insinuations against the regime and against Mao himself...

In 1964, Mao drew up a list of 39 artists, writers, and scholars for denunciation. He branded them "reactionary bourgeois authorities," a new category of class enemies. Prominent names on the list included the most famous playwright in the Ming Mandarin genre, Wu Han, and Professor Ma Yin-chu, who had been the first leading economist to advocate birth control. For this he had already been named a rightist in 1957. Mao had subsequently realized that birth control was necessary, but he resented Professor Ma for showing him up and making it clear that he was wrong.

The list was not made public, and the 39 people were not purged by their Party organizations. Mao had the list circulated to officials down to my mother's level with instructions to catch other "reactionary bourgeois authorities." In the winter of 1964-65, my mother was sent as the head of a work team to a school named "Ox Market." She was told to look for suspects among prominent teachers and those who had written books or articles.

My mother was appalled, particularly as the purge threatened the very people she most admired. Besides, she could plainly see that even if she were to look for "enemies" she would not find any. Apart from anything else, with the memory of all the recent persecutions few had dared to open their mouths at all. She told her superior, Mr. Pao, who was in charge of the campaign in Chengdu, how she felt.

Nineteen sixty-five passed, and my mother did nothing. Mr. Pao did not exert any pressure on her. Their inaction reflected the general mood among Party officials. Most of them were fed up with persecutions, and wanted to get on with improving living standards and building a normal life. But they did not openly oppose Mao, and indeed went on promoting his personality cult. The few who watched Mao's deification with apprehension knew there was nothing they could do to stop it: Mao had such power and prestige that his cult was irresistible. The most they could do was engage in some kind of passive resistance.

Mao interpreted the reaction from the Party officials to his call for a witch-hunt as an indication that their loyalty to him was weakening and that their hearts were with the policies being pursued by President Liu and Deng. His suspicion was confirmed when the Party newspapers refused to publish an article he had authorized denouncing Wu Han and his play about the Ming Mandarin. Mao's purpose in getting the article published was to involve the population in the witch-hunt. Now he found he was cut off from his subjects by the Party system, which had been the intermediary between himself and the people. He had, in effect, lost control. The Party Committee of Peking, where Wu Han was deputy mayor, and the Central Department of Public Affairs, which looked after the media and the arts, stood up to Mao, refusing either to denounce Wu Han or to dismiss him...

On 10 November 1965, having repeatedly failed to have the article condemning Wu Han's play published in Peking, Mao was at last able to get it printed in Shanghai, where his followers were in charge. It was in this article that the term "Cultural Revolution" first appeared. The Party's own newspaper the *People's Daily*, refused to reprint the article, as did the *Peking Daily*, the voice of the Party organization in the capital. In the provinces, some papers did carry the article. At the time, my father was overseeing the provincial Party newspaper, the *Sichuan Daily*, and was against reprinting the article, which he could sense was an attack on Marshal Peng and a call for a witch-hunt. He went to see the man in charge of cultural affairs for the province, who suggested they telephone Deng Xiaoping. Deng was not in his office, and the call was taken by Marshal Ho Lung, a close friend of Deng's and a member of the Politburo. It was he who my father had overheard saying in 1959: "It really should be him (Deng) on the throne." He said not to reprint the article...

Over the next three months there was intense maneuvering, with Mao's opponents, as well as Zhou, trying to head off Mao's witch-hunt. In February 1966, while Mao was away from Peking, the Politburo passed a resolution that "academic discussions" must not degenerate into persecutions. Mao had objected to this resolution, but he was ignored.

In April my father was asked to prepare a document in the spirit of the Politburo's February resolution to guide the Cultural Revolution in Sichuan. What he wrote became known as the "April Document." It said: The debates must be strictly academic. No wild accusations should be allowed. Everyone is equal before the truth. The Party must not use force to suppress intellectuals.

Just as this document was about to be published in May, it was suddenly blocked. There was a new Politburo decision. This time, Mao had been present and had got the upper hand, with Zhou En-lai's complicity. Mao tore up the February resolution and declared that all dissident scholars and their ideas must be "eliminated." He emphasized that it was officials in the Communist Party who had been protecting the dissident scholars and other class enemies. He termed these officials "those in power following the capitalist road," and declared war on them. They became known as the "capitalist-roaders." The mammoth Cultural Revolution was formally launched.

Who exactly were these "capitalist roaders"? Mao himself was not sure. He knew he wanted to replace the whole of the Peking Party Committee, which he did. He also knew he wanted to get rid of Liu Shao-chi and Deng Xiaoping, and "the bourgeois headquarters in the Party." But he did not know who in the vast Party system were loyal to him and who were followers of Liu and Deng and their "capitalist road." He calculated that he controlled only a third of the Party. In order not to let a single one of his enemies escape, he resolved to overthrow the entire Communist Party. Those faithful to him would survive the upheaval. In his own words: "Destroy first, and construction will look after itself." Mao was not worried about the possible destruction of the Party: Mao the Emperor always over-rode Mao the Communist. Nor was he fainthearted about hurting anyone unduly, even those most loyal to him. One of his great heroes, General Tsao Tsao of the first century, had spoken an immortal line which Mao openly admired: "I would rather wrong all people under Heaven; and no one under Heaven must ever wrong me." The general proclaimed this when he discovered that he had murdered an elderly couple by mistake — the old man and woman, whom he had suspected of betraying him, had in fact saved his life.

Mao's vague battle calls threw the population and the majority of Party officials into profound confusion. Few knew what he was driving at, or who exactly were the enemies at this time. My father and mother, like other senior Party people, could see that Mao had decided to punish some officials. But they had no idea who these would be. It could well be themselves. Apprehension and bewilderment overwhelmed them.

Meanwhile, Mao made his single most important organizational move: he set up his own personal chain of command that operated outside the Party apparatus, although — by formally claiming it was under the Politburo and the Central Committee — he was able to pretend it was acting on Party orders.

First, he picked as his deputy Marshal Lin Biao, who had succeeded Peng Dehuai as defense minister in 1959 and had greatly boosted Mao's personality cult in the armed forces. He also set up a new body, the Cultural Revolution Authority, under his former secretary Chen Boda, with his intelligence chief Kang Sheng and Mme. Mao as its *de facto* leaders. It became the core of the leadership of the Cultural Revolution.

Next, Mao moved in on the media, primarily the *People's Daily*, which carried the most authority as it was the official Party newspaper and the population had become accustomed to it being the voice of the regime. He appointed Chen Boda to take over on 31 May, thus securing a channel through which he could speak directly to hundreds of millions of China.

Starting in June 1966, the *People's Daily* showered the country with one strident editorial after another, calling for "establishing Chairman Mao's absolute authority," "sweeping away all the ox devils and snake demons" (class enemies), and exhorting people to follow Mao and join the vast, unprecedented undertaking of a Cultural Revolution.

In my school, teaching stopped completely from the beginning of June, though we had to continue to go there. Loudspeakers blasted out *People's Daily* editorials, and the front page of the newspaper, which we had to study every day, was frequently taken up entirely by a full-page portrait of Mao. There was a daily column of Mao's quotations. I still remember the slogans in bold type, which, through reading in class over and over again, were engraved into the deepest folds of my brain: "Chairman Mao is the red sun in our hearts!" "Mao Zedong Thought is our lifetime!" "We will smash whoever opposes Chairman Mao!" "People all over the world love our Great Leader Chairman Mao!" There were pages of worshiping comments from foreigners, and pictures of European crowds trying to grab Mao's works. Chinese national pride was being mobilized to enhance his cult.

The daily newspaper reading soon gave way to the recitation and memorizing of *The Quotations of Chairman Mao*, which were collected together in a pocket-size book with a red plastic cover, known as "The Little Red Book." Everyone was given a copy and told to cherish it "like our eyes." Every day we chanted passages from it over and over again in unison. I still remember many verbatim...

One day my deputy headmaster, Mr. Kan, a jolly, energetic man, was accused of being a capitalist-roader and of protecting the condemned teachers. Everything he had done in the school over the years was said to be "capitalist," even studying Mao's works — as fewer hours had been devoted to this than to academic studies.

I was equally shocked to see the cheerful secretary of the Communist Youth League in the school, Mr. Shan, being accused of being "anti-Chairman Mao." He was a dashing-looking young man whose attention I had been eager to attract, as he might help me join the Youth League when I reached the minimum age, fifteen.

He had been teaching a course on Marxist philosophy to the sixteen-to eighteen-year-olds, and had given them some essay-writing assignments. He had underlined bits of the essays which he thought were particularly well written. Now these disconnected parts were joined together by his pupils to form an obviously nonsensical passage which the wall posters claimed was anti-Mao. I learned years later that this method of unconnected sentences had started as early as 1955, the year my mother suffered her first detention under the Communists, when some writers had used it to attack their fellow writers...

The deputy headmaster, Mr. Kan, had been devoted to the Party, and felt terribly wronged. One evening he wrote a suicide note and then slashed his throat with a razor. He was rushed to hospital by his wife, who had come home earlier than usual. The work team hushed up his suicide attempt. For a Party member like Mr. Kan to commit suicide was regarded as betrayal. It was seen as a loss of faith in the Party and an attempt to blackmail. Therefore no mercy should be shown to the unfortunate person. But the work team was nervous. They knew very well that they had been inventing victims without the slightest justification. When my mother was told about Mr. Kan she cried...

Chapter 16: "Soar to heaven, and pierce the earth." Mao's Red Guards (June–August 1966) **1**

Under Mao a generation of teenagers grew up expecting to fight class enemies, and the vague calls in the press for a Cultural Revolution had stoked the feeling that a "war" was imminent. Some politically well-attuned youngsters sensed that their idol, Mao, was directly involved, and their indoctrination gave them no alternative but to take his side. By the beginning of June a few activists from a middle school attached to China's most renowned universities, Qinghua in Peking, had got together several times to discuss their strategies for the forthcoming battle and had decided to call themselves "the Red Guards of Chairman Mao." They adopted a quotation by Mao that had appeared in the People's Daily, "Rebellion is justified," as their motto.

These early Red Guards were "high officials' children." Only they could feel sufficiently secure to engage in activities of this kind. In addition, they had been brought up in a political environment, and were more interested in political intrigues than most Chinese. Mme. Mao noticed them, and gave them an audience in July. On 1 August, Mao made the unusual gesture of writing them an open letter to offer his "most warm and fiery support." In the letter he subtly modified his earlier saying to "Rebellion against reactionaries is justified." To the teenage zealots, this was like being addressed by God. After this, Red Guard groups sprang up all over Peking, and then throughout China.

Mao wanted the Red Guards to be his shock troops. He could see that the people were not responding to his repeated calls to attack the capitalist-roaders. The Communist Party had a sizable constituency, and, moreover, the lesson of 1957 was also still fresh in people's minds. Then, too, Mao had called on the population to criticize party officials, but those who had taken up his invitation had ended up being labeled as rightists and had been damned. Most people suspected the same tactic again — "enticing the snake out of its haunt in order to cut off its head."

---

[1] Ibid., pp. 358-378.

If he was to get the population to act, Mao would have to remove authority from the Party and establish absolute loyalty and obedience to himself alone. To achieve this, he needed terror — an intense terror that would block all other considerations and crush all other fears. He saw boys and girls in their teens and early twenties as his ideal agents. They had been brought up in the fanatical personality cult of Mao and the militant doctrine of "class struggle." They were endowed with the qualities of youth — they were rebellious, eager to fight for a "just cause," thirsty for adventure and action. They were also irresponsible, ignorant, and easy to manipulate — prone to violence. Only they could give Mao the immense force that he needed to terrorize the whole society, and to create a chaos that would shake, and then shatter, the foundation of the Party. One slogan summed up the Red Guards' mission: "We vow to launch a bloody war against anyone who dares to resist the Cultural Revolution, who dares to oppose Chairman Mao!"

All policies and orders had hitherto been conveyed through a tightly controlled system which was entirely in the hands of the Party. Mao now discarded this channel and turned directly to the masses of the youth. He did this by combining two quite different methods: vague, high-flown rhetoric carried openly in the press and conspiratorial manipulation and agitation conducted by the Cultural Revolution Authority, particularly his wife. It was they who filled out the real meaning of the rhetoric. Phrases like "rebellion against authority," revolution in education," "destroying the old world so a new one could be born," and "creating the new man" — all of which attracted many in the West in the 1960s — were interpreted as calls for violent action. Mao understood the latent violence of the young, and said that since they were all well fed and had had their lessons stopped, they could easily be stirred up and use their boundless energy to go out and wreak havoc.

To arouse the young to control mob violence, victims were necessary. The most conspicuous targets in any school were the teachers, some of whom had already been victimized by work teams and school authorities in the last few months. Now the rebellious children set upon them. Teachers were better targets than parents, who could only have been attacked in an atomized and isolated manner. Teachers were also more important figures of authority than parents in Chinese culture. In practically every school in China, teachers were abused and beaten, sometimes fatally. Some school-children set up prisons in which teachers were tortured. But this was not enough on its own to generate the kind of terror that Mao wanted. On 18 August, a mammoth rally was held in Tiananmen Square in the center of Peking, with over a million young participants. Lin Biao appeared in public as Mao's deputy and spokesman for the first time. He made a speech calling on the Red Guards to charge out of their schools and "smash up the four olds" — defined as "old ideas, old culture, old customs, and old habits.

Following this obscure call, Red Guards all over China took to the streets, giving full vent to their vandalism, ignorance, and fanaticism. They raided people's houses, smashed their antiques, tore up paintings and works of calligraphy. Bonfires were lit to consume books. Very soon nearly all treasures in private collections were destroyed. Many writers and artists committed suicide after being cruelly beaten and humiliated, and being forced to witness their work being burned to ashes. Museums were raided, palaces, temples, ancient tombs, statues, pagodas, city walls — anything "old" was pillaged. The few things that survived, such as the Forbidden City, did so only because Premier Zhou Enlai sent the army to guard them, and issued specific orders that they should be protected. The Red Guards only pressed on when they were encouraged.

Mao hailed the Red Guards' actions as "very good indeed!" and ordered the nation to support them.

He encouraged the Red Guards to pick on a wider range of victims in order to increase the terror. Prominent writers, artists, scholars, and most other top professionals, who had been privileged under the Communist regime, were now categorically condemned as "reactionary bourgeois authorities." With the help of some of these people's colleagues who hated them for various reasons, ranging from fanaticism to envy, the Red Guards began to abuse them. Then there were the old "class enemies": former landlords and capitalists, people with Kuomintang connections, those condemned in previous political campaigns like the "rightists" — and their children...

A wave of beating and torture swept the country, mainly during house raids. Almost invariably, the families would be ordered to kneel on the floor and kowtow to the Red Guards; they were beaten with the brass buckles of the Red Guards' leather belts, they were kicked around, and one side of their head was shaved, a humiliating style called the "yin and yang head," because it resembled the classic Chinese symbol of a dark side (yin) and a light side (yang). Most of their possessions were either smashed or taken away.

It was worst in Peking, where the Cultural Revolution Authority was on hand to incite the young people. In the city center theaters and cinemas were turned into torture chambers. Victims were dragged in from all over Peking. Pedestrians avoided the spots because the streets around echoed with the screams of the victims.

The earliest Red Guards groups were made up of high officials' children. Soon, when more people from other backgrounds joined, some of the high officials' children managed to keep their own special groups, like the "Pickets." Mao and his camarilla took a number of steps calculated to increase their sense of power. At the second mass Red Guard rally, Lin Biao wore their armband, to signify that he was one of them. Mme. Mao made them the guards of honor in front of the Gate of Heavenly Peace in Tiananmen Square on National Day, 1 October. As a result, some them developed an outrageous "theory of the bloodline," summed up in the words of a song: "The son of a hero father is always a great man; a reactionary father produces nothing but a bastard!" Armed with this "theory," some high officials' children tyrannized and even tortured children from "undesirable" backgrounds.

Mao let all this happen in order to generate the terror and chaos he wanted. He was not scrupulous about either who was hit or who were the agents of violence. These early victims were not his real targets, and Mao did not particularly like or trust his young Red Guards. He was simply using them...

Producing a yin-and-yang haircut for "bourgeois elements" (anti-Maoists), China 1966

But Mao's insidious encouragement of atrocities was undeniable. On 18 August, at the first of the eight gigantic rallies which altogether were attended by thirteen million people, he asked a female Red Guard what her name was. When she answered "Bin-bin," which means "gentle," he said disapprovingly, "Be violent" (yao-wu-ma). Mao rarely spoke in public, and this remark, well publicized, was naturally followed like the gospel. At the third mammoth rally, on 15 September, when the Red Guards' atrocities were reaching their zenith, Mao's recognized spokesman, Lin Biao, announced, with Mao standing next to him: "Red Guard fighters: The direction of your battles has always been correct. You have soundly, heartily battered the capitalist-roaders, the reactionary bourgeois authorities, the bloodsuckers and parasites. You have done the right thing! And you have done marvelously!" At that, hysterical cheers, deafening screams of "Long live Chairman Mao," uncontrollable tears, and howled pledges of loyalty took possession of the crowds filling the enormous Tiananmen Square. Mao waved paternally, generating more frenzy...

When Lin Biao called for everything that represented old culture to be destroyed, some pupils in my school started to smash things up. Being more than 2,000 years old, the school had lots of antiques and was therefore a prime site for action. The school gateway had an old tiled roof with carved eaves. These were hammered to pieces. The same happened to the sweeping blue-glazed roof of the big temple which had been used as a Ping-Pong hall. The pair of giant bronze incense burners in front of the temple were toppled, and some boys urinated into them. In the back garden, pupils with big hammers and iron rods went along the sandstone bridges casually breaking the little statues. On one side of the sports field was a pair of towering rectangular tablets made of red sandstone, each twenty feet high. Some lines about Confucius were carved on them in beautiful calligraphy. A huge rope was tied around them, and two gangs pulled. It took them a couple of days, as the foundations were deep. They had to get some workers from outside to dig a hole around the tablets. When the monuments finally crashed down amid cheers, they lifted part of the path that ran behind them.

All the things I loved were disappearing. The saddest thing of all for me was the ransacking of the library: the golden tiled roof, the delicately sculpted windows, the blue painted chairs...Bookshelves were turned upside down, and some pupils tore books to pieces just for the hell of it. Afterward, X-shaped white paper strips with black characters were stuck on what was left of the doors and windows to signal that the building was sealed.

Books were major targets of Mao's order to destroy. Because they had not been written within the last few months, and therefore did not quote Mao on every page, some Red Guards declared that they were all "poisonous weeds." With the exception of Marxist classics and the works of Stalin, Mao, and the late Lu Xun, whose name Mme. Mao was using for her personal vendettas, books were burning all across China. The country lost most of its written heritage. Many of the books which survived later went into people's stoves as fuel...

By then "denunciation meetings" were becoming a major feature of the Cultural Revolution. They involved a hysterical crowd and were seldom without physical brutality. Peking University had taken the lead, under the personal supervision of Mao. At its first denunciation meeting, on 18 June, over sixty professors and heads of departments including the chancellor, were beaten, kicked, and forced to kneel for hours. Dunce caps with humiliating slogans were forced onto their heads. Ink was poured over their faces to make them black, the color of evil, and slogans were pasted all over their bodies. Two students gripped the arms of each victim, twisting them around behind his back and pushing them up with such ferocity as almost to dislocate them. This posture was called the "jet plane," and soon became a feature of most denunciation meetings all over the country.

I was once called by the Red Guards in my form to attend such a meeting. Horror made me feel very chilly in the hot summer afternoon when I saw a dozen or so teachers standing on the platform on the sports ground, with their heads bent and their arms twisted into the "jet plane" position. Then, some were kicked on the back of their knees and forced to kneel, while others, including my English-language teacher, an elderly man with the fine manner of a classical gentleman, were forced to stand on long, narrow benches. He found it hard to keep his balance, and swayed and fell, cutting his forehead on the sharp corner of a bench. A Red Guard standing next to him instinctively stooped and extended his hands to help, but immediately straightened up and assumed an exaggeratedly harsh posture, with his fists clenched, yelling: "Get back onto the bench!" He did not want to be seen as soft on a "class enemy." Blood trickled down the teacher's forehead and coagulated on the side of his face.

He like other teachers, was accused of all sorts of outlandish crimes; but they were really there because they were graded, and therefore the best, or because some pupils had grudges against them...

Chapter 19: "*Where there is a will to condemn, there is evidence.*" My parents tormented (December 1966–1967)1

A capitalist-roader was supposed to be a powerful official who was pursuing capitalist policies. But in reality no official had any choice about which policies they pursued. The orders of Mao and those of his opponents were all presented as coming from the Party, and the officials had to obey all of them — even though in doing so they were obliged to carry out many zigzags and even U-turns. If they really disliked a particular order, the most they could do was engage in passive resistance, which they had to try hard to disguise. It was therefore impossible to determine whether officials were capitalist-roaders or not on the basis of their work.

---

[1] Ibid., pp. 415-425.

Many officials had their own views, but the Party rule was that they must not reveal them to the public. Nor did they dare to. So whatever the officials' sympathies were, they were unknown to the general public.

But ordinary people were the very force Mao now ordered to attack capitalist-roaders — without, of course, the benefit of either information or the right to exercise any independent judgment. So what happened was that officials came under attack as capitalist-roaders because of the positions they held. Seniority alone was not the criterion. The decisive factor was whether a person was the leader of a relatively self-contained unit or not. The whole population was organized into units, and the people who represented power to ordinary people were their immediate bosses — unit leaders. In designating these people for attack, Mao was tapping into the most obvious pool of resentment, in the same way that he had incited pupils against teachers. Unit leaders were also the link in the chain of the Communist power structure which Mao wanted to get rid of.

It was because they were leaders of departments that both my parents were denounced as capitalist-roaders. "Where there is a will to condemn, there is evidence," as the Chinese saying has it. On this basis, all unit leaders across China, big and small, were summarily denounced by people under them as capitalist-roaders for implementing policies that were alleged to be "capitalist" and "anti-Chairman Mao." These included allowing free markets in the countryside, advocating better professional skills for workers, permitting relative literary and artistic freedom, and encouraging competitiveness in sports — now termed "bourgeois cups-and-medals mania." Until now most officials had had no idea that Mao had disliked these policies — after all, the directives had all come from the Party, which was led by him. Now they were told, out of the blue, that all these policies had come from the "bourgeois headquarters" within the Party...

In the meantime, the Rebels in my father's department stepped up their assaults on him. Being one of the most important in the provincial government, the department had more than its share of opportunists. Formerly obedient instruments of the old Party system, many now became fiercely militant Rebels, led by Mrs. Shau under the banner of 26 August.

One day, a group of them barged into our apartment and marched into my father's study. They looked at the bookshelves, and declared them a real "diehard" because he still had his "reactionary books." Earlier, in the wake of the book burning by the teenage Red Guards, many people had set fire to their collections. But not my father. Now he made a faint attempt to protect his books by pointing at the sets of Marxist hardbacks. "Don't try to fool us Red Guards!" yelled Mrs. Shau. "You have plenty of 'poisonous weeds'!" She picked up some Chinese classics printed on flimsy rice paper.

"What do you mean, 'us Red Guards'?" my father retorted. "You are old enough to be their mother — and you ought to have more sense, too."

Mrs. Shau slapped my father hard. The crowd barked at him indignantly, although a few tried to hide their giggles. Then they pulled out his books and threw them into huge jute sacks they had brought with them. When all the bags were full, they carried them downstairs, telling my father they were going to burn them on the grounds of the department the next day after a denunciation meeting against him. They ordered him to watch the bonfire "to be taught a lesson." In the meantime, they said, he must burn the rest of his collection.

When I came home that afternoon, I found my father in the kitchen. He had lit a fire in the big cement sink and was hurling his books into the fire.

This was the first time in my life that I had seen him weep.

Book burning during the Cultural Revolution. 'Poisonous weed' into the fire!

3. The Chinese Cultural Revolution from Up Close: The testimony of a Soviet eyewitness[1]

Introduction by G. Schnehen

A. Shelokhevtsev, a Soviet sinologist, came to the People's Republic of China in early 1966. He had spent almost a year trying to get an entry visa for China, and one day he was successful.

After that he spent some months in Beijing studying at a pedagogical insti-tute. He lived in a students' dormitory and was one of the few foreign students to be allowed to study in China at the time. He was assigned a Chinese tutor by the name of Ma to lead him through his studies and also to keep a watchful eye on him. In his book (which meanwhile was removed from a library of a German state parliament), which is full of firsthand accounts and experiences of what went on during the Cultural Revolution, he also mentions the death of the famous Chinese novelist, playwright and poet, Lao She. At the height of the Cultural Revolution Lao's apartment was stormed by Mao's Red Guards and ransacked. They smashed everything judged "bourgeois" and "poisonous weed" to pieces, and in the end forced him to burn his own books on the floor of his living room of his living room which he stubbornly refused to do. Lao then myste-riously disappeared. In a leaflet issued by the local Red Guards some days later, they proudly described the "struggle session" they had with him and his wife. By chance, Shelokhevtsev got hold of it and read it. His conclusion: Lao She was either murdered by the Red Guards or committed suicide due to his humiliation.

In October 2014, I sent his report about Lao She's fate to a German Maoist organization, MLPD. Here is an excerpt of the answer I received from them, which was also publicized in their journal Red Flag.

> Undoubtedly, Shelokhevtsev's "testimony" you let us have was moti-vated by his intention to denigrate the Chinese Cultural Revolution. In 1965, Shelokhevtsev was sent to Beijing by the Communist Party of the Soviet Union as a sinologist...He was anything but a "neutral observer" and "eyewitness".[2]

Obviously, they had not even read the testimony. Shelokhevtsev was alleg-edly "sent to China by the Communist Party of the Soviet Union" — something they freely invented which was reason enough for them to suspect that he had been sent to China as a spy in order to denigrate the Great Proletarian Cultural Revolution as they call Mao's mass purges. So he can't be taken seriously.

---

[1] *Chinesische Kulturrevolution aus der Nähe. Augenzeugenbericht eines sowjetischen Beobachters*, A. Schelo-chowzew, Stuttgart/Germany 1969

[2] https://www.rf-news.de/rote-fahne/2014/die-grose-proletarische-kulturrevolution-in-china-und-ihre-bewertung-2013-ein-briefwechsel.

Here are some excerpts describing what Shelokhevtsev saw during his stay in Mao's China in 1966, the first year of the Cultural Revolution:

On the Eve of the Catastrophe

He who spends his time studying the Chinese language and its characters and is also familiar with the culture, the history, the economy and, more generally, with the everyday life of this huge subcontinent, is usually called a sinologist. All sinologists thrive to come to China one day, but it has not been so easy recently, especially during the last eight years. Having tried to get hold of a visa for almost a year, I was successful in the end and boarded the international express train Moscow–Beijing on 2 February, 1966. Smoothly, the train set into motion leaving the frozen figures of the relatives behind...[1]

The bus was packed with Red Guards. I got on the bus and was immediately offered a seat. I refused at first, but then someone lifted me on to a seat. So apparently, these people were used to violence.

"Where have you been?" I asked my neighbor after I had taken a little breather.

"On a revolutionary mission. Every day we go to Wangfuching to establish the revolutionary order over there. Today it was our group's turn."

"And this bus — who does it belong to?"

"We have confiscated it from an institution for the purpose of the Revolution," the Red Guard replied.

"But don't you know that your laws do not allow Chinese people to talk to foreigners?"

"Maybe it was like that up to the Cultural Revolution, but for us Red Guards this is meaningless, and we also need to propagate the Revolution!"

Since early in the morning, he told me, they had been touring the central districts of the city to confiscate "superfluous" furniture, luxuries, and valuables.

"What are you doing with the stuff? Do you dispose of it?"

"No," he said, "we take it to the commission shops and then sell the furniture — the valuables, however, are brought to the authorities..."

When we had passed through Hsintsiekou, a lively shopping district, the bus slowed down a little. Here not just the sidewalks, but also the street itself was packed with confiscated furniture, beds, cupboards, deckchairs, suitcases, and other objects...An incredible collection of old stuff. A

---

[1] A. Schelochowzew, ibid., p. 9.

small furniture shop to which the Red Guards had brought the confiscated objects, had filled the whole street with them. Astonishingly, there were many people who were buying the furniture which had just been stolen from other people.

"The great epoch of Mao Zedong reigns with us, and we all are now making revolution," my Red Guard neighbor amiably explained to me.

"We do not make much fuss with all the riffraff now," he declared.

"Our main enemies are the degenerates within the Communist Party," a girl standing next to him added.

"They've forgotten that we all are obliged to our sun — Chairman Mao. We confiscate their luxury items, thus helping them to purify their consciousness."

"But who buys the stuff?" I couldn't help asking.

"Revolutionary comrades," my neighbor told me without much thinking.

"Objects are not so important, the consciousness is important, the ideas," the girl added.

"If someone follows Mao's ideas, if he really adopts them sincerely, if he opens all his soul to them, then things are not important for him, then he is the master of things. But the misfits in the Party are alien to the ideas of our Chairman!"

"But how do you identify Chairman Mao's enemies?" I asked, "and how can you be so sure that nobody escapes?"

"We are many. The pupils march forward, the little leaders of the Revolution. They know everything what's going on in their neighborhoods. That's why we can always be absolutely sure."[1]

The Bloodbath[2]

In the evening, a deafening roar again sounded from the stadium of the university. A meeting of Red Guards who had just returned from the city was dedicated to "evaluating the results of the day as well as to the exchange of revolutionary experience." Several thousand had gathered there. When I stepped out of my canteen after dinner, it was empty all around. Next to the entrance of the residential building for lecturers with families two women, who were standing there, shouted something to me. I went to them.

"Look at what is going on here! How terrible! Two hours ago they left. Come over here, look at that!"

"Who is 'they'?"

---

[1] Ibid., pp. 206f.
[2] Ibid, p. 207ff

"The Red Guards!"

They led me to a staircase unlit for reasons of economy. It was a four-storey brick house, elegant by Beijing standards. There was not only gas in it, one had to prepare the food also on stoves heated by coal briquettes.

"Who lives here?" I asked in front of the entrance to the apartment they invited me to enter.

"The apartment owner was a member of the Party office of the faculty. He was taken away long ago."

This used to be a modest two-room apartment. Everything in it was turned from bottom to top, the beds overturned, the chest and the cupboard as well; linen and clothes lay untidily around, and on the ground of the other one a pile of ashes smoked on the cement floor.

The women told me how it started in the first place. The Red Guards had come to them around midday. They were twelve people altogether. Two "revolutionary" lecturers had joined them as eyewitnesses. Among the Red Guards nobody had studied at the faculty where the apartment owner used to lecture. They started confiscating the furniture. They pulled the pieces apart, dragged them to the yard and then drove them away in their trucks. After that they started their "re-education program".

"Where are the portraits of Chairman Mao? Why are there no portraits of him?" they asked the underage son of the landlord. Then they turned to his sister and his mother, slapping them in the face. The Red Guards tore down the pictures from the wall — reproductions, photographs — and stepped on them with their feet. Debris from the frames lay on the floor, pictures torn to shreds.

"And where are Mao Zedong's works?" they shouted. Fortunately, a small volume of selected works was found. They put them aside, the remaining books, however, were declared "bad ones." The apartment owners were forced to pile up the domestic library on the floor to burn it. I saw the ashes of the books on the concrete floor in the second room. The Red Guards then turned to the dishes and clothes, smashing bowls and plates.

"A bowl with dragon patterns on it is a feudalistic bowl!"Bang, on the floor!

"A bowl with small flowers and roses is a bourgeois, petty bourgeois bowl!" Bang, on the floor.

"Where is Mao Zedong's bust?" the Red Guards asked, stepping with their feet on porcelain, statuettes of fishermen, of a peasant girl and of poets that had been on one of the shelves of the professor. The aquarium with the goldfish was thrown out of the window: a relic of feudalism! The girls tore jackets and pants of European cut into pieces and after that the skirts of the housewife. "Foreign slaves and traitors!" they shouted. Meanwhile the boys went to the balcony and started to smash the pots with the cacti:

"Needless luxuries!"

On the balcony they discovered the cat, which had crawled into a corner:

"Look at this bourgeois!" shouted one of the Red Guards, grabbed the cat at the tail and smashed its head against the wall. He wanted to throw it into the yard, but the girls protested. "Why not put the carrion into the storeroom and lock it up, so that the bourgeois riffraff may enjoy the smell."

The whole family was begging for mercy, but the Red Guards were adamant and hung a lock in front of the storeroom, so that they couldn't get rid of the stench of the corpse. At this point the eyewitnesses came in, the two lectures, saying:

"That's not necessary," they started telling them. "We're gonna take the second room away from them to let a revolutionary family from the activists move in. If the dead cat stays in the room, the new family will also have to smell the stench."

This argument worked. So they threw the cat out of the window.

"Did they steal anything from you?" I asked the landlady.

"Yes, a few things: my husband's fountain pen, his and my wristwatch, my glasses, notepads, paper and notebooks...This is not so important but they stole his manuscripts and his letters. They said they were going to look into our crimes soon..."

On the floor I noticed broken records.

"We love Russian songs," the woman said sadly. "We've had these records for quite a long time. They smashed them on my son's head. They became very angry when they saw our Soviet records. Then they searched for Soviet newspapers and journals, but we didn't have any. Already in 1961 my husband had secretly burned them."

She told me how the Red Guards, after having dealt with the objects, then proceeded to deal with the people. At first they demanded that they should break away from the arrested head of the family. But she and her son refused to write such a slander. They also refused to denounce his "rotten ideas" and did not want to show the Red Guards in writing their "gratitude" for the liberation from the shackles of the old customs and for the transition to a new life. They spent almost an hour to talk them into it. Then they put all of them with their backs to the wall and asked them:

"Are we fighting well against the old customs? Are we spreading Mao Zedong's ideas well?"

Having received no answers, they again started to slap them in the face and pushed their necks to the wall.

"We've endured it for a long time and thought they would leave for a meeting," the boy said to me.

"But after having made up their minds, they decided to leave five people here to continue 'fighting' with us. We gave in...I told them: 'You're very good at spreading Mao Zedong's ideas! You're fighting well against the bourgeoisie!' Then they stopped beating us and left for the meeting. They threatened to come back but did not say exactly when. That's why we don't clean up. Let everything lie around!"

"But why did you call me of all people after all what happened?" I asked in amazement.

"Oh, we don't care about anything now," she said in despair. "We only wanted you to know what is happening here."...[1]

When I had listened to their lofty 'revolutionary' phrases, I simply asked them:

"Tell me, why is the Revolution necessary? What is its aim?"

The Red Guards were unable to answer as their revolution is not for the individual and not for the Chinese people either. Their revolution lacks purpose and meaning. They answered:

"The Revolution is necessary so that the people and the country stay revolutionary."

What does this tautology mean? Principally, the 'Revolution' is necessary to enable China to remain pro-Mao, overexcited, aroused, and destitute. Only in such chaos can a great people like China be held at the leash of the personality cult, which has been discredited for a long time.

And then there is another stimulus for national chauvinism: China has Mao Zedong! The greatest, the wisest, the most revolutionary, the sun-like...Is there anywhere in the world a similar leader? Isn't he himself the object of national pride, a pretext for arrogance and vanity? Mao Zedong was capable of transferring the hurt national feelings of the Chinese, which had been downtrodden over centuries of humiliation and suppression to himself, and he could change them into an instrument for the glorification of his own person...[2]

---

[1] Ibid.
[2] Ibid., p. 258.

The Death of Lao She[1]

One of the combat divisions of the Red Guards had just combed through one of the districts of the capital, looking into every nook and cranny of every house. So they also came across Lao She's house which they entered. In the apartment of the old writer they sensed "indignation and revolutionary anger." The writer's lifestyle seemed to be a mixture between "feudalism and capitalism." In his apartment the walls were decorated with pictures of Chinese paintings, and in the midst of this "feudalistic" rubbish no room at all was left for a portrait of Mao Zedong. In his house a valuable collection of old Chinese porcelain was exhibited, but "not even one bowl with a red flag on it!." In the end, the house was filled with "poisonous literature," as they called the writer's library. Snorting with bitterness, the leaflet enumerated the old Chinese editions, mentioned an "enormous quantity" of literature "in foreign languages" — proving that Lao She had been a "foreign slave," and, to top it all: in his library were also found poisonous books in Russian language!

Lao She — great Chinese patriot, murdered by Mao's Red Guards

The writer had treated the intruders with disrespect, reason enough for them to "struggle with him in the spirit of the Cultural Revolution." First the Red Guards forced him to stand up and gave him some warnings. The young boys then lectured him about the greatness of Mao Zedong "Thought," in an attempt to tear him away from his "counter-revolutionary past." Now he should destroy all objects being of a feudalistic, bourgeois, or foreign culture in his house. But, alas, the writer had answered with "counter-revolutionary silence." Then the Red Guard held a conference, noticing that he had exposed himself and that it was their revolutionary duty "to help him to revolutionize himself." They then resorted to decisive

---

[1] Ibid., pp. 276ff, the author refers to a Red Guard leaflet describing their "struggle session" with the famous Chinese writer and playwright Lao She in his apartment. In his satiric novel 'Cat City' he thoroughly exposes Great-Han-Chauvinism and makes fun of it. The book was banned by Mao Zedong's cultural officials.

action. In front of the helpless apartment owners, they started to tear the collection of pictures to shreds, smashed the porcelain of which there was so much left that the whole floor was covered with a layer of broken glass.

The ceremony also required "fighting with words," and during a pause for breath, the looters addressed their victims with an admonishing speech. Politely and circumstantial, but not without pride, in their leaflet the Red Guards underlined having explained to the writer that the rotten bourgeois culture he used to live in was powerless before the splendor of Mao Zedong's ideas and would be turned to dust just like the stupid pots."

Lao She could not stand the shameless hypocrisy and started to speak. What he literally said, the Red Guards have not disclosed to the public. According to them, he had "boasted of his services to the Chinese culture" and had called them barbarians in a "demagogic" way. He had ended his speech by saying that they did not know what they were doing, but one day, when having grown up, they would regret it. His final remark was seen as a direct insult to Mao Zedong's ideas and had showed his reluctance to conscientiously learn "revolutionary lessons." To help him, the Red Guards said, the best way to understand the "Cultural Revolution" would be to honestly take part in it himself. To make a start, they suggested to him to burn his books on the floor right in front of them. But Lao She did not move an inch. "In view of his age and his physical condition" they offered to help collect the books and to put them on a pile, but he did not make a move... Then the Red Guards grabbed him under the arms to make him burn his books. The leaflet denied any use of force or insult. On the contrary: the Red Guards swore they had been models of polite and correct behavior.

Then the unforeseen happened: "In a fit of counter-revolutionary malice" his wife threw herself on the Red Guards, scratching and biting them, and like a "mad dog," she did not allow them "to help him burn his books." To preserve the valuable life and the health of the "revolutionary comrades," they were obliged to use force: quickly, they bounded his wife with ropes but Lao She, irrespective of her "counter-revolutionary behavior," tried to defend her, therefore finally exposing himself as an enemy of the "Cultural Revolution." An apotheosis of hostility was his following action: "Blinded by his class hatred," the old writer took his life.

"Through his mean black suicide he thought he could damage our revolutionary cause, but he only succeeded in finally exposing himself as a feudalistic and bourgeois character and as a class enemy as well, a spreader of poison and as a foreign slave." ...

In the last passages of the leaflet they expressed their conviction that the victory of the "Cultural Revolution" would be quick and indispensable in spite of the many intrigues of all its enemies who, in their baseness, would not even stop at provoking suicide. I could not believe at first that behind this shameless demagogy of lofty phrases there was the gruesome truth of a reckoning, but, since then, Lao She has kept silent, which means that he probably is no longer with us...

The fate of Tien Han[1]

Under the conditions of the "Cultural Revolution" with its terror, acts of violence, bitter power struggles at the top and at the anarchistic resistance from the bottom, the cultural life of the People's Republic of China lost all meaning. Literary journals and new books were no longer published. The available paper was used to produce many millions of the program, the repertoire of theaters was reduced to a couple of "revolutionary" plays, which, due to Jian Qing's (Mao's wife — GS) participation in their creation, remained untouched. The Chinese cinematography began to release promotional movies praising Mao Zedong, his encounters with the Red Guards, on the Chinese-Albanian friendship or showing films about the A-bomb.

Tien Han wrote the text for China's national anthem, yet he was persecuted by Mao's Red Guards and called a "bourgeois writer."

Gradually, the central press, which now was completely under the control of Mao Zedong's followers, started to publicize Red Guard material about the convicted party officials formerly in charge of Chinese culture. Thus, the charges leveled against Tien Han, Hsia Yen, Ou-yang Shan, Sha Ting, Cha Shu-li, Hua Tsuen-wu and many others were made public.

The sentences passed were in standard manner. The entire activity of the writers was denied from beginning to end, and not a single good word

---

[1] Ibid., pp. 282-288.

was said about them. The charges were standardized as well: anti-Party, anti-socialist activity, bourgeois ideology, revisionism, etc. Behind it there is a single real cause: various types of resistance against the introduction of the personality cult of Mao Zedong.

The present state of Chinese cultural life knows no precedent. Creative activity has become impossible. The own traditions are condemned, and the progressive literature of the thirties as well and also all those things created after the liberation during the time of the People's Republic of China. Mao Zedong's personality cult has completely crushed all areas of artistic activity. The country has become a cultural desert. The damage done to the people and their culture is immeasurable. Hunting down cultural officials — that's what the "Cultural Revolution" is about.

On 8 December, 1966, when I was already back in Moscow, the Beijing radio station, captured by units of the Red Guards, announced some arrests made by them. According to this message, Red Guards from Beijing arrested a group of well-respected officials of the PR of China on 4 December. Among the arrested was also Peng Chen. On 6 December, one of the leading newspapers, the Kuangming-yipao, devoted an entire page to the condemnation of Tien Han. From these materials we can learn why he had been subjected to public humiliation, persecution and finally incarceration. His situation became worse, his life was in danger, and, moreover, the silence about his situation gave his prosecutors a free hand -reason enough to talk about him, all the more so because his pursuers have leaked some valuable information...

Tien Han was China's most popular dramatist, poet and scriptwriter after the "May 4th Movement." He was born on 12 March 1898 in a peasant family in the village of Tienshiatsun east of Changsha in Hunan province... In 1932 he became a member of the Communist Party of China...In late 1935, he was arrested by the reactionary Kuomintang regime. After his release from prison in Nanking in 1937, he was put under police supervision. The outbreak of the national liberation war against Japan gave him freedom. Without hesitation Tien Han joined the rows of the patriotic theater movement. Under the leadership of the Party and also joined by Chou En-lai he directed the Shanghai Theater Group "Save the Homeland" and also the theater troupe of Wuhan "Resistance against the Enemy." During the guest performances in Nanking, Changcha, Chunking, Kueiling, and in other cities these performances led to an upswing of the patriotic movement in Chinese theater. Therein lies is greatest merit...After the proclamation of the People's Republic of China in 1949, Tien Han was elected into the All-China Political Consultative Council and became a delegate to the National People's Congress in the first and second legislative period. At present (1966 — Ed.). he is Deputy Chairman of the All-China Association of Literature and Artists and also Chairman of the Union of Chinese Theater Professionals.

The front page of the Kuangming-jipao newspaper dated December 6 is titled with a saying of Mao Zedong:

"All the erroneous ideas, all the poisonous herbs, all monsters and demons must be subjected to discussion. Under no circumstances, are they allowed to develop freely."

The ominous meaning of this saying reveals the fate of Tien Han completely. In a message to the editor of the Kuangming-jipao compiled by the group Mao Zedong, the veteran of the Chinese culture was officially confronted with the following allegations:

"On the eve of the Liberation, this chameleon has wormed his way into the Party. For more than ten years, Tien Han has usurped the leading position in China's theatrical life. Hiding behind a "red banner," he has wholeheartedly supported the counter-revolutionary, revisionist line of the leading Department for Propaganda and Agitation at the Central Committee of the Communist Party of China and of the former Ministry of Culture of the People's Republic of China, he has come out against the Red Flag and has fought furiously against the Party, against socialism, and Mao Zedong Thought...After the start of the Cultural Revolution he, together with a bunch of counter-revolutionary and revisionist elements, openly opposed the great instructions of Chairman Mao on the Cultural Revolution on the basis of a common agreement..."

The Maoists disclosed not a few of Tien Han's biting remarks directed against them:

"Tien Han has insulted Mao Zedong Thought for quite some time; he has condemned the movement for a study close to life of the works of Chairman Mao and their application, the movement for the propaganda and the implementation of Mao Zedong's ideas, and has said that 'one could not live a decent life based on his thoughts'. He has slandered Mao Zedong's ideas, as if they were no universal truths being correct and applicable everywhere, even beyond the four seas. In 1958 he said that our Party 'is still very young, is lacking the necessary experience, and that we can only move forward very slowly and carefully based on the Marxist principles.' Everywhere he had his dirty hands in it. He eagerly tried to erase the shine of Mao Zedong's ideas. All serious anti-Party statements were invariably pinpointed against Mao Zedong Thought..."

The Kuangming-jipao used information from wall newspapers which had been posted at the Association of Chinese Theatrical Producers. Now Tien Han has been arrested by Red Guards. His life is in danger...

But even from the demagogic and evil interpretations by the Red Guards, everybody could see that Maoist "revolutionization" met with the resistance of the Chinese intelligentsia. The mass terror exercised by the Red Guards in 1966 was caused by this resistance, as there was no other way than this to implement Mao Zedong's directives.

Although Tien Han was arrested in December, they had started to mock him much earlier. In September the Red Guards openly demanded to do away with the former national anthem, which had been composed and written by Tien Han, the "Black Bandit" and to replace it with "The East is Glowing...," a song on Mao Zedong. In the central streets one could read appeals to the "revolutionary comrades" to actively participate in the struggle against the condemned literary and artistic officials to which Tien also belonged.

On Saturday and Sunday they let him go together with the other condemned lecturers from the Pedagogical College. But now they have posted an appeal in the streets to "visit him at any time during the night or the day" at his home, in order to "fight with him where he lived." The organizers of the reckoning were afraid of their victims getting even a one-minute rest...

In September, every time when I visited the students at the Beijing Institute for Languages, I had to walk past the desecrated grave of the great Chinese artist Chi Pai-shi. The Red Guards no longer met him among the living, so they expressed their disrespect towards him this way. This abomination became widely known because many foreigners used to live there.

Similar acts of vandalism were numerous. At the Beijing conservatories the Red Guards threw pianos out of the windows and destroyed "foreign musical instruments." They forced the pianists to declare in writing that they wouldn't touch any keys anymore, and if they refused, their fingers were broken. (It reminds one of what the Chilean fascists did to Victor Jara, the Chilean freedom singer, who was put in a concentration camp by Augusto Pinochet's henchmen after the bloody fascist coup of 9/11 in 1973, where he then started to sing his freedom songs. Shortly afterwards, his hands were broken. Some days later he was shot. Mao Zedong, by the way, was a supporter of General Pinochet — Ed.). This happened to Liu Shi-kun, the winner of the Tchaikovsky competition in Moscow. By pretending to fight the old customs, the Red Guards in reality revived the practice of medieval intolerance and cruelty against dissenters.

Note:

Tien Han was arrested in 1966 during the Cultural Revolution by Kang Sheng, Mao's long-time loyal executioner. He was put into one of Mao's infamous prisons where he died on December 10, 1968.

4. Peter Vladimirov on Mao's first "Cultural Revolution" in 1943–1944, also called the chengfeng

The Cultural Revolution did not come as a bolt out of the blue. There were precursors: one of them was the so-called chengfeng campaign Mao had launched in the special area of the Communist Party of China as early as 1943 — the second of his infamous purges. The first was launched a year earlier allegedly to "improve styles of writing".

During *cheng feng* party members were asked to study 22 carefully selected documents Mao thought vital to become a good and loyal party soldier. The campaign lasted several months. Countless self-criticism assemblies were held, and those party members who were critical of Mao Zedong's policies or his life-style were either purged from the party or re-accepted after having voiced extensive and humiliating public self-criticisms.

Even the libraries in the Yenan special area were purged: from dissident literature so that only the selected material written by Mao Zedong and his ghost writers remained there for ordinary party members to study.

Peter Vladimirov, a Soviet TASS correspondent and a military man as well, was sent to the area by the Communist International to follow the developments in the special area where the Chinese Communist Party headed by Mao Zedong had retreated after the Long March.

Commenting on Mao, his *cheng feng* campaign and his relationship to culture and the arts in general, he wrote the following in his diary on March 17, 1944:

The idea that Mao Zedong is one of the continuers of the Marxist-Leninist philosophy is being propagated here in every way possible. His name is ever more frequently being ranked with the classics of scientific communism.

The invalidity of such claims can be proved without going into the essence of Mao Zedong's theoretical investigations.

Marx, Engels, and Lenin were men of great culture, who possessed enormous knowledge virtually in all branches of the humanities and natural sciences. They knew many ancient and modern languages and read the work of geniuses of mankind in the original. They studied the development of society in all its stages, being outstanding scholars in such fields of learning as history, philosophy, sociology, theoretical economics, and aesthetics.

Lenin pointed out: "But it would mean falling into a grave error for you to try to draw conclusions that one can become a Communist without assimilating the wealth of knowledge amassed by mankind. It would be mistaken to think it sufficient to learn communist slogans and the conclusions of communist science, without acquiring that sum of knowledge of which communism itself is a result."

How can one be a continuer of what one does not know properly? Up to now most of the works of Marx, Engels, and Lenin have not been translated into Chinese. Mao Zedong did not find it necessary to learn any European language.

In this connection the following words of Lenin assume a special meaning:

"Marxism is the system of Marx's views and teachings. Marx was the genius who continued and consummated the three main ideological currents of the 19th century, as represented by the most advanced countries of mankind: classical German philosophy, classical English political economy, and French socialism..."[1]

On March, 27, 1944, he made an entry about Mao's relationship to culture and intellectuals, who later, during the Cultural Revolution, would become his main target:

The intellectuals were hardest hit by cheng-feng. A special zeal was shown to purify them "spiritually." Most, even really gifted people, were charged to learn from semi-literate agitators. Strong recommendations were made for physical re-education measures to develop a correct class consciousness in them. This kind of indoctrination was partly due to the scornful attitude to scientific knowledge and education in general. The value of the intellectuals was proclaimed only in words. In practice they were subjected to a most severe "spiritual purification." As an educational measure, they were forced to do manual work, often useless and insulting (like the obligatory sock-knitting). The scarce cadre of party intellectuals were reduced to the role of technical executors like clerks, messengers, unskilled workers, officer's attendants, etc.

Mao Zedong is hewing out the forest of millennial trees of one of the greatest national cultures of the world. His sermons on proletarian culture are a distortion of Marxist principles. Here culture is far from being enriched with revolutionary élan. The ancient opera loved by Mao Zedong has been flourishing in Yenan for ten years now, while not a single good novel has been produced here, nor a collection of short stories, nor songs of the kind of our famous songs of the Civil War period.

In Yenan they do not even speak of a culture lofty, multiform, and morally pure: They won't understand and won't take it seriously. Although it was Mao Zedong who started cheng-feng from the "analysis of proletarian art."

Hostility to living thought clearly shows in the Chairman of the CCP Central Committee. This already presupposes a cultural stagnation. The words about the value of the intellectuals for the revolution are only words. In reality the true intellectuals are being replaced by uneducated people crammed with dogmas. The severe conditions of the revolutionary and later anti-Japanese struggle are no justification for such a policy.

This unjustifiable offensive attitude towards the intellectuals engenders difficulties in the management of the economy, as well as weakens the struggle against bourgeois ideology. The cheng-feng policy is already a

---

[1] from Peter Vladimirov, *The Vladimirov Diaries, Yenan, China: 1942–1945*, New York, 1975.

norm of party life and does harm to the party. This harm ever more perceptibly makes for the vulgarization of Marxism.

The highly educated party intellectuals bear the responsibility for the training of cadres. With years, as a result of cheng-feng, this part of the intellectuals has been either ousted or itself turned into dogmatists.

Even the learned secretaries of the Chairman of the Central Committee have an education which clearly falls short of their duties and responsibilities.

Thus, disregard for the cultural legacy of the world's past and the sum total of philosophical knowledge leads to a scantiness of knowledge and disregard for, and the primitiveness of, the teaching process (studies in the so-called higher institutions of learning in Yenan are conducted, at most, five to six hours a week).

Party dogmatism becomes a testimony to political maturity and loyalty. "Marxism in reality" assumes the disguise of omniscience, dogmatism, and scorn for genuine knowledge and culture.

By culture they gradually begin to understand the small amount of the required reading of historical novels, amateur plays with a political content, simple poems, which again are a primitive rehash of political slogans, and, of course, the selection of writings included in the list of "The 22 Documents".

By his utterances on proletarian culture the Chairman of the Central Committee proclaimed cheng-feng (Mao's talks in 1942). The party is being deprived of Marxism for the sake of "Marxism in Reality" (later to become Mao Zedong Thought — GS), which is nothing but a dogma subject to learning by rote. Henceforth art is fettered to the cheng-feng ideas. It has become a rule of political life that everything outside the ideas of cheng-feng (Mao Zedong's "Marxism in Reality") is to be subjected to "purification."[1]

---

[1] Ibid., pp. 210-213.

6. THE FATE OF A YENAN REVOLUTIONARY INTELLECTUAL[1]

Introduction (G. Schnehen)

Wang Shiwei (real name Shu Han) was a young Communist who came to Yenan, the special area of the Chinese Communist Party in North China, in 1937 at the age of thirty-one. He had joined the Communist Party of China in 1926. Soon he began translating some of Marx' and Lenin's works into Chinese at the Yenan

Central Research Institute. But very soon he also wrote some essays and articles in the journals and papers, including wall newspapers, which were highly critical of the way the area was run by the leading Party officials. These essays were still published when Mao Zedong had already launched his first campaign allegedly to Rectify the Three Styles of Writing in February of 1942.

The writer Wang Shiwei (1906–1947)

At the early stage of this campaign, which was a political and not so much a literary one, the young intellectuals to whom Wang belonged were officially encouraged to speak their minds openly and to freely voice their opinions. But soon afterwards repression set in, and those who had taken the bait, were subju-

---

[1] From Dai Qing, "*Wang Shiwei And 'Wild Lilies*

gated to extensive "struggle sessions" and even to physical repression and murder for their criticism. When this first rectification campaign began in February 1942 after Mao Zedong had given his landmark speech on culture, artists and other intellectuals felt encouraged to speak their mind, among them not just Wang but also many other people.

Ding Ling, as Dai Qing reports in her book Wang Shiwei and 'Wild Lilies,' was the first to publish an article on women's rights in Yenan titled Thoughts on March 8 (International Women's Day) that criticized the party leadership around Mao for their unfair treatment of women in the area. Mao Zedong was enraged. Soon afterwards she was dismissed as an editor of a magazine. Some days later Wang Shiwei published his Wild Lilies. Wang attacked dancing events and excessive partying the Yenan Party leadership used to indulge in, he condemned their privileges in eating and clothing, etc. Dai Qing writes:

> Wang attacked dancing and the parties that the leadership became noted for, while soldiers died at the front. He parodied Mao's style. He implied that the three classes of clothing and five classes of food, which differentiated people at different levels of rank, represented unjustified privilege, indeed class, a charge that struck Mao's rawest nerve.[1]

When Mao Zedong had finished reading an article by Wang Shiwei published in the wall newspaper *Arrow and Target*, he declared: "Our ideological struggle now has a target."[2]

He now demanded tighter party control over the press and to reorganize the official paper *Liberation Daily* where those articles were still allowed to be published.[3] His next step: He created a special commission headed by his ghost writer Chen Boda to supervise what was going on in the area, what was written in wall newspapers and magazines and to check how far dissent had already reached out to ordinary party members. He must have known that Wang had already become very popular due to his open and courageous criticisms, his wall newspapers and articles in the local press, and for many dissatisfied people, especially for many students, he had already become some sort of a star and a hero. When Mao had issued his directive on how to voice an opinion, young writers now had to abide by certain writing rules if they wanted to still have a voice in *Liberation Daily*. And, what is more: ten people from artist but also from non-artist groups who enjoyed Mao's trust were named to implement the new directives among the writing community.

Shortly after that, the witch-hunt against Wang and his followers was in full swing. Multiple "struggle sessions," reminiscent of the Cultural Revolution in the late 1960s, were organized to defame the criticism of these writers and to slander them personally. Wang was made an "ideological criminal" and his group was

[1] Dai Qing, *Wang Shiwei and 'Wild Lilies'*, London and New York 2015, p. XXII.
[2] Ibid., p. 37.
[3] Ibid.

called the "Five -Member -Anti-Party -Gang." Kang Sheng, who was in charge of the secret service in the area and who was a close associate of Mao Zedong — he had arranged his marriage by the way — recommended to organize "struggle sessions" for each member separately to prevent their views from becoming too popular and to turn public opinion more easily against them.

Allegedly, Wang had committed four major "crimes." He was suspected of being:

1. A member of the "Five -Member -Anti-Party -Gang";

2. A counterrevolutionary;

3. A Trotskyite spy;

4. A "hidden Kuomintang spy".

On April 1, 1943, Wang was finally imprisoned. He spent four years there, and, of course, was not allowed to write essays or to translate Marxist classics into Chinese. Instead, now he had to work in a labor camp.

In 1947, when the Special Area had to be dissolved under pressure from Chiang Kai-shek's forces, Wang was secretly executed during the troop withdrawal, obviously on orders from high above. Later Mao denied any wrongdoing. he had not given the order to liquidate him, as he "still needed him." Whether this is true remains doubtful. It seems that the military crisis was used to get rid of him so as not to allow more critical voices to be heard.

In 1982, forty years later, when Mao was already dead (he died on September 9, 1976) and Deng Xiaoping had taken over, a decision was taken to finally rehabilitate Wang. The main charges against him were dropped and his widow Liu Ying, then 85 years of age, received the following message from the party leadership:

No evidence turned up during the re-investigation proved that Wang Shiwei was ever involved with a Trotskyite organization. Thus, the conclusion against Wang Shiwei as a counter-revolutionary spy should be rectified and therefore Wang, who was executed during the (civil) war, should be rehabilitated.[1]

Liu was given 10,000 yuan as "consolation money" — which she refused to accept.

1. From Wang Shiwei's Works

a) Wild Lilies (excerpts)

---

[1] Dai Qing, *Wang Shiwei and "Wild Lilies," Rectification and Purges in the Communist Party 1942-1944*, London and New York, 2015, p. 190.

Wild Lilies was a series of essays written by the Marxist writer and poet Wang Shiwei during his stay in Yenan/North China between 1937 and early 1943 until his imprisonment. Here the excerpts.

pp. 6f:

So deep down what is missing in our lives? The following short conversation might be revealing.

During the New Year Holiday, as I was returning from a friend's home one evening, there were two young female comrades walking in the dark ahead of me chatting animatedly in a low voice. We were some ten feet apart. I walked lightly and listened attentively.

"At the drop of a hat, he'll talk about other people's petty bourgeois egalitarianism; yet himself has his own doctrine of privilege. No matter what the occasion he makes sure of his special privilege. He is constantly taking care of his special interests. But with lower level comrades he could care less whether they're healthy or frail, sick or dead!

"Hmmh! Crows are black wherever you see them.[1] Our comrade XX is like that too!

"They talk a good line: class friendship. Ha! Shit! They don't even have normal human sympathy; when they meet people they put on the smiles, but it's all superficial — not from the heart. You never really know what they're thinking. If someone offends them slightly, they glare at you, adopt the grandiose air of a department head and lecture you!

"High or low, leaders are all alike. Our section chief, so-and-so, is all respect and honor to the higher-ups, but he's haughty towards us. Often when comrades are sick, he doesn't even bother to call. *But* once, when an eagle snatched a small chicken of his, you should have seen the big fuss he made over that weighty matter! Since then every time the eagle shows up, he screams and yells, throwing clods of dirt at the bird — that selfish, self-seeking jerk!"

Silence fell for a moment. On the one hand, I admired these female comrades' eloquence, on the other, I felt a daze as if I had lost something.

"There are too many comrades who get sick; it makes people very sad. But in fact, if you're sick, you wouldn't want that sort of man visiting you. He would only make you feel worse. Nothing in his voice, facial expression, or attitude would inspire any confidence that he had the slightest concern or affection for you.

---

[1] This idiom was evidently intended by Wang as a parody of Mao Zedong's literary style (Dai Qing).

"In the last two years I have changed jobs three or four times. From department heads to section chiefs to unit heads, there are just too damn few cadres who really care about us.

"Yeah, you're not wrong! He hasn't a bit of affection for others, so naturally no one feels affection for him. If they want to do mass work, they're bound to fail."

The female comrades continued their animated whispers, but as I had come to turn off the path I could hear no more. This conversation may perhaps be biased and exaggerated and its "image" may not be universally accepted; but we cannot deny that it can serve as a mirror.

Deep down, what is missing in our lives? Look in the mirror.

pp. 18-20:

Egalitarianism and Hierarchy.

I've heard that a certain comrade has already used the same topic in an essay for his organization's wall newspaper. The result was that he was criticized and attacked by that organization's "department head" ultimately becoming partially demented. I hope this is baseless hearsay. But even unseasoned youngsters have really gone mad, and so, I'm afraid, it is not completely impossible that an adult could go mad as well. Although I don't feel my nerves are as "healthy" as some other men, I feel I still have enough vitality to not sink into madness under any circumstances. Therefore I will dare to follow that certain comrade and speak on egalitarianism and hierarchy...

Many people have lost their priceless health and so we should not speak in terms of "according to one's value" and "indulging." On the contrary, men with a heavier responsibility ought to share the life-style of lower level comrades (a national virtue that truly ought to be fostered) and by doing so, the lower levels will feel heartfelt affection for them. Only this can weld an ironclad unity...

I am not an egalitarian, but the three classes of clothing and five grades of food are not necessarily reasonable and needed — this is especially true with clothes...These should all be allocated according to need. If, on the one hand, the ill can't get a bowl of noodles and the young eat two bowls of congee a day (party members, when asked if they really had enough to eat, must still set an example and say "I'm full!"), while, on the other hand, there are some rather healthy "big shots" who receive unnecessary and unreasonable perks, such a situation makes subordinates see their superiors as belonging to another species; not only do they not feel affection for them, but ... if one is forced to think about it, this cannot but result in trouble...

Could it be perhaps that always talking about "love" and "warmth" is an effect of "petty bourgeois sentimentality"? I await your criticism.

—March 17, 1942

b) *Politicians, Artists* by the same author (excerpts)

pp. 90-93

Our revolutionary work has two aspects: to reform society and to reform people — people's souls. The politician is a strategist and tactician of the revolution. He is a unifier, organizer, promoter, and leader of the revolutionary force; his duty is primarily to reform the social system. The artist is the "engineer of the soul" whose duty is primarily to reform people's souls (mind, spirit, thought, consciousness — here all one thing).

The darkness and filth in people's souls is the product of the inequality of the social system; before the social system has been fundamentally changed, a fundamental change in the human soul is impossible. The process of reforming the social system is also the process of reforming the human soul. The former expands the sphere of the latter, the latter speeds the completion of the former. The work of the politician and the work of the artist are mutually supplementary and interdependent.

The politician is primarily the commander of the material force of the revolution; the artist is primarily the instigator of its spiritual force. The former is a sober and cool-headed person good at carrying out the actual struggle to eliminate filth and darkness and to realize purity and brightness; the latter, however, is often more passionate and sensitive, good at exposing filth and darkness and indicating purity and brightness and so, from a spiritual level, replenishing the revolution's fighting power...

But apart from the truly great politician, none can avoid some desire to use these skills for their own reputation, position, and profit and thus to harm the revolution. Here we demand that the sharp claws of the cat will only be used to catch the rat and not to grab the chickens. Here is drawn the dividing line between the good politician and the self-seeking one. We must especially guard against the cat that cannot catch rats, but is expert at snatching chickens.

As for the defects of artists in general, the most important are arrogance, partially unsociability, and eccentricity; they are poor uniting with their own ranks to the point of mutual disdain and infighting. Here we demand of the engineers of the soul first reform their own souls to become pure and bright. To purge one's soul of the filth and darkness within is a difficult and bitter process, but it takes us along a great road that must be traveled...

Bravely but appropriately we should expose all filth and darkness; wash them out. This is just as important as praising brightness; even more important. The work of exposure and cleansing is not just negative work, because as darkness decreases light will naturally increase. Some people think revolutionary artists should "close ranks," that if we expose our own defects this will provide the enemy with an opening for attack. This is a short-sighted view; our camp today has already grown so strong that it is not afraid to expose its own defects, though it still has not strengthened itself enough. Correct use of self and mutual criticism is the necessary method of consolidating its strength...

There are few politicians who are arrogant; when they talk about artists their mouths float up in sarcastic smiles. There are as well a few artists who are conceited; when they mention politicians they, too, shrug their shoulders. In fact, objectively they both have some truth. It would be best if each took the other as a mirror in which to inspect themselves. Don't forget: we all are old China's children carrying filth and darkness.

The truly great politician certainly has a truly great soul sufficient to remold and cleanse by personal example the darkness and filth in the soul of others; here the great politician is also the great artist. The artist who truly has a great soul is also certainly able to unite, organize, mobilize, and lead the revolutionary forces; here the great artist is also the great politician.

Finally, with cordial sincerity and ardent hope, I respectfully call out in a thin voice to my comrade artists: Assume more fully the great mission of transforming the soul and first focus on doing work among ourselves and our own camp. Especially in China, reform the social system; it not only determines the speed at which the revolution will be completed but also will influence the success or failure of revolutionary work.

2. The Witch-Hunt Against Wang Shiwei and His Comrades[1]

a) Mao gives the go-ahead

Having been informed of Wang's and other comrades' critical articles published in *Arrow and Target*, Mao was quick to respond. One night, he went to the Central Research Institute where Wang was working, reportedly saying:

> Our ideological struggle now has a target.[2]

At a meeting held in late March of 1942, he gave a speech on the necessity to restructure *Liberation Daily*, telling his audience:

> Some people do not take the correct standpoint. This refers to the conduct of carrying out the absolute egalitarian concept through cold satire and innuendo. Recently, quite a few people demanded egalitarianism. This is an unrealistic illusion.[3]

---

[1] Dai Qing's remarks are in small print.
[2] Dai Qing, ibid., p. 37, quoting Li Yan, "Some Views".
[3] Ibid., p. 38.

Then Mao told his secretary Hu Qiaomu to talk to Wang Shiwei. They had two talks altogether. After that Hu also wrote a letter to Wang telling him what Mao wanted to be corrected:

What Chairman Mao wishes you to correct is your incorrect standpoint. The article is full of unfriendly feelings towards the leaders and is provocative in winning ordinary people's support to attack them. Such conduct is definitely not allowed among party members, no matter whether you are a politician or an artist. The more this kind of criticism draws some comrades together into opposition, the more dangerous it becomes to the party.[1]

Despite these efforts on Mao's part, Wang's coworkers at the Research Institute continued to support him in his efforts to democratize life in Yenan.

b) The "April 3 Decision"

This prompted Mao and his circle to take further steps to quell the emerging dissident movement. On April 3, the Propaganda Department of the Communist Party of China issued a decree called "April 3 Decision." Some days later, Mao gave another speech to make his point: "The youth are dissatisfied and have uneasy feelings. There is also a problem of policy in the literary and artistic circles."[2]

In this speech it was not explicitly mentioned but later in 1945, at the 7th Party Congress held in Yenan, when Wang had been behind bars for two years already, Mao became more explicit, saying:

The party can only proceed if there is one unanimous thought; otherwise, there will be diverse ideas. The party cannot proceed if Wang Shiwei keeps declaring himself as king and autocrat. Wang Shiwei was the one who started the whole thing of putting up wall newspapers that attracted so many people outside Yan'an's south gate in 1942. He was the "general commander" and defeated us. We admit that we were defeated. That's why we will carry out this Rectification Movement thoroughly right now.[3]

When Mao said this, the so-called Campaign for the Rectification of the Three Styles of Work initiated by him in February 1842 was already three years old. This campaign was originally targeted against Mao's adversaries in the party leadership, especially against Wang Ming, but also against Bo Gu, the former elected General Secretary of the Chinese Communist Party, and against other "dogmatists" who had studied in the USSR in the thirties and who supported the Soviet system and leadership and its struggle against Nazi Germany. But this campaign was now also used to fight young Yenan intellectuals who had mean-

---

[1] Ibid., quoting Li Yan, "Some Views"
[2] Ibid.
[3] Ibid., p. 39.

while gained a lot of support in the Special Area — reason enough to fight back and to conduct mass purges to get rid of the challenge.

The first establishment hit by Mao's vengeance was the Central Research Institute where Wang was working.

Dai Qing writes:

> On April 7, the "thorough rectification" started at the Central Research Institute.[1]
>
> First various meetings were held at the call of the Propaganda Department of the CP of China to win back the support of the cadres in the institute and to make the main critic repent his "sins." Further talks were held with Wang Shiwei to make him admit his "errors." He simply could not understand why he of all people was being criticized for his endeavors to improve the party and the state of affairs in the Special Area. He felt to be treated unjustly.

c) The involvement of Kang Sheng, head of Mao's secret police

Soon the "Central Social Department" — Mao Zedong's secret service — got involved. Some of their people were sent to the Research Institute to spy on Wang Shiwei and his comrades, among them a man called Li Yan who was ordered to take notes on what Wang did and said. The wall newspaper *Arrow and Target* was closed and no more wall newspapers were allowed to be put up. The Research Institute, where mainly translations were done, got a new head: Mao Zedong's private secretary Chen Boda even though he did not know any foreign languages. Mao did not know any, either.

d) The Forum on Literature and Art

Then Mao gave an important speech at the Forum on Literature and Art on what kind of "errors" should be avoided in creating artistic works. A military man and confidant of Mao called Wang Zhen, the commander of the Garrison Headquarters, was told to head the "rectification study group" among artists, even though he totally lacked any qualifications in the field. Days later, another forum on "Democracy and Discipline in the Party" was organized at the Central Research Institute, the hub of the critics. Wang's articles were disseminated as study materials, and head of departments made speeches to attack Wang Shiwei directly. The next day, on May 28, the first mass meeting was held attracting thousands of listeners. Since there was no hall large enough to seat the huge audience, the struggle session was moved to the sports ground. For the first time, Wang was called "anti-Party" and also a "Trotskyite." A speaker called Liu Xuewei stood up and "exposed his Trotskyite ideas," arguing:

> He slandered the leading organ of the party (i.e., the Politburo now solely dominated by Mao Zedong and his inner circle after Wang Ming had

---

[1] Ibid.

seriously fallen ill and had been sent to hospital) by believing that some members were corrupt; he said that the Rectification Movement was "a unification under the leadership of Chairman Mao..."[1]

Wang was present and tried to defend himself after various speeches against him had been made:

> If you read my article on national forms of literature published in *Chinese Culture*, you would know that I have firmly supported the United Front... How can I have Trotskyite thought?...I said that I hated the Trotskyites who organized against Stalin....[2]

This was the last time Wang Shiwei attended a forum or conference. When another "special meeting" was organized against him on June 23 — a meeting called "Meeting to Criticize Wang Shiwei" — he was no longer there. Other critics preferred to engage in humiliating self-criticisms and "regretted" their "failures" openly "to get rid of the ideological burden" and "to start to remold their views".[3] Many former friends and comrades of Wang were among them and were now turning against him to save their skins.

In June, the Literature and Arts Forum issued a resolution on "the Trotskyite Wang Shiwei":

> 1. We unanimously agree that Wang Shiwei's fundamental thought and activities are Trotskyite. It is anti-proletarian and harmful to the Communist Party and the revolutionary cause. All revolutionaries and their sympathizers should firmly oppose it.

> 2. We unanimously agree that Wang Shiwei's 'Wild Lilies' and 'Politicians, Artists' are propaganda reflecting his incorrect thought. It is inappropriate for the Literature and Art column of *Liberation Daily* and *Spring Rain* to print them instead of exposing and criticizing them.

> 3. We unanimously agree that the criticism of Wang Shiwei by the Central Research Institute and *Liberation Daily* is necessary and correct. It is of great educational significance to all literary circles and ourselves; therefore, we unanimously support this struggle.[4]

From then on repressive measures were taken against the poet: he was dismissed from the Literary Resistance Association. To quell dissent in general, Mao Zedong drafted rules on "Methods of Soliciting Articles for the *Liberation Daily*. Having been sympathetic or just friendly with Wang now became anathema and a scar printed on someone's forehead.

---

[1] Ibid., p. 45.
[2] Ibid., p. 48, quoting Wen Jize, "Diary of a Struggle." Wen participated in the meetings.
[3] Ibid., p. 50.
[4] Ibid., p. 114, document 2.2.

3. Arrest and Execution

Wang was arrested on April 1, 1943. At that time the spy mania was running high in Yenan. Spies were seen everywhere, so that it does not come as a surprise that Wang was now called a "Trotskyite spy," later also a "Kuomintang spy" — an agent of the archenemy.

Vladimirov, the Soviet observer in the area, made this entry in his diary:

> April 23, 1943
>
> Cheng-feng and the "spy" arrests are aggravating the general tension in Yenan.[1]

A fortnight earlier he had a talk with the former elected General Secretary of the Chinese Communist Party, Po Ku (Bo Gu) elected at the 6th Party Congress in 1928 who had been pushed aside by the Maoists during the Long March. Vladimirov:

> In a talk with me Po Ku used sharp words about Kang Sheng. He called him "a politically alien figure" in the Chinese Communist Party. He was outraged with the surveillance system introduced by Kang Sheng.[2]

He had this to say about Mao Zedong's spy chief (entry dated August 9, 1942):

> The question suggests itself whether Kang Sheng is not a Japanese agent. He is decidedly opposed on an active struggle against the Japanese occupiers and is inciting Mao Zedong to withdraw all troops from the Japanese front into the rear.[3]

Following his arrest by Kang Sheng's "Central Social Department" (= the secret service of the CP), they brought Wang in for questioning on various occasions. An eyewitness called Ling Yun had this to say about the first round of questioning Wang was subjected to:

> The first attempt was carried out soon after Wang's arrest at the detention office of the Central Social Department at Hou Gou, near Zao Yuan (Mao Zedong's residence in Yenan -Dai Qing). Wang did not say a word to anyone and bowed entering the room, but proceeded directly to Lenin's portray and bowed deeply...The people at the Central Social Department were quite polite to Wang and did not use later methods (Cultural Revolution methods, Dai Qing), such as "extorting a confession," "tricking one into a confession" or taking turns in interrogation.[4]

We do not know whether this is true since Ling was working for Kang's secret police at the time. The interrogators seemed to have focused on Wang's earlier sporadic contacts with some Trotskyites to promote the thesis that he was in

---

[1] Peter Vladimirov, *The Vladimirov Diaries, Yenan, China: 1942-1945*, New York, 1975, p. 113.
[2] Ibid., p. 111.
[3] Ibid., p. 46, entry dated August 9, 1942.
[4] Dai Qing, ibid., p. 54.

fact a "Trotskyite spy" which was later denied by the leaders of the Communist Party of China themselves who rehabilitated him in the early eighties.

Four months after Wang's arrest, in August of 1943, Kang Sheng gave a speech to a training class revealing the methods by which he used "to expose anti-party people" and "other enemies." Maybe his two-year stay at the Communist International in the USSR where similar methods were used to "catch Trotskyite spies" in the late thirties had helped him develop such tricks.

There the number one spy-catcher, a member of the Soviet Politburo called Nikolai Yezhov, the head of the Soviet secret service NKVD, who was later executed for this behavior of framing and executing innocent people, used similar methods, maybe even more brutal ones. Yezhov later admitted having had close relations to the German military attaché, a Mr. Koestrin in Moscow, who gave him orders for a military coup against the Soviet government.

Here is an excerpt of Kang's speech in somewhat greater detail:

> The first phase was from the time Mao gave his speech in March to the anti-Wang Shiwei meeting held on June 23. At the time, the policy of our leadership was to stress the democratic aspect of the April 3 decision by calling on people to speak out boldly, by advocating the publication of wall newspapers, and by supporting criticism of against leaders. We neither immediately counteracted nor suppressed some of the incorrect criticisms.[1]

This tactic of luring the snake out of its den is reminiscent of Mao Zedong's later campaign against Chinese intellectuals launched in 1957: first they were told to discuss freely and openly and to speak their mind, and, having done that, they were later reprimanded, called "rightists" and repressed. The expert on Maoist China, Roderick MacFarquahar:

> For a brief six weeks in the early summer of 1957, Mao Tse-tung invited his country's academic, artistic and managerial intelligentsia to criticize his regime...The intelligentsia responded enthusiastically.[2]

The result: open-air meetings were organized by intellectuals to criticize leading party officials. The "righists" had come out into the open and now they could be attacked for their "false ideas".

But let us continue with Kang Sheng's speech in August of 1943. He seems to have invented this strategy against people deemed disloyal and "unreliable" in relation to the leadership of the Communist Party. Kang in his speech to the trainees:

> At that time the incorrect thoughts of many party members were revealed. Comrades on the front line would be frightened to death once

---

[1] Ibid., p. 146, document 2.5, abstract of Kang Sheng's Report to a Training Class, August 1943. It is the original transcript of his speech made at the time and, according to Dai Qing, and has not been revised.

[2] Roderick Mac Farquahar, Ed., *The Hundred Flowers*, Paris, 1960, p. 3, quoted by William B. Bland, in ibid., p. 86.

they discovered how those counter-revolutionaries acted, how much hatred they had for the revolution, and how they expressed their ideas in literature. I am not sure if comrades from the front lines have read *Wild Lilies* and *Politics, Artists*. These things must be read in order to carry out rectification.[1]

People who honestly tried to improve life in Yenan by criticizing inequality and discrimination of women, the authoritarianism of heads of departments and the decadent lifestyle of the party leadership, were given the label of "counter-revolutionaries" and "Trotskyites" just like at the time of the Great Terror in Moscow in the year of 1937 when thousands were defamed, vilified and executed on trumped-up charges, thrown into prison and even killed for having voiced some minor dissent. This criticism was not addressed by the leaders but immediately slandered "anti-party" or "hatred for the party." Kang Sheng adding also these phrases:

> One thing you don't know is the letter Cheng Quan wrote to Chairman Mao. The letter was written to Mao three days after the chairman gave his speech on the problem of stereotyped writing in party. Cheng Quan also followed the stereotyped tendency. That bastard's hatred toward the party was beyond our expectations.[2]

This comrade had written a letter to Mao thinking he was open to criticism and discussion. But what happened? He was called a "bastard" and a "counter-revolutionary"! And the proof for the crime was there for everybody to see: The confidential letter he had written to Mao said it all and was subsequently handed over to Mao's most trusted lieutenant and collaborator: Kang Sheng. What a breach of trust!

Now Wang was behind bars and so many others were also incarcerated for having "incorrect thoughts." Wang's comrades, among them Pan and Zong, allegedly belonging to the "Five Member Anti-Party Gang" were also victimized. Dai Qing writes that more than 200 party members and non-party members were arrested together with Wang in one single night to "prevent these internal traitors" from making contact with Hu Zong-nan, a KMT general who would soon arrive in Yan'an as the head of a delegation on April 1, 1943[3], which clearly was just a pretext. Kang is admitting their arrest in the same speech but also gives us some valuable insight in how the "struggle" against dissent in the party should be organized in future to win the upper hand:

> We arrested Pan and Zong on April 1, 1943 (the day when Wang Shiwei was also arrested; their full names were Pan Fang and Zong Zheng — GS). That was another round of attack in the struggle. Another triangle. This struggle is fairly meticulous. Some comrades at the party school found out

---

[1] Dai Qing, ibid.
[2] Ibid., p. 147.
[3] Ibid., p. 33.

about Wu Xiru's problem first. That struggle was extremely circuitous. We began by attacking Li Guohua, not Wu. Later on, Li owned up. But this was only the ideological phase. After quite a few go-arounds, we shifted the focus to political struggle. That struggle was very circuitous and meticulous. Chairman Mao has said these four lines (1) cure the illness to save the patient; (2) when a melon is ripe, the stem will surely fall off, don't pick melons that are not yet ripe, when a melon is ripe, it will just drop off; in struggle it won't do to be rigid; (3) one's accomplishments are revealed in the details; (4) welcome progress. We appreciated Yu Bingran's progress. These four lines were actualized through the intense struggles in Yan'an although they seemed simple.[1]

This is From the handbook of a highly experienced secret service agent and a loyal executioner of Mao Zedong's will. The same tactics to quell any dissent in the but was later applied during the Cultural Revolution but even before that during the many campaigns launched by Mao and his entourage in the 1950s. One could summarize the main approach this way:

(1) An excessive personality cult aroung the "leader" is necessary to suppress criticism in the first place. Many ordinary people and party members will abstain from criticism if the leader is revered and said to be "wise" and "humane".

(2) For people who are cultured, critical thinkers and who insist on their own views and whose backs have not been broken yet, a whole series of meetings are needed to make them feel isolated, guilty and weak so that they give up their resistance in view of the many "comrades" who criticize them now, too. These meetings must go on for some time until the "melon is ripe and falls off" (Mao Zedong).

(3) If they still don't give up their resistance, harsher measures need to be put into practice: labeling them "counter-revolutionaries," "anti-party elements," "Trotskyites," "bourgeois elements" or even vicious "spies" and "enemies" in order to expose them properly, to expose their "true nature".

(4) If they still keep firm, they need to be arrested and put into special re-education and labor camps. The leaders who are most outspoken need to be executed one way or the other to set an example and to create widespread fear according to the saying: "Punish one — educate a thousand." If the crime comes to light one day, then put the blame on those people who were directly involved in the killing, wash your own hands in innocence and pose as "a humane leader".

In prison Wang was also used, or should I say abused, for "foreign affairs purposes" in the following manner:

> At the end of the summer in 1943, a group of Chinese and foreign journalists...were invited by Mao Zedong to visit Yan'an, where they requested a meeting with "that writer." Wang Zhen, who received the guests, agreed immediately and a few weeks later, Wang Shiwei met with the journalists.

---

[1] Ibid., p. 155.

According to a memoir by Wei Jingmeng, then a journalist for the KMT Central News Agency and now a "national policy consultant" on Taiwan:

'When Wang Shiwei met us, he immediately confessed: "I'm a Trotskyite." The only expression I saw on his expressionless face war fear.

He said over and over again: "I'm a Trotskyite. I attacked Mao. So I deserve to be executed. I should have been executed a thousand times. But Mao is so magnanimous. He doesn't want me to die. He allows me to work. I am working diligently and have realized the great principle that labor is holy. I am extremely grateful for his mercy."[1]

This was what they had told him to tell the visitors. So not only was he robbed of his freedoms but was also abused by the party leadership to create the impression that there were no illicitly imprisoned dissenters in Mao's prisons, and the most famous one, Wang Shiwei, had himself confessed to his errors and had even lauded Mao for his leniency! The case was thus closed for the foreign press and no more inquiries followed.

Wang Shiwei was killed in 1947 when the Special Area had to be given up under the pressure of Kuomintang forces. It is not known who killed him. David E. Apter and Timothy Cheek, who wrote the introduction for Dai Qing's book *Wang Shiwei and 'White Lilies'* say that:

[H]e was executed probably on orders from Kang Sheng, who could hardly have acted on his own initiative, either by Li Kenong as Guilhem Fabre would have it or, as Dai Qing and Wen Zize suggest, by Xu Haidong or He Long (a high commander — GS).[2]

Dr. Li Zhisui, Mao's personal physician, remembers what Mao himself once confided to him about the Wang Shiwei case. Mao made these remarks in connection with his campaign "Let a hundred flowers bloom, let a hundred schools contend" (summer of 1957):

We're going to single out hundreds of rightists. We won't kill anyone, though, because if we were to kill anyone we would have to kill them all. This is a rule we laid down during the rectification campaign in Yanan in the early 1940s, when Wang Shiwei launched an attack on the party and published *Wild Lilies.* When we investigated, we discovered that Wang was a Trotskyite and a secret agent, but I insisted that he not be killed. It was when we were retreating from Yanan under Guomindang attack that our security forces executed him. They were afraid he might try to run away. I criticized them for killing him."[3]

Let's remember: When Mao Zedong ordered his expedition unit to destroy the leadership of the area of Shensi, west of Yenan, during the Long

---

[1] Ibid., pp. 64f.
[2] Ibid., p. XIX, introduction.
[3] Dr. Li Zhisui, *The Private Life of Chairman Mao*, ibid., pp. 204f. In the German edition this passage has been omitted by the translators.

March in 1935, he later claimed innocence saying that he had nothing to do with the massacre that had cost the lives of many leading comrades, and he got away with it. The same tactics he used during the Futien massacre. The people of his militia were to blame, they had allegedly not followed his orders and killed the wrong people. And why should he have acted in a different way this time when, again, he was putting the blame on his "security forces" who had "ignored his orders"?

Vladimirov writes in his Yenan diary that since mid-July 1943 Mao had been vested with unlimited powers by the Politburo so that nobody could ignore his orders anymore:

The Politburo has vested Mao Tse-tung with unlimited powers. From now on the Chairman of the Central Committee of the CCP has the decisive vote at the Secretariat of the Central Committee. This means that Mao Tse-tung will have the last word in everything. As he decides, so it will happen. In fact, the party organs now discharge purely technical functions at his side.[1]

How could an underling, a usual army commander or even Kang Sheng have acted on his own without prior consent of the Chairman in this important matter? It does not make sense.

4. Liu Ying, Weng Shiwei's Wife (by Dai Qing)

Wang Shiwei, as with many intellectuals in his time, explored all sorts of ways and struggled bravely to rescue the country and to achieve socialism! Shiwei was an intellectual with acute and sharp insight on society. He had his own idiosyncratic view of the various facets of human nature. From his perspective, human nature had a glorious aspect, but also an ugly side. Although internal forces have a great impact on the development of human nature, he believed the role of external forces in shaping and guarding the human condition cannot be ignored. He also thought that socialism was the best system for controlling this ugly and vicious side of human beings...[2]

On Dai Qing (G. Schnehen)

Dai Qing had trained at an elite military academy, and was first employed as a missile technician, then as an agent for military intelligence. She was the columnist with the most devoted following in one of China's largest dailies, and in 1989, she was prisoner in the infamous Qin-Cheng Prison. Her story was concealed by the Chinese Communist Party for half a century.

---

[1] Peter Vladimirov, ibd., p. 133, entry dated July 20, 1943.
[2] Dai Qing, ibid., p. 191, *A Few Words on the Commemoration of Shiwei*, Nov. 13, 1992.

7. Pol Pot's Four-Year Plan — Documentation and Analysis

Pol Pot (nom de guèrre), Saloth Sar

I. Documentation (David Chandler)
Introduction
The Party's Four-Year Plan

II. Analysis and Conclusion (G. Schnehen)
Introduction
1. Principles of Economic Planning According to Marxism
2. Did Pol Pot's Plan Follow Marxist principles?
3. Were the Experiences of Other Socialist Countries Taken into Account?
4. A Regime of Genocide?
    a) Exhausting the labor force
    b) Genocide against minorities
    c) The proportions of the crimes
5. Who Supported the Regime?

I. DOCUMENTATION[1]

English translation by David P. Chandler

INTRODUCTION

Is it necessary for Kampuchea to have a multi-year plan? Are the circumstances right for making a plan? Do we have the qualities and the resources? We have been liberated for a little over a year. What capital have we accumulated?

According to documents from other countries, after a war, they had three-year plans in order to prepare the economy.[2] At the end of their three-year plans, they first prepared their own five-year plans. After the destruction of the war, therefore, they first prepared the economy for three years. They didn't prepare the five-year plan until the three years were completed.

Now we want to build the economy quickly, and build socialism quickly. Should we wait three years before we start a plan? On reflection, it is clearly too long to wait for three years until 1979; doing so, would interfere with our strategy. We must create the resources and character to leap forward. It isn't necessary to wait three years like them.

Immediately, as requested by the Party, we prepare the Plan to build our economy.

What qualities do we have? What are the difficulties? What things are easy? What is our situation in relation to the truth? If we are masters of our situation, we will have a clear direction and form definite beliefs.

---

[1] From: David P. Chandler et al, *Pol Pot Plans the Future. Confidential Leadership Documents from Democratic Kampuchea, 1976-1977*, Yale University, New Haven/Connecticut/USA, 1988; main extracts of the plan, but tables not included, only numbers of tables mentioned, pp. 50-115.

[2] It is not clear which countries and documents they have got in mind. It says "after a war." Which war? The Soviet Union prepared its first five-year plan 11 years after the Great October Revolution of 1917, in 1928. Under Lenin (up to 1922) Soviet Russia only had a ten-year electrification plan called GOELRO; China started in 1953 with its first five-year plan after bitter arguments within the party leadership, four years after the proclamation of the People's Republic of China on October 1, 1949. After WW II, the German Democratic Republic started with planning in 1948, three years after the war (a two-year plan); Albania under Enver Hoxha had its first two-year plan five years after liberation (1944), covering the years 1949 and 1950. It seems that the "planners" are not very well informed about the developments in other formerly socialist or semi-socialist countries.

According to observations, we began preparing our economy at the end of 1975 and the beginning of 1976. This is a very short period of time. These are the easy and difficult tasks we have observed.

Easy Tasks

Social Aspects

Our society is basically a collective society, and we are in the process of continuing our revolution. Truly, we are not preparing ourselves to destroy the people's democratic revolution; we are not preparing ourselves as a step toward socialism. In fact, our society is already a socialist society, both in the countryside and in the cities.[1] In our society nowadays, we can see new relations of production; these are collective. There are no longer the oppressive characteristics of the old society. Because the new relations are good, the new production force is good, and indeed, the entire production force is collective, no matter how we allocate the forces of human beings, livestock, and equipment.

This good situation is our foundation. We have leaped over the neo-colonial, semi-feudalist society of the American imperialists, the feudal-ists and capitalists of every nation, and have achieved a socialist society straight away. The situation is completely different from other countries. For example, when China was liberated in 1949, the Chinese were prepared to end the people's democratic revolution before they prepared to carry out the reforms leading to socialism. A long period of time was required. In 1955 they started the peoples' communes.[2] Take the example of Korea, liberated in 1945. Not until 1958 did they establish cooperatives consisting of between twenty and thirty families. After liberation, it took them a long time to reach socialism. They didn't carry out a genuine socialist revolution until 1958. They needed fourteen years to make the transition. North Vietnam did the same. Now a similar situation applies in South Vietnam. They need a long period of time to make the transition.

---

[1] This is presumptuousness and a fallacy. Without the political power of the proletariat firmly established, there can be no socialism. In Cambodia the proletariat was not in power, but an organization of a few intellectual adventurers educated in Paris neither representing the inter-ests of the urban proletariat nor the mass of the small Cambodian peasants. The Marxists had been purged from the Party, the CPC (Communist Party of Cambodia), before Pol Pot became party leader. The small Cambodian peasants (the then majority of the Cambodian population) for example had no wish to work as slave laborers for an organization called "Angka" in coop-eratives into which they were driven by force. Socialism cannot be built by simply declaring socialism or by brute force against the will of the majority of the population. This is wishful thinking and contradicts the laws for building socialism.

[2] In fact, the peoples' communes were only started in the summer of 1958 by a decision taken at the party conference of Peitaho, initiated by Mao Zedong. Before that there had only been relatively small agricultural cooperatives. The name "people's communes" was used for the first time then.

As for us, we have a different character from them. We are faster than they are. If we examine our collective character, in terms of a socialist system, we are four to ten years ahead of them. We have new relations of production; nothing is confused, as it is with them.

Party Leadership

Certainly our Party doesn't hesitate. We didn't go through a period of land reform or social change. Instead, we leaped from a people's democratic revolution into socialism. Our line is correct, both in terms of strategy and tactics. The line has filtered down into the entire Party and is experienced continuously.

Natural Resources

These are such things as land, livestock, natural resources, water, sources such as lakes, rivers and ponds. Our natural characteristics have given us great advantages compared with China, Vietnam, or Africa. Compared to Korea, we also have positive qualities.

Difficult tasks

In addition, we have a certain number of difficulties.

1. Industrial Base

As for industries of all types, heavy and light, there are hardly any, especially in the field of heavy industry. There are no minerals or power resources. There is a little light industry, but this is dependent on foreigners for raw materials. In a word, our industry is weak. Because our industrial base is weak, our technology is also weak. The Chinese are different from us. They have a larger industrial base in both light and heavy industry. The same is true of Korea, although to be sure this was provided by the Japanese colonialists. Nonetheless, it's an industrial base; they were smelting steel long before (liberation). North Vietnam is similar. After liberation, they had minerals, iron, coal etc.

Compared to other countries, in industrial terms, we are extremely weak. Moreover, we don't use old workers, because if we used old workers without carefully selecting and purifying them first, there would be many complications politically, which would lead to more difficulties for us.

2. We have no foreign assistance to help us

We have no assistance from outside for industry or agriculture. North Vietnam, after liberation in 1954, was greatly assisted by China and Russia. The same is true at present. China and Korea, after liberation, were greatly assisted by Russia. Broadly speaking, other (socialist) countries were greatly assisted by foreign capital after liberation. For us, at present, there is some Chinese aid, but there isn't very much compared with other countries. This is our Party's policy. If we go and beg for help we would certainly obtain some, but this would affect our political line. It's not easy to ask the Russians. Vietnam goes around begging from them. We don't follow them. This is because, if we asked help from them, a little or a lot, there would be political conditions imposed on us without fail.

3. Capital, various types of production, cash resources, and financial resources are scarce.

We discarded old money because we didn't wish to entangle ourselves with old affairs. We raise this issue to show that we lack capital. If we allowed foreign (investors) to move in, we'd have capital, but we would become politically entangled.

Analysis and Conclusion

To conclude, we are strong in terms of political force, collective force, and land. We are weak in materials and techniques. In this situation, can we build the country quickly by stressing independence, mastery and self reliance? Do we need foreign assistance? Do we need to delay and wait until some qualities are formed before preparing the plan? Alone, will we be able to succeed? And can we move quickly as the Party line suggests? We raise the problems so as to analyze and solve them.

After examination, we see that combining virtues and defects and using advantages as the basis, because technology is not the decisive factor; the determining factors of a revolution are politics, revolutionary people and revolutionary methods. Lenin carried out a revolution in difficulties and with empty hands. But we had a clear line and a firm standpoint. We made a revolution, and we beat our enemies. Building the country in economic terms is the same thing. At present, the revolutionary force of the Party and the people is a very strong force. This force will transform our land, which is our most important resource, so as to produce harvests rapidly. On the other hand, even though truly we have strength, our Party is strong and our people are strong. If we fight in the wrong direction, our movement would not be strong. For example, if we fought in the industrial fields we would not be strong, because we lack industrial characteristics. We fight in the field of agriculture because we have agricultural resources. We'll move to other fields when the agricultural battle is finished. By the speed of the movement, we can see that the battle is a rapid one. We stand on agriculture as the basis, so as to collect agricultural capital with which to strengthen and expand industry. We'll solve the conflict by standing on agricultural capital, in accordance with our stand on independence, mastery, and self-reliance. We don't solve the problem as some other countries do. Our characteristics are different. Our line is different. Our philosophy is different. Our standpoint is different, and so solving problems takes different methods.

Can we succeed or not?

We see that we have the qualities to succeed totally. We succeeded in 1975 and also in 1976. The year 1977 will be even more successful. This is speaking only of agriculture. As for industry, we can also make some progress. We can observe that in the year just passed, we have administered the country well. In the future, as long as we have agricultural capital with which to purchase factories and individual machines, we can certainly succeed, because we have the line. For example, take a tractor-producing factory: if we had different types of lathes and furnaces, we would be able to produce tractors ourselves. We will succeed with heavy industry, too, as long as we have the capital to do so. As for rubber, if we have the capital, we can buy machines or factories with it, so as to expand the rubber industry and achieve other developments as well. If we begged from other people, all of these problems would be even more difficult.

To sum up, if we have plentiful agricultural capital, we can rapidly strengthen and expand our industries. According to our present qualities, our resources, we can build our country along the lines laid down by the Plan, in the direction of independence and mastery. Only with economic independence can we be assured of economic independence and of our capacity to defend our country.

According to the above account, we conclude that we can accomplish (the Plan). We must unite together on this issue. If we don't unite, our work will be haphazard and hesitant, and we will descend into intellectualism. If we don't unite, the Plan has no meaning, and we would revert to our original confusion.

The world is looking at us, and analyzing us according to their points of view. They can say we are to the left, because we neglect small producers and petty bourgeoisie. Others are jealous of us, take issue with us and are provocative. Our revolutionary movement is a new experience, and an important one in the whole world, because we don't perform like others. We leap from a people's democratic revolution to a socialist revolution, and quickly build socialism. We don't need a long period of time for the transformation. Ours is a new experience, and people are observing it. We don't follow any book. We act according to the actual situation in our country.

PART ONE. THE PARTY'S FOUR-YEAR-PLAN TO BUILD SO-CIALISM IN ALL FIELDS, 1977–1980 [1]

Why did we choose a four-year period? Why not one, two, three, or five years? We chose four years for the following reasons:

1. We want to stop in 1980 in order to begin a second fouror five-year plan in 1981. This reason is of secondary importance.

2. The important reason is that we wanted to have a rather long period of time to arrange our direction and strategy. One year at a time is too short. A one-year period would be to apply the methods of combat to a long-term strategy.

The building of socialism must have the Plan as its pattern. Can we make the Plan or not? We have already decided that we must make the Plan. Without the Plan, we cannot build socialism as a unifying theme; we wouldn't know what to do, or what to buy. On the other hand, with the Plan, we know what to do, how much to do, what to buy, and how much to buy. At the end of four years' work, there will be some concrete achievements, and we'll know what we have to do for the next Plan. This is the only way to achieve strategic direction, transforming our economy from primitive to modern agriculture.

In this way, we won't stumble on the way. We accumulate capital and apply it in the right direction. We don't scatter. There is a direction common to the entire country, identical for each zone. If we have no plan as a unifying theme we would have no mastery in the task of building socialism. Instead we would be moving around in circles, doing a little of this, a little of that, changing all the time. If we thought of something, we'd do it; if we needed to ask for something, we'd ask for it, because there was no Plan, no program. This is not the correct way to proceed; it's a way of falling apart, and certainly we would encounter difficulties of confusion and complications. Not only would this slow down our advance; it would be an obstacle in the way of our combat in all fields.

Therefore, there must be a plan to cover every aspect, so we can rapidly serve the revolution and the task of building socialism efficiently.

Economics, Finance and Capital
- Building socialism in agriculture

Objectives

---

[1] TABLES omitted intentionally. The general idea is clear.

1. To aim to serve the people's livelihood, and to raise the people's standard of living quickly, both in terms of supplies and in terms of other material goods;

2. To seek, gather, save, and increase capital for agriculture, aiming to rapidly expand our agriculture, our industry, and our defense rapidly. All this is to be to the limits and possibilities of each year and of the four-year period as a whole.

About Rice Production

Objective

To produce rice for food to raise the standard of living of the people, and in order to export so as to obtain capital for imports, which we need.

Thus paddy and milled rice are our capital base. Besides rice, we have other agricultural products such as rubber, corn, beans, fish, and other forest products. These products are only complimentary. For 100.000 tons of milled rice, we would get $20 million; if we had 500,000 tons, we'd get $100 million. We must increase rice production in order to obtain capital. Other products, which are only complimentary will be increased in the future.

Plans for production, obtaining capital, and for total expenditures in the period 1977–1980

Rice fields

As of June 1976, there were more than 2.4 million hectares of rice fields, including lowland and upland fields, fertile, first-class fields and other not so fertile.

Because of problems with rice-growing areas, we have taken into account only 1.42 million hectares, or 58% of the total, as the area to be harvested once a year, figuring that this area produces an average of three tons per hectare. Please read TABLE 1.

Fertile, first-class fields produce rice twice a year.

We have allocated only a very small amount of hectares to this kind of field, but the amount of hectares should increase on a yearly basis. Production should be between six and seven tons per hectare for both harvests, according to the soil, and zone and the region. Read TABLE 2.

Governing rations

From 1977, the ration for the people will average 13 *thangs* or 312 kilograms of *padi* per person per year throughout the country. Thus rice production, taking into account the availability of rice-fields, can be calculated as in TABLE 3...(tables 1 — 37 following).

There are a number of problems related to the production of rice.

A. The water problem

Increase the degree of mastery over the water problem from one year to another until it reaches 100 percent by 1980 for first-class rice land and reaches 40-50% for ordinary rice land.

TABLE 38: Plan for solving the water problem

In order to gain mastery over water there must be a network of dikes and canals as the basis. There must also be canals, reservoirs, and irriga-tion pumps stationed in accordance with our strategy. We can observe that there is the possibility that we'll achieve the above goal for first quality rice land — 525,000 ha in 1980 as long as we grasp and tightly maintain our direction.

In our second plan from 1981 onward we can increase first quality rice land to over one million hectares and gain mastery over water to 100 percent; and in over one million hectares of ordinary rice land, we can gain mastery over water from 50 to 60 percent.

B. The fertilizer problem

TABLE 39: Plan for production of all types of fertilizer...

The reserves of fertilizer in Stung Meanchey are to be given to the army, offices, and ministries that need it.

C. Agricultural Chemicals

TABLE 40: Plan for the production of agricultural chemicals...

D. Experimenting with Different Seed Strains, 1977–1980
- Choose good seeds that yield greater harvests. Organize research to find seeds that have high quality, high yields, durability and strong straight stalks; seeds that are easy to work with and easy to harvest.

- An area must be set aside for experiments in order to increase rice production, according to the types of seed chosen, fertilizer, and weather conditions. Together with this, we must set up a meteorological station.

E. Agricultural Tools

These should be modified, as time goes on, in the direction of modernization and mechanization. Examples: irrigation pumps, mechanical plows, and machines for broadcasting, planting, transplanting, harvesting, and threshing, as well as instruments for transporting, digging, collecting, and pouring. They should also include rice-milling equipment, chemical sprays and so on.

TABLE 41: Plan for the production of agricultural tools...

F. The Problem of Energy

The important thing is to serve the first quality land that is harvested twice. It is a matter of serving agriculture. We must use electric-powered engines, and we can burn gas, charcoal, and use wood to make steam.

TABLE 42: Plan to generate energy for agriculture...

Three Other Cereals

A. *Request:* It is important to set these crops aside for consumption and also for feeding animals. Crops for export are beans of all types, especially, and certain quantities of corn.

B. *Types:* Red corn, green beans, red beans, peanuts, etc. We also include all types of root crops in this group as well.

TABLE 43: Plan for the production of corn, beans, and sesame...

Industrial Crops

A. *Request:* A portion should be set aside to increase our industrial base. Another portion should be exported. Goods for export include rubber, kapok, coconuts and so on.

B. *Types:* These include rubber, cotton, jute, coconut, sugar-cane, kapok, tobacco, Khmer dyes, lacquer and so on.

TABLE 44: Plan for production of industrial crops...

Fruit

A. *Requirements:* Primarily to support individual units; also for export.

B. *Types:* The important fruits in our country are bananas, paw-paws, mangoes, oranges, lemons, custard apples, pineapples, jackfruit, mangosteen, durian, pepper, coffee, and so on.

C. Directions for production:

  1. Look after existing gardens.

  2. Grow more fruit in co-operatives, factories, families, offices, ministries, and units. Grow individually and collectively, in tune with the Plan and the proper place.

Vegetables

A. *Requirements:* Everyone should be self-supporting 100% throughout the year in terms of fresh, dry, and preserved vegetables.

B. *Types:* These include cabbages, egg-plants, tomatoes, pumpkin, cucumber, beans, lettuce, garlic, onions, potatoes (all types), mushrooms, chillis, capsicum, mint (all sorts), ginger, bamboo, and so on.

C. Directions for production:

  1. Look after existing gardens.

  2. Grow new vegetables according to plans in co-operatives and families, factories, offices, ministries, units, collectives and on an individual basis.

Trees and Forest Products

A. *Plants:* bamboo, hollow bamboo, ferns, teak, etc.

B. *Trees:* Cultivate older forest trees, and grow new ones such as srol, tbeng, koki, etc.

The organization must be such as to permit work in co-operatives, army units, and other public units.

Forest Crops Useful for Insecticides and Medicine

A. *Types:* sdau trees, quinine, manioc, strychnine, cardamom, medicinal pepper, rattan, camphor, grapes, and trees useful for Khmer medicine, etc.

B. *Directions for expansion:* Seek more information from the masses, and from traditional healers, so as to attain abundance. Plan according to the available possibilities.

Forest by-products

A. *Types:* liquid, solid, and root resins; vines; samrong dye, honey, bees' wax, varnish, etc.

B. *Possibilities for expansion:* Organize resources for use inside the country as a basis, and then export small quantities. Make arrangements for raising bees systematically.

Animal Husbandry

A. Draft animals: oxen, buffalo, horses

1. raising on co-operatives

2. raising as a state industry, i. e. Northeast, West, Northwest, Region 103, 106, etc.

B. Animals for meat and milk: oxen, pigs, hens, ducks, turkeys, pigeons, rabbits, French hens, sheep, and goats.

C. Providing for these animals' needs:

1. Food: grass, hay, chaff, etc. We need also to produce food mixtures, such as banana chaff, rice dust, potato flour, fish meal, etc.

2. Medicines must be prepared to prevent animal diseases.

TABLE 45: Plan to raise more draft animals nationally during the period 1977–1980...

TABLE 46: Plan to raise meat stock...

TABLE 47: Plan to produce food and medicine for animals...

Fish and Other Water Creatures

A. Fresh water fish: fresh, dried, prahoc (preserved), paok, (preserved), smoked, fish sauce, fish meal

B. Other fresh water creatures: eels, lobsters, turtles, frog, etc.

TABLE 48: Plan of production of fresh water fish and other creatures...

C. Salt water fish: fish, crab, prawn, salt water fish sauce

TABLE 49: Plan of production of salt water fish and other creatures; selling price in batch and volume of fish sauce in liters...

PART TWO. BUILDING SOCIALISM IN THE INDUSTRIAL SECTOR

A. Request

1. Prepare the basic economic conditions for producing various equipment in order to simultaneously achieve independence — master our economy; for instance, various agricultural tools and raw materials to avoid carrying others and buying from them forever. So we strive to become our own masters step by step. Standing on this first request we must consider heavy industry, i.e., we must prepare to establish the accompanying conditions step by step.

2. Serve the people's livelihood (requirements) such as clothing, mosquito nets, blankets, crockery and industrial foodstuffs such as fish sauce, soy sauce, bean paste, and other commodities necessary for the people's livelihood.

3. Increasingly develop agricultural equipment that will even more ease the people's labor and expand the productive forces.

B. On the leadership criteria to build socialism in the industrial sector we stand on agriculture as the base in order to expand industry.

Within this industrial sector, we first of all pay attention to light industry that directly serves the people's livelihood. Together with this we also prepare the conditions for heavy industry.

The experience in other countries is that they take heavy industries as the base, as in the USSR, Eastern Europe, Korea. In the USSR and Eastern Europe their industry has a firm base but agriculture is weaker. In Korea they turned back to agriculture in time after they had made heavy industry and have resolved the problem the best. The Chinese were first concerned about heavy industry but later on turned back to agriculture and light industry. Now light industry has advanced while heavy industry and agriculture also have a firm base. In North Vietnam there are also a number of heavy industries but they are not yet firm. Light industry also has no strong base and neither does agriculture.

General observation shows that others have followed the Soviet experiment in general outline. Turning to us, we stand on our situation and our direction. Our economy stands on agriculture now. But should our industry stand on heavy or light industry? In accordance with our situation we must divide the capital we have earned through agriculture into two:

- first for light industry and
- second for heavy industry.

We walk on two legs, i.e., we operate light industry together with heavy industry, so that heavy industry serves light industry. If we don't operate heavy industry together with light industry, we'll still be carrying foreigners.

But we must expand light industry to master it step by step from the start, because if we do not operate light industry, our people's livelihood will still be carrying that of others; such as plates, pots, water bowls, spoons, scarves, mosquito-nets, mats, foodstuffs. Formerly they bought everything from foreign countries, from liniment to Maggi sauce.

We can only earn capital from agriculture, because we have no other capital, unlike other countries, where their first plan includes a lot of foreign aid capital.

So we expand light industry as well as heavy industry, but in stages: sometimes we stress heavy industry a lot because by then the livelihood of our people will have been raised and advanced to a certain level.

I. The Plan To Build Light Industry

Framework: Center, Zone, and some Regions

A. Types of Light Industry

1. Various textile industries — sacks.

2. Various foodstuff industries — cigarettes, sugar, edible oils, vermicelli.

3. Paper industries — educational and office stationary.

4. Industries producing goods of everyday use. Clothing, mosquito nets, blankets, mats, shoes, hats, tables, cupboards, chairs, plates, pots, pans, serving spoons, spoons, water bowls, water pitchers, jars, thermoses, glasses, bottles, (big and small) teapots, cups, toothbrushes, toothpaste, combs, scissors, cleaning materials, hygiene soap, towels, medical equipment, muslin, cotton wool, alcohol, knives, axes, sickles, plows, tailoring, leather, etc.

5. The bicycle industry and bicycle spare parts.

B. Plan for Light Industry Production

1. *The sector directly serving the people:* such as tailoring, clothing, scarves, mosquito nets, blankets, shoes, plates, pots, serving spoons, spoons, water bowls, water pitchers, soap, toothpaste, towels, muslin, alcohol, etc. Produce from 60 to 100 percent from 1977 to 1980.

2. *Other parts:* organize to build also, but step by step in this Four-Year Plan, especially:

Muslin for mosquito nets: We must produce 5 million meters per year.

Cotton: Find a way to buy cotton looms so that we have one or several production lines to serve the common needs, such as for blankets, clothing material, dresses (sampor), scarves, muslin, etc.

Tailoring: Must be set up as factories in every important location.

II. THE PLAN TO BUILD HEAVY INDUSTRY

A. Types of Heavy Industry

- various machine tool industries producing tools for agriculture aiming evermore at greatly increasing the production forces and evermore easing the direct demands of the people's force
- ferrous and various other non-ferrous metal industries
- the chemical industry
- coal and various mineral industries
- the electrical power industry
- various construction industries
- the petroleum industry
- rubber and all kinds of rubber processing industries
- the salt industry, etc.

B. Direction of Construction

We must postpone ferrous metals for the time being for two reasons: first, we have no capital with which to buy an iron-smelting factory; second: we haven't yet grasped the technology. If we wait to make an iron-smelting factory first, we will have to wait longer. So we must expand various machine-tool industries by buying iron from others for the time being, and then gradually set up an iron-smelting factory.

1. Machine-tool Industries to Serve Agriculture

The important direction is to expand industries that serve agriculture in order to even more strongly increase the production forces and to even more ease demands in the direction of people's toiling forces. Whenever our agriculture has advanced, we'll have much capital to expand all sectors of industry ever more progressively and quickly.

TABLE 50 (on machine production, additional purchases from abroad, chemical industry, mineral industries and coal, electrical power industry...)

TABLE 51 (on salt, marine salt..)

III. COMMUNICATIONS, TRANSPORT, AND TELECOMMUNICATIONS

Request:

- To serve the building of socialism in agriculture and industry so that they progress hand in hand. It is the means of communication and transport that give appropriate speed to agriculture and industry.

- To suitably serve internal and external trade according to the Party's increasingly lofty requests.

- To punctually provide for increasingly high living standards of the people.

Transport is a bridge, a vein connecting things to one another. Standing on this request, we must organize in such a way that they go hand in hand, throughout the country, in the zones, regions, districts, sub-districts and co-operatives.

1. Water Transport

A. River and Sea Routes

1. Lakes, rivers, streams, canals

2. The sea — first, near to the shore

TABLE 52: Plan to build motorized boats and ships throughout the country...

We must organize resources to simultaneously master sectors like timber and saw-milling. Some zone and regions must simultaneously set up their own workshops or factories to build these 10–100 ton ships as well. So saw-milling and planning machinery must be produced and bought for the whole country and the large zones.

B. Wharves

1. Sea Wharves

Sea wharves must be strengthened and expanded step-by-step each year to master the increasing import and export requirements. So we must also have the mechanical equipment for this work, such as irrigation pumps, cranes, big and small, forklifts, construction machinery, warehouses, customary regulations, buoys, meteorology, radio, water, electricity, etc.

2. River Wharves:

The major ones are Phnom Penh, and we must also consider Tonle Bet, Neak Leung, Kompong Cham, Chihe, Peamchikong, Stung Trang, Krauch Chmar, Kratie, Kompong Chnang, Kompong Thom, Kompong Kheang, Phnom Penh, Kompong Plouk, etc.

- We must look after and beautify water routes; must start from 1977.

2. Railways

A. We must extend the old railway lines and add more carriages. This must be administered realistically and be mastered from now on.

B. Must extend a new railway line from Phnom Penh to Kompong Som. Must have a clear annual plan until this new railway is finished (1977–1979).

C. Wood for trains. Organize forces to cut down rubber trees not Klong-theng. It is more economical to use rubber trees.

TABLE 53: Yearly plan of railway transport...

3. Road Transport

A. Direction for Building up Road Transport

1. Repair all national highways and bridges.

2. Repair all provincial roads and bridges.

3. Repair and beautify all large and small roads through the bases.

4. Strengthen and extend roads alongside reservoirs, dams, and canals.

So we must organize various resources and be masters according to the year (in stone, rubber, metal stone crushers).

TABLE 54: Yearly plan for road-building...

Must organize to produce all types of land transport equipment and be masters in serving the movement punctually from one year to the next.

1. Equipment repaired by the people: ox-carts, buffalo-carts, horse-carts, bicycle-carts, trailers for use in co-operative.

2. Mechanical and various semi-mechanical equipment, tractor and trailer, motorcycle and trailer, car and trailer, etc.

TABLE 55: Plan to produce transport equipment...

This percentage represents the yearly target for transportation so that it increases in capacity each year. Zones and regions will help with transportation whenever the co-operatives cannot do enough.

The higher level has the duty to transport and gather goods to be exported from zones and regions to Phnom Penh and Kompong Som port, and to transport imports from Kompong Som port and Phnom Penh to the zones and regions, otherwise Phnom Penh and the regions cannot transport the full quantity.

Request: Transportation must meet 100% of the annual need.

4. Civil Aviation

A. *Domestic:* Prepare various resources, planes and pilots in order to start this work from 1978, especially the Phnom Penh-Siem Reap route for guests.

B. *International:* Prepare engines, administration, strengthen and expand civil aviation (with foreign planes).

5. Telecommunication and Postal Services

Prepare resources and repair as new so that these can be used gradually from the end of 1977 on, especially in Phnom Penh, the receiving and broadcasting of telecommunications.

IV. TRADE

A. Types of Trade

1. Domestic Trade
   - must have definite annual plans for the volume of goods
   - all types of goods
   - relations between organizations of state and state, state and co-operative

2. Overseas Trade
   - must have definite annual plans for the volume of goods
   - different types of goods

Exports: rice, rubber, various cereals, minor crops, timber, fish, artisan products

Imports: screws and nuts, spare parts, agricultural and industrial machinery, necessary goods for the livelihood of the people, goods for national defense.

B. Organizational Direction

1. Prepare and be complete masters every year of the machinery trade and big and small warehouses in the bases.

2. Fix the volume of goods collected from the bases — master completely the annual volume of imports and exports.
   - Seek and select markets for complete mastery over each type of goods for one or many years.
   - Meticulously consider the quality of goods in accordance with international regulations.

V. TOURISM (importantly Siem Reap — Angkor)

A. Request

It is important to serve the political influence of the Party. Must organize:
   - hotels, water, electricity
   - communication routes — especially aviation, Siem Reap airfield
   - place to relax and visit — the regions of Angkor (Wat), Angkor Thom, Banteay Srei, the system of dikes, irrigation channels, canals, rice fields, vegetable gardens, fishing areas, Bareay Tuk Thla, etc.

- various artisanry
- organization and administration

B. *Method of Procedure:* Prepare the resources step by step from 1977 onward.

VI. TECHNOLOGY AND THE SCIENCES OF ECONOMICS, AGRICULTURE, AND INDUSTRY

A. Request

Serve agricultural and industrial production by simultaneously but rapidly building up the ranks of our nation's technicians.

B. Method

1. Experimental Offices in the Bases

- agriculture: zones, regions, districts, co-operatives, state work sites
- industry: in important factories method is to go from small to big, from assembly in important places and then spreading out simultaneously.

2. *Actuality of poly-technical schooling:* Center and zones. Method is to build some technical workshops of various kinds going step-by-step from small to big, from few to many, for practical work and study of theory at the same time.

VII. FINANCE: ACCUMULATION AND CREATION OF CAPITAL

A. Request

There must be capital to serve the construction of the country in the fields of agriculture and industry which are being expanded every year and in every plan.

- To provide for what is necessary to the people's living conditions which are rising every year.
- To serve national defense which is increasing every year.

So this capital must be seriously attended to, accumulated and economized from all things and increased to the maximum as planned.

B. Plan to Accumulate Capital

Our capital has come from the export of various agricultural products — especially rice.

TABLE 56: Plan to accumulate capital from various products...

PART TWO. FIELDS OF SOCIAL ACTION, HEALTH, AND RAISING THE PEOPLE'S LIVING STANDARDS

Request

Pay attention to the improvement of social action, health, and raising the people's living standards, every year and in every plan, in order to nurture, strengthen, and increase our people's physical force. This leads to an improvement in political forces and consciousness. To increase mechanization greatly is to ease greatly the workload on people's living standards within the context of strengthening and expanding the socialist system is to prevent the socialist system becoming tattered or becoming private and capitalist again. Therefore, increase it within the framework of the collectivist system.

Example:

The people customarily eat whatever they like, buy whatever they like to eat, so long as they have the money. So only those who have money are free to buy whatever they like to eat. In the socialist part of the world at present the problem has been posed that too strong an emphasis on collectivization leads to a disappearance of the individual or family nourishment. That's why they allow some privateness and still use money. As we see, this path does not completely repress capitalists. They already have socialism as a base but they have not gotten clear from the capitalist framework; China and Korea are examples. Here we don't mention the revisionists. Within this group the capitalist and private sectors are in the process of daily strengthening and expanding their base in every aspect. So long as the capitalist system exists, it will strengthen itself and expand and become an obstacle to the socialist revolution.

As for us, we organize collective eating completely. Eating and drinking are collectivized. Dessert is also collectively prepared. Briefly, raising the people's living standards in our own country means doing it collectively. In 1977 there are to be two desserts per week. In 1978 there is one dessert every two days. Then in 1979 there is one dessert every day, and so on. So people live collectively with enough to eat; they are nourished with snacks. They are happy to live in this system.

Therefore we organize so that an absolutely clear collectivism is absolutely clear, without capitalist vestiges (tails); otherwise we are afraid that it will arise again. If there are still capitalist vestiges there is still privacy. These vestiges, together with the capitalist standpoint, bring danger for the collective system and the socialist system whether in the short term or the long term, whether by war or by peaceful means.

Where to build, strengthen and expand socialism in the field of health

A. Build, strengthen, and expand the ranks of low and medium-qualified staff in various techniques:

- Build, strengthen and expand them in the framework of the center, zones, regions, districts, co-operatives, and factories.

B. General and special disease hospitals:

- Build them in the framework of the center, zones, regions, districts, co-operatives and factories.

TABLE 57: Plan to build, strengthen and expand hospital staff and hospitals...

C. Factories and Center producing medicine and medical instruments

1. Do it according to the popular methods and on the theme of correcting and advancing them and simultaneously following industrial methods.

2. Follow modern science.

3. Produce special medicine for people and animals to be protected against smallpox, cholera, etc. in Chrouy Changvar.

4. Produce muslin, cotton wool, glasses, plates, and various medical instruments.

Working direction: Prepare to proceed to a concrete plan starting from 1977.

TABLE 58: Plan to produce medicine throughout the country during 1977–1980...

D. Eradicating malaria in all forms:

TABLE 59: Plan to eradicate malaria...

E. General hygiene:
- Establish an organization and instigate a mass movement for general hygiene in every field
- Household hygiene and villages
- Water, food, clothing
- Sweeping and washing up, etc.

RAISING THE STANDARD OF LIVING OF THE WORKER-PEASANT PEOPLE

1. People's Villages
- Peasant co-operative villages
- Workers' villages

Procedures to build up people's villages

There must be maps and diagrams as clear plans to begin with and start work, step-by-step each year.
- Build a neat, clean, and proper house for each family.
- With watering places for people and for animals.
- Places for animals to live in, have roofs
- hygienic toilets
- sheds for fertilizer
- carpentry workshops
- kitchen and eating houses
- schools and meeting places
- medical clinics
- vegetable gardens, large and small. Villages and homes must be located in the tree glades and among all sorts of crops; villages and homes must not have just the sky above and the earth below them.
- barbers and hairdressers
- rice barn/warehouses
- a place for tailoring and darning, etc.

2. Material Necessities for the People
- On a co-operative, family, and individual basis

- Clothing — scarves
- Bed supplies — mosquito nets, blankets, mats, pillows
- Materials for common and individual uses: water pitchers, water bowls, glasses, teapots, cups, plates, spoons, shoes, towels, soap, toothbrushes, toothpaste, combs, medicine (especially inhalants), writing books, reading books, pens, pencils, knives, shovels, axes, spectacles, chalk, ink, hats, raincoats, thread, needles, scissors, lighters and flint, kerosene, lamps, etc.

Procedures

- We must produce and, to start with, import some things in order to serve the people's livelihoods to the maximum each year.
- We must provide the people with 50–100 percent of their material necessities from 1977 on.

3. The People's Eating Regime

Food: Rice, vegetables, fish, meat, preserved fish (paok, prahoc), salt, fish sauce, soy sauce, etc.

Desserts: Fruits, sugar, cakes, beans, and various things, etc.

TABLE 60: Plan of the ration system throughout the country (1977: 1 dessert once every 3 days, 1978: 1 dessert once every 2 days, 1979: daily dessert, 1980: daily dessert...)

Note: Fish and meat must be set as follows, each week:
- meat two times
- fresh fish, two times
- dried fish, preserved fish (prahok, poak) three times

Warm rice and side dishes and fresh vegetables are the basic ration.
- Organize, nominate and administer people to take responsibility for cooking tasty and high-quality food and desserts; i.e, there must be a separate group, not people taking turns, who are responsible for cooking and making desserts and consider it a high revolutionary duty.

4. The Working and Resting Regime

- Three rest days per month. One rest day in every ten.
- Between ten and fifteen days, according to remoteness of location, for rest, visiting, and study each year.
- Two months' rest for pregnancy and confinement.
- Those under hospitalization (are considered) according to the concrete situation.

This system must be applied throughout the country from 1977 onward. Resting time at home is nominated and arranged as time for tending small gardens, cleaning up, hygiene, and light study of culture and politics.

5. The regime for studying culture, science and technology to nurture politics and consciousness

- Nominate and organize a daily and weekly timetable for cultural, scientific and technological education at the level necessary to serve the concrete movement.
- Set times for livelihood meetings of the people's organizations — political study and consciousness building according to the time set.

6. Care Center for Infants and Children, for the Aged and Disabled

- Organize child-care centers in various bases; in co-operatives, factories, offices, ministries, military units.
- Organize centers to look after and educate children and lead them in increasing production according to the concrete situation in various bases, co-operatives, factories, offices, ministries, military units.
- Organize centers to look after and educate the aged and disabled and where they can be involved in the light production activities according to the concrete situation in various bases.

This is to be implemented from 1977 on, with meticulous organization and responsibility.

PART THREE. THE FIELDS OF CULTURE, LITERATURE, ART, TECHNOLOGY, SCIENCE, EDUCATION OF THE PEOPLE, PROPAGANDA, AND INFORMATION

I. The Fields of Revolutionary Culture, Literature, and Art of the Worker-Peasant Class in Accordance with the Party's Proletarian Standpoint

A. Continue to struggle to abolish, uproot, and disperse the cultural, literary, and artistic remnants of the imperialists, colonialists, and all of the other oppressor classes. This will be implemented strongly, deeply and continuously one after the other from 1977 onward.

B. Continue to strengthen and expand the building of revolutionary culture, literature and art of the worker-peasant class in accordance with the Party's proletarian standpoint. Organize work towards continuously and progressively strengthening and expanding them as assigned annually, from 1977 to 1980 to meet the requests of worker-peasant masses for the nurturing of culture, political awareness, and consciousness. Especially the strengthening and expanding of songs and poems that reflect good models in the period of political/armed struggle and in the revolutionary war for national and people's liberation, in the period of national-democratic revolution, and songs that describe good models in the period of socialist revolution and the building of socialism.

II. Field of Education, Instructing of the People, Propaganda and Information

A. Education System

- Primary education — general subjects — three years
- Secondary education — general subjects — three years, technical subjects — three years
- Tertiary education in technical subjects — three years

B. Daily education methods

- Half study, half work for material production
- In primary education it is important to give attention to abolishing illiteracy among the population.

C. Set plan for the educational system

- Primary education: from 1977 onward
- Secondary education especially in the technical part must simultaneously begin to some extent from 1977.

In our educational system there are no examinations and no certificates; it is a system of learning through the collective and in the concrete movement of the socialist revolution and the building of socialism in the specific bases, especially the co-operatives, factories, and military units.

B. General subjects

- reading and writings
- arithmetic

- geography (importantly that of the nation)
- history of the revolutionary struggle of the people, the revolutionary struggle of the nation, the revolutionary struggle for democracy, the revolutionary struggle for socialist revolution and the struggle to build socialism
- natural science, physics, chemistry (as base)
- the Party's politics, consciousness and organization

C. Build, strengthen and expand the ranks of educational cadres

We must choose (people with) backgrounds that adhere to the revolutionary movement and have the quality to grasp the Party's educational line and are able to apply it concretely and continuously strengthen and expand their own capacity in the concrete movement.

2. Instruction of the People, Propaganda and Information

A. *Radio Broadcasting:* organize general listening sessions using loudspeakers for all important places and mobile work brigades.

B. *Films:* of the revolutionary movement's present and past, especially the present. Organize many groups to produce many films to show to the people in general.

C. *Art:* Step-by-step (a little is enough) in order not to disturb the productive forces raising production.

D. *Newspapers:* pictorial magazines, political magazines and general knowledge.

Procedures:

- Be careful in building, strengthening and expanding the ranks by choosing (people of) backgrounds close to the revolutionary movement who can apply the Party's policy to instruct the people and disseminate propaganda and information.
- Organize printing in foreign languages, especially English, starting from mid–1977 onward.

3. Scientific Technology

A. Workshop or place for experimentation in co-operatives and important factories.

B. Technical schools at primary and secondary level in important traders, such as

- rice and other cereals
- rubber and other industrial crops
- forestry and fruit trees
- animal breeding
- fresh and salt-water fish
- river and sea water
- energy
- medical knowledge, etc.

C. Poly-technical school with practical primary and secondary levels

Procedure:

Organize these simultaneously from 1977 onward, according to the Plan and its annual program.

II. ANALYSIS [1]

Introduction

Can we call Pol Pot's four-year plan (1977–1980) a genuinely scientific plan for the building and management of a socialist economy or is it something completely different?

At first sight one gets the impression that this document has not much to do with the planning of a socialist economy at all but has a lot more to do with the attempt by an over-ambitious group of people to win control over an entire country and its people with, at that time, around 10 million inhabitants. The entire political, social, economic, cultural, and above all, the private life of the Cambodians, is scheduled to be put under one minutely elaborated ambitious Plan to 'build genuine socialism,' in order to prevent the reemergence of capitalism, to win total independence from the outside world and to control practically everything — starting with the economy and the country's resources and ending with the way people should spend their meager 12-day annual holidays or how many desserts they are entitled to eat in the big dining halls where meals are to be eaten collectively like in Mao Zedong's 'People's Communes' in the late 1950s. Everything is to be put under the control of 'Angka,' the Communist Party led by Pol Pot and his entourage, which has already abolished money so as to make the people completely dependent on what the 'organization' (Angka)

[1] by G. Schnehen

hands out to them to keep them alive. People work collectively in co-operatives, spend their spare time collectively and use the buildings provided by Pol Pot also collectively where they are under the watchful eyes of unit leaders making sure that nobody goes astray.

For the authors of the Plan communism can only work properly if a powerful organization such as Angka is in a position to control all spheres of live to make sure that the entire life is run under its control and that everything is done collectively and uniformly. Private life is anathema and harbors the danger that capitalism will one day raise its ugly head again and creep in surreptitiously. This needs be prevented at all costs!

Apart from that, socialism needs to be built very quickly. No transitional periods are allowed anymore, because there is already socialism having proclaimed it. Other countries that tried to build socialism after the war allegedly made the mistake to allow such periods being far too long. So taking advice from them is not necessary, will lead to dependence and begging, and since we know better and do not need any textbooks to tell us how socialism can be erected in a backward country ravaged by a prolonged war. we will go our own way and try something completely different, thus winning complete independence, autonomy and an ideal society. We control the people, the people are with us, they are happy with us, and this is to our advantage, so we can take the risk of making such a human experiment never tried before. We will go down in history as the true communists.

If one compares such an undertaking with what some other countries did that started building socialism following a revolutionary upheaval (in Russia for instance after 1917) or after the Second World War (after 1945), the difference clearly springs to mind. With the possible exception of China under Mao Zedong in the late 1950s, such 'socialist planning' has never been attempted and never and nowhere been put into practice. Long transitional periods were always permitted to take place before the planning of the economy was even envisaged, and the planning itself gained a very different character from the Cambodian model. It was more or less confined to the national economy, to production, and did not go far beyond that sphere.

Let's deal with the Soviet 'model' to begin with.

The first attempt at planning the economy was done under Lenin in the early twenties with the plan to electrify backward Russia after the Civil War had come to an end in 1921/1922. It was called GOELRO (State Commission for the Electrification of Russia) which envisaged the building of 30 power plants all over Russia stretching over a period of ten years. It was a German scientist who helped Lenin and his team to draft the plan laying the foundation for the industrialization of the huge country.

Lenin said at the time. "Communism — that's Soviet power, plus the electrification of the whole country.[1]

However, real overall planning of the entire national economy only began in 1928, eleven years after the October Revolution with the first five-year plan, also affectionately called 'Pyatiletka' by the ordinary Russians. So the transitional period needed to lay the foundations and create the preconditions for the plan lasted approximately twelve years. Only then was the first economic plan put into practice, ending in 1933 and leading to double-digit growth rates as far as industrial development was concerned.

Why did the Soviet Union wait so long to introduce the first economic plan, why was it not started right after the October Revolution in 1917 or at least in 1918? The Maoist Pol Pot would have liked doing it much earlier "and without delay." The answer is very simple: Certain preconditions must exist to plan an entire economy. If they do not exist, planning is bound to fail. Here are only five of them:

(1) The majority of the means of production must be controlled by the new popular state. In Soviet Russia Lenin's first government issued the Decree on Nationalization to make sure that this was the case.

(2) No debt repayments. All the debt incurred by former governments must be annulled to make sure that the financial means do not go into debt repayment but into economic reconstruction.

(3) A united governing party must exist. If there is disunity at the top, permanent strife will render the planning and ruling of the economy sooner or later futile.

(4) It is necessary to have exchange between town and village. If there is a lack of commodities and commodity exchange between the urban and the rural areas, no planned economy is possible. Then only shortages are going to be distributed equally among the people. The villagers must be provided with cheap industrial goods and the workers in the towns with enough foodstuffs and textiles. So both spheres, town and countryside, need a certain standard of commodities, and there also must be an alliance between peasants and workers, between town and village.

(5) Qualified technical cadres need to be trained to make sure that the new factories work properly. Trained factory directors must be able to lead an enterprise, they must know how to organize and to do good bookkeeping. A certain cultural level is necessary to have qualified staff at one's disposal to run an enterprise smoothly and efficiently. If most people are still illiterate, planning will come to nothing, it will then be reduced to a command economy, where everything is decreed from the top to make things work.

---

[1] *Große Sowjet-Enzyklopädie*, Vol. 1, Berlin 1952, p. 700; Great Soviet Encyclopedia.

These are just some of many other preconditions for sound economic planning. If the conditions do exist, then the next stage can be envisaged: You need a competent planning body with capable people who have an understanding of the economy. But not everything can be decreed from above: central planning has to be propped up from below as well. Reliable data need to be provided for the authorities to get the required information needed for setting up provisional plans.

The result of all the prep work: the drafting of a provisional plan which will then have to be revised permanently, corrected and supplemented by new data and new figures. In the Soviet Unit two different drafts competed against one another, a soft one and a hard one setting the targets much higher than the first. Then, after a period of experimenting and trial and error, it is up to the new socialist government and the new legislature to discuss the plan and finally adopt and sign it into law. After the implementation of the plan, it becomes law for each and every productive and administrative unit as well as for the people working in these spheres. Maybe it will be necessary to revise the plan after a certain period of time, if for example it turns out that the figures were set much too high or much too low. This must be done in close cooperation among the governing. The central authorities always need the assistance of the base to make everything work smoothly. This is the essence of democratic socialism. Surely, the plan is going to be sabotaged by certain elements of society who want to set the clock back and who favor the old anarchic capitalist way of handling a national economy, and this resistance, of course, needs to be overcome. So not just the thousand and one technical obstacles must be overcome but also social obstacles.

It turns out that planning an entire economy is a very complicated issue and cannot be achieved at will and over night. Scientific institutes are needed being equipped with well-qualified personnel to watch over the implementation of the plans. In Russia no blueprints were available, the country could not benefit from the experience of other socialist nations as there had not been any. But later, after the end of the Second World War, when numerous other country started to introduce socialism, the Russian experience became a valuable source of knowledge to benefit from, some sort of treasure trove, to avoid mishandling things and making unnecessary mistakes and to progress more easily and swiftly toward real socialism.

So it turns out that there were good reasons to wait more than ten years before economic planning got under way in the Soviet Union, also involving the new nations that had joined the Union in late 1922 when the USSR was founded.

However, the Maoist Pol Pot and his planners did not want to wait that long. After "liberation" as they called their seizure of power in Cambodia in April 1975 after the collapse of the US-sponsored Lon Nol regime, only a little over a year had passed before they started working on their first plan, covering a period of four years. In the 'introduction' to the document it says:

Is it necessary for Kampuchea to have a multi-year plan? Are the circumstances right for making a plan? Do we have the qualities and the resources?[1]

So they realized that certain preconditions had to exist to make a plan, but not knowing them or not wanting to know them, they, of course, answered the question in the affirmative. Now they wanted to build the country and socialism quickly. They couldn't wait:

Now we want to build the country quickly, and build socialism quickly.[2]...We don't need a long period of time for the transformation. Ours is a new experience, and people are observing it. We don't follow any book...[3]

In the document other countries are briefly and superficially discussed that had waited much longer. The Soviet example is not mentioned, explicitly mentioned are only China, Korea (North Korea that is) and Vietnam. They regret that genuine socialist revolutions had allegedly only taken place in Korea and North Vietnam without going into much detail. They themselves claim to have organized a genuine socialist revolution and felt very confident, because their party, the Communist Party of Kampuchea (CPK), was said to be very strong and that it was on the right path:

Our line is correct, both in terms of strategy and tactics.[4]

So they knew full well, that their way of handling the economy was an experiment never done before. They didn't want advisers, they didn't want to take the experience of other socialist countries into account, they wanted the 'Great Leap Forward' into 'socialism' and therefore they also needed the plan to do everything systematically and according to their own deliberations. They didn't want to waste time. Now was the time to act quickly and to build 'real socialism' which, according to the party leaders, was tantamount to collectivism, to having big co-operatives, big dining halls attached, a strict labor regime, state-owned factories and the political power fully in their own hands.

The plan now takes a completely different character than the usual plans drafted in the Soviet Union or in other socialist countries. It is not just a plan for the reconstruction of the economy alone but something different: a plan to reconstruct the whole social life in Cambodia, not just the economic life, but also the private life of the people. According to the authors this was needed to make sure that capitalism could not raise its

---

[1] David P. Chandler et al, ibid. p. 45.
[2] Ibid.
[3] Ibid., p. 49.
[4] Ibid., p. 46.

head again. The whole life under the control of 'Angka,' life in co-opera-tives and eating halls, the control over people's private life, about how they should spend their short 12-day annual holiday, etc., was also part of the plan.

Whereas in socialist countries, such as the Soviet Union, the five-year plan was restricted to the national economy, Pol Pot's plan (which by the way had Mao Zedong's approval) had a much wider scope: it was a project to plan practically everything and anything: the economy, the cultural life, the social life, the political life, and the private life as well. The plan was officially called 'The Party's Four-Year Plan to Build Socialism IN ALL FIELDS, 1977–1980'.[1] It is criticized that in some socialist countries (they don't name them) privacy was not forbidden and even money (!) was still allowed, which they deeply regret:

Only those who have money are free to buy whatever they like to eat. In the socialist part of the world at present the problem has been posed that too strong an emphasis on collectivization leads to a disappearance of the individual or family nourishment. That's why they allow some privacy and still use money. As we see it, this path doesn't completely repress capital-ists.[2]

So according to Pol Pot's planners, it was a must not just to give up money but also to collectivize the whole life (private and public) so as not to allow the capitalists creeping back into the system. Only full-scale collectivization would guarantee that capitalism would not come back one day (it came back sooner than expected though, after only three and a half years). Full spectrum control and dominance was the rule of the day. So also eating and drinking had to be collectivized, and the amount of desserts for a peasant or worker had to be fixed for the four-year period:

As for us, we organize collective eating completely. Eating and drinking are collectivized. Dessert is also collectively prepared. Briefly, raising the people's living standards in our own country means doing it collectively. In 1977, there are to be two desserts per week. In 1978 there is one dessert every two days. Then in 1979, there is one dessert every day, and so on. So people live collectively with enough to eat, they are nourished with snacks. They are happy to live in this system.

Therefore, we organize so that an absolutely clear collectivism is abso-lutely clear, without capitalist vestiges (tails), otherwise we are afraid that it will arise again. If there are still capitalist vestiges there is still privacy. These vestiges, together with the capitalist standpoint and view, bring danger for the collective system and the socialist system whether in the short term or in the long term, whether by war or by peaceful means.[3]

---

[1] Ibid., p. 50. My emphasis.
[2] Ibid., p. 107.
[3] Ibid., pp. 107f.

Nobody should have any doubts about their absolute and resolute determination to put the whole country under their wings. Their idea of socialism was completely different from that in the Soviet Union: Pol Pot's 'socialism' was conceived to be a system of full-scale collectivism, of absolute control over the individual whose private life became a thing of the past; socialism was eating collectively in big dining halls, not in families. Children were to address their parents using the term 'comrade,' not Mom or Pa and were also asked to spy on them, if necessary. Apparently, only this way could conspiratorial talks in the family apartment be avoided. Socialism was tantamount to the total absence of a private life.

Socialism was to become totalitarianism.

Mao Zedong was enthusiastic, he welcomed the Angka leaders in Beijing in 1975 and provided a generous credit worth one billion (in dollars) to support the project — the biggest credit ever granted in the history of the People's Republic of China.

In the Soviet Union, however, family life and private life was respected, but the vast majority of the means of production was collectivized and the land put into public ownership. There were hardly any people's communes (only if people wished to live that way), but so-called "artels" which were much smaller and allowed privacy.

Here we have the difference between socialist planning in the Soviet Union under Stalin and 'socialist' planning in Pol Pot's Kampuchea. Pol Pots' model was China in the late 1950s and early 1960s, when, on the initiative of Mao Zedong, the 'People's Communes' were established nationwide, also with huge dining halls and the absence of private dwellings. These dwellings were often even destroyed if peasants refused to join the communes. This difference should be noted and not blurred, as they are two completely different things. The Soviet planners took Marxism to heart, Pol Pot's people took Maoism to heart — a perversion of Marxism.

1. Principles of Economic Planning According to Marxism

Four important principles or requirements are maybe worth mentioning:

(1) The basic principles of economic planning need to be strictly observed, among them the primacy of developing heavy industry and machine building, especially if only an insignificant industrial base exists in a certain county. Heavy industry takes precedence over light industry, consumer goods production and agriculture — in order to lay a solid and reliable basis for socialist industrialization but also for the defense of a prospective socialist country. Without a firm

industrial basis, no healthy socialist economy can be built in the long run.[1] And such a country must also be able to defend itself against all attempts to sabotage or to end socialism by means of foreign intervention and instigating war.

(2) The experiences made by other friendly socialist countries gained while building socialism must be taken into account to avoid the typical mistakes planners are prone to make when intending to build socialism. Therefore Foreign advisers should be allowed to enter the country to assist in drawing up long-term or short-term plans and to help the plan to become a reality. Close cooperation on an international scale is a must to be successful. Socialist Planning is a science like other natural sciences and must be treated like that and Without international cooperation and exchange of views there can be no science.

(3) Planning must take the national characteristics of a given country into consideration, its traditions, culture, psychology, religion and the balance of power between the new regime and its enemies. No plan affecting the entire country and the life of a socialist nation can be forced upon the majority of the people. If people do not want a planned economy, then one must abstain from the whole project and wait until a later date when the majority is prepared to accept such an important undertaking. The same holds true with agricultural collectivization which also cannot be forced upon farmers. Maybe a nationwide referendum should be held to find out what people think in this regard.

(4) the people must be involved during all the various stages from drawing up such a plan to implementing it. No plan can be made in a conference room on a drawing board just involving some very clever experts.

There are some other essential principles for the successful and proper construction of a socialist economy like for example the harmonious and proportional development of each and every branch of industry, the development of socialist emulation, the validity of the plan indices for the directors of enterprises and their staff who are now state employees and who have to guarantee that their plans will be realized successfully to enhance the living standard of the people.

2. Did Pol Pot's Plan abide by these Principles?

Was the first requirement mentioned — prioritization of heavy over light industry — adhered to?

PART TWO of the document states:

---

[1] Cp. A. Koryagin, *Vorwiegende Steigerung der Produktion von Produktionsmitteln – unerlässliche Voraussetzung für den stetigen Aufstieg der Volkswirtschaft*, in: *Neue Welt*, Jahrgang 11, June 1953, p. 1,363 (Predominant increase of the production of means of production – essential precondition for a steady rise of the national economy). Koryagin: *The stormy growth of the production of means of production, especially in machine building, constitutes the foundation for uninterrupted progress and perfection of the entire socialist production, including the production of consumer goods*, ibid., p. 1,375.

On the leadership criteria to build socialism in the industrial sector we stand on agriculture as the base in order to expand industry.[1]

As to the relationship between heavy and light industry we find the following remark there directly below:

Within this industrial sector, we first of all pay attention to light industry that directly serves the people's livelihood. Together with this we also prepare the conditions for heavy industry...But should our industry stand on the heavy or light industry? In accordance with our situation we must divide the capital we have earned through agriculture into two:

- first for light industry and

- second for heavy industry.[2]

Which branches of the light industry should get special attention? Heavy industry? No, It's the textile industry, light industry.

B. Plan for Light Industry Production: 1. The sector directly serving the people: such as tailoring, clothing, scarves..., towels...[3]

The capital accumulated in agriculture should go there first, only after that to the heavy industry. But heavy industry was to be expanded in the second four-year plan period following up on the first — starting in 1980.

The primary law of the development of capitalism allegedly also has validity for the building of socialism according to Pol Pot and his planning staff. England at that time, by the way, needed more than a whole century to develop its light industry, especially textiles. So the most important law of constructing a socialist national economy, the building of a solid heavy industrial sector, is thrown into the winds and the capitalist law is favored. But explicitly, Pol Pot and his advisers do not want to follow any model, they want to go their own way (although unconsciously they follow the capitalist development law).

Ours is a new experience, and people are observing it. We don't follow any book. We act according to the situation in our country.[4]

Only after less than four years, the path taken by the Cambodian Maoists turned out to be a complete failure. The regime collapsed in January 1979 and the ambitious plan came to nothing.

3. Were the experiences of other socialist countries taken into account?

The section on BUILDING SOCIALISM IN THE INDUSTRIAL SECTOR states:

---

[1] David P. Chandler et al, ibid, p. 96.
[2] Ibid.
[3] Ibid., p. 97.
[4] Ibid., p. 49.

The Chinese were first concerned about heavy industry but later on turned back to agriculture and light industry. Now light industry has advanced while heavy industry and agriculture also have a firm base... General observation shows that others have followed the Soviet experiment in general outline. Turing to us, we stand on our situation and our direction. Our economy stands on agriculture now.[1]

So the Soviet experience was ignored and so were those countries that had followed the Soviet example after liberation from Nazi fascism in 1945. Instead, they turned to Mao Zedong's China in the late 1950s when the principles of the first Marxist Chinese five-year plan (1953 through to 1957) were reversed and agriculture and light industry were favored over heavy industry.

The example of the little Balkan country of Albania under the leadership of Enver Hoxha was also ignored, even though the conditions after the liberation of Albania in late 1944 were very similar to those in Cambodia in 1975.

[T]o make agriculture in 'Democratic Kampuchea' a success, hundreds of thousands of people were evacuated from the big and medium-sized cities and resettled in the countryside to work in the newly created rice cooperatives as manual laborers without regard for their lives and that of their families. The 'new people' were at first warmly welcomed on the day of their arrival in the countryside, but later, the niceties ended and they had to adapt to a harsh labor regime never experienced before in their life time. For those who resisted and went on the rampage, special re-education camps were installed. The reign of terror had only just started.

Brute force was used to bend their will, with many people simply beaten to death when they had the audacity to oppose the new regime and the living conditions created by them. And also child labor was widely used to ensure that the norm was fulfilled.

Small wonder that the labor productivity in the new cooperatives remained low, as there was no motivation for the 'new people' and the others to function as mere dispossessed slave laborers.

The new regime could have learned from the Soviet Union where an unprecedented enthusiasm was seen during the first Soviet five-year plan which was fulfilled after only four years.

Socialism cannot be built by force. Socialism can only be erected by free people voluntarily who have come to the conclusion that the new system is their own system — a system they can benefit from.

4. 1950 - A Regime of Genocide?

a) Exhausting the labor force

---

[1] Ibid., p. 96.

To implement what they called the 'Super Great Leap Forward' and to achieve the over-ambitious target of getting three tons of rice per hectare out of the rice-lands, which was twice as much as had been achieved under the monarchist Siha-nouk regime in the past, two things were essential:

        (1) the resettlement program to gain new laborers from the cities and

        (2) a strict labor regime.

The resettlement program is not explicitly mentioned in the document but we learn from certain tables that it did exist. For example: In table one on 'population and rice-land in Kampuchea 1977' the population figure of Battambang and Pursat in the Northwest of the country is given as 1,790.000. Below the table we find the comparative figure for 1968 which only amounts to only 908,000. the almost doubling of the figure was obviously due to the evacuation of Southern urban areas that had taken place before 1977.[1] Around 800,000 must have been sent to the Northwest, emptying some cities in the South.[2]

The exodus from Phnom Penh, April 1975

This was done intentionally to win enough capital from rice exports according to the maxim of 'agriculture first,' as agriculture was considered to be the primary source of capital accumulation. The urban dwellers who were sent to the rice-lands were not in the least prepared to undergo such a labor regime. They had completely different jobs before. Now, all of a sudden they and their children found themselves being rice pickers in the paddy fields.

---

[1] David P. Chandler et al, ibid., p. 52.
[2] David P. Chandler et al, ibid., p. 52.

The working regime is mentioned in PART TWO of the Plan below the title of 'raising the standard of living of the worker-peasant people':

The Working and Resting Regime

- Three rest days per month. One rest day in every ten.

- Between ten and fifteen days, according to the remoteness of location, for rest, visiting, and study each year.

- Two months' rest for pregnancy and confinement.

- Those under hospitalization (are considered) according to the concrete situation.

The system must be applied throughout the country from 1977 on. Resting time at home is nominated and arranged as time for tending small gardens, cleaning up, hygiene, and light study of culture and politics.[1]

No mention is made of the daily working hours but we have reason to assume that at least ten hours per day was the minimum demanded from them.

One of the survivors of the Cambodian genocide, Mr. Ouk Villa, whose report is given below, had this to say about the labor regime he himself had experienced as a nine-year-old boy.

In late 1975 my family was separated. My two sisters were sent to the mobile youth group far away from us. They were forced to work day and night, but they weren't fed enough and dressed in rags. As for me, I was sent to the child group center, which was about a kilometer from my family. I had to carry manure to the rice fields, and I was badly treated because I was accused of being lazy...

All children had to get up early in the morning or they were kicked and pulled by the unit leaders. We never received any education because schools, money, markets, books, postal services, and religions were banned. The living conditions of the new people grew more desperate and seemed more physically and mentally arduous than the conditions of slaves in the Middle Ages. We were taught only about hard work and faithfulness to the government.[2]

His testimony is corroborated by another survivor, a woman called Roeun Sam, who succeeded to escape to Thailand in 1979 to find some food for her starving family. This is what she said about her work in the fields as a child laborer and about what she experienced one day:

They put me together with others of my age and had me work in the field to watch the cows. Every day I watched the cows, and after I had fed them at night, I went to the place where the children lay on the ground to sleep. We didn't have a roof, wall, or bed. We slept on the ground. I worked

---

[1] Ibid., p. 112.
[2] Kim DePaul, ed., compiled by Dith Pran, with an introduction by Ben Kiernan, *Children of Cambodia's Killing Fields. Memoirs of Survivors,* Yale University, 1997, p. 116.

hard and got so little to eat. We only had one meal a day, at lunch. Angka measured each serving, only about a cup and a half, which was mostly broth and maybe two tablespoons of rice. They also gave us a small piece of salt to suck on as we ate. Sometimes we didn't even get salt. We fought each other for it.

One day, as I was watching the cows eat grass, I noticed that a few of my cows were missing. I smelled something like a dead animal. My cows were running toward the smell, and I followed them. By the time I got there, the cows were licking the dead body's clothes. Some were standing there sniffing. It was a human body that had just been killed. You could see her long black hair and the string around her hands...This was a place where they took people to kill...[1]

Child labor

There was also a plan for the ration system, of course, as mentioned in the above document. Without going into all the details for the various tables, those for the daily rations should be mentioned here to give a broad idea about what hard-working people were given to eat by Angka in the communal dining halls. Table 60 provides some details about what the New People and the old people working the rice-lands were entitled to.[2]

Note: The workforce is subdivided into four categories: No. 1 probably being the more hard working group, No. 4 the least hard working one, maybe women's work. Warm rice, side dishes and fresh vegetables are to be the basic ration.

---

[1] Ibid., pp. 74f.
[2] David P. Chandler et al, ibid., p. 111.

Types of food	1977	1978	1979	1980
1. Rice — 4 systems for workforces				
No. 1	3 cans	same	same	same
No. 2	2.5 cans	same	same	same
No. 3	2 cans	same	same	same
No. 4	1.5 cans	same	same	same
2. Two side dishes: soup/dried food	same	same	same	same
3. Dessert	lx every 3 days	lx ev. 2 days	daily	daily

As all money had been abolished shortly after the takeover of power by the Khmer Rouge, nobody was able to buy something extra on the black market or in a shop to supplement his or her ration.

If we can believe the survivors' testimonies, plans for the future and reality were probably miles apart from each other. But even if we take the Plan as a starting point, the nutrition provided by Angka seems very scarce. And moreover, the table does not tell us what the hard-working children were entitled to get as a ration.

Sopheap K. Hang who was a child when the Khmer Rouge took power tells us that the labor regime got worse as time went by:

> Many months passed. Things got harder and harder. Angka made the city people work from early dawn to midnight. The food portion was cut to half a spoon of rice and half a spoon of green beans. The city people couldn't stand the suffering and the torture that Angka forced on them. Some of them committed suicide by hanging from trees, strangling themselves with ropes around their necks, or by suffocation.[1]

As far as children, disabled people and the aged were concerned, we find these instructions in the four-year plan for the years 1977–1980:

> Organize centers to look after and educate children and lead them in increasing production according to the concrete situation in various bases, co-operatives, factories, offices, ministries, military units.

> Organize centers to look after and educate the aged and disabled and where they can be involved in light production activities according to the concrete situation in various bases.[2]

Children were not treated as human beings having rights and a childhood, but were seen as a production force, and disabled and older people didn't fare

---

[1] Kim DePaul et al, ibid., p. 31.
[2] David P. Chandler, et al, ibid., p. 112.

any better. Survivors who were children at the time keep telling us that they did not get any schooling or basic education. Educated people, even educated children, were suspiciously looked upon as Teeda Butt Mam tells us, especially if they were from 'bourgeois' Phnom Penh, a city considered to be the 'class enemy':

> We were from Phnom Penh. I was afraid of who I was. I was an educated girl from a middle-class family. I could read, write and think. I was proud of my family and my roots...

> I was always hungry. I woke up hungry before sunrise and walked many kilometers to the worksite with no breakfast. I worked until noon. My lunch was either rice porridge with a few grains or boiled young bananas or boiled corn. I continued working till sunset. Every night I went to sleep dirty and hungry. I was sad because I missed my mom...

> They kept moving us around, from the fields into the woods. They purposely did this to disorientate us so they could have complete control. They did it to get rid of the 'useless people,' those who were to old or too weak to work, those who did not produce their quota. We were cold because we had so few clothes and blankets. We had no shoes. We were sick and had little or no medical care. They told us that we 'volunteered' to work fifteen hours or more a day in the rain or in the moonlight with no holidays...[1]

We can guess what the planners had in mind when talking about 'education': indoctrination with the ultra-leftist slogans of 'The Organization,' the CPK that is. The Plan for the years 1977–1980 all sound very 'revolutionary'. The following remarks discuss how to educate the youth in the not too distant future:

> In our educational system there are no examinations and no certificates. It is a system of learning through the collective and in the concrete movement of the socialist revolution and the building of socialism in the specific basis especially the co-operatives, factories, and military units.

> *General subjects:* reading and writing, arithmetic, geography (importantly that of the nation), history of the revolutionary struggle of the people, the revolutionary struggle for the nation, the revolutionary struggle for democracy, the revolutionary struggle for socialist revolution and the struggle to build socialism. Natural science, physics, chemistry (as base). The Party's politics, consciousness, and organization.[2]

Teeda Butt Mam's education was probably considered 'bourgeois' and 'counter-revolutionary,' and one gets the impression that kids with such a family background were intentionally made to work hard to get rid of them in the long run by feeding them badly, starving them to death or by driving them into suicide. Such a suicide could then be used also against their parents. Teeda again:

---

[1] Ibid., p. 15, testimony of Teeda Butt Mam.
[2] David P. Chandler et al, ibid., p. 114.

I wanted to commit suicide but I couldn't. If I did, I would be labeled 'the enemy' because I dared to show my unhappiness with their regime. My death would be followed by my family's death because they were the family of the enemy.[1]

b) Genocide against minorities

What exactly is a "genocide"?

According to the UN Genocide Convention it is an attempt "to destroy, in whole or in part, a national, ethnic, racial or religious group."[2]

At the time of the rule of the Khmer Rouge, more than 20 minorities used to live in Cambodia, among them the Vietnamese, the Chinese, the Muslim Cham, the Thai, the Lao, the Sáoch, the Kola (Shan), and many more.[3]

Hardest hit by the persecutions was the Vietnamese minority. Before the American puppet regime of General Lon Nol was installed in Cambodia in 1970, the Vietnamese minority counted about 400,000 people. Immediately after his takeover, 200.000 were expelled from the country and sent back to Vietnam. Pol Pot continued with this policy expelling 100,000 after the victory of the Khmer Rouge over the Lon Nol regime in April 1975.[4] Ben Kiernan says:

In more than a year's worth of research in Cambodia since 1979, I was not able to find a single Vietnamese resident who had survived the Pol Pot years there. However, plenty of eyewitnesses from other ethnic groups, including Khmers who had married Vietnamese, testified to the terrible fates of their Vietnamese spouses and neighbors. This was a campaign of systematic racial extermination.[5]

At a special conference held on 20 May 1975, all military and civilian officials of the new regime are said to have been given the following instructions:

1. Evacuate people from all towns.

2. Abolish all markets.

3. Abolish Lon Nol regime currency and withhold the revolutionary currency that had been printed.

4. Defrock all Budddhist monks and put them to work growing rice.

5. Execute all leaders of the Lon Nol regime beginning with the top leaders.

6. Establish high-level cooperatives throughout the country with communal eating.

---

[1] Ibid.

[2] www.culturalsurvival.org/publications/cultural-survival-quarterly/survival-cambo-dians-ethnic-minorities.

[3] Ibid.

[4] Ibid.

[5] Ibid.

7. EXPEL THE ENTIRE VIETNAMESE MINORITY POPULATION.

8. Dispatch troops to the borders, particularly the Vietnamese border.[1]

(There is no official document of the meeting though. In an interview Ben Kiernan had with a former political commissar of the regime by the name of Sin Song in Phom Penh on August 12, 1980, he was given the information. Song's immediate superior was a participant of the meeting and had told him about the eight points).

Kiernan also says that the persecutions extended to the Khmer Krom, ethnic Khmers born in Vietnam who had resettled to Cambodia. After the overthrow of the regime, 200,000 had returned to their former native areas:

> Heng Samrin, the leader of the successor government in Cambodia after the downfall of Pol Pot, who was also interviewed by Kiernan, told him that the Vietnamese who had not fled the country were forbidden to leave from mid-1976, when the first massacres began. The first official directive came on 1 April 1977, when Pol Pots headquarters started a nationwide campaign against the remaining Vietnamese population. The order was called 'Directive from 870'.[2]

> Kiernan conducted interviews with survivors in 1980 who told him of the massacres against the Vietnamese minority.

> The Muslim minority of the Cham also fell victim to Pol Pot's perse-cutions, according to Kiernan. In 1975 there were 250,000 Chan people of which around 90,000 had died, he tells us. The pogroms had started in the SW area of Cambodia. First women had to cut their hair short (which reminds us of scenes during Mao's Cultural Revolution), then they were forbidden to sing their Sarong songs and had to wear a black pajama. No reli-gious activities were allowed anymore. Korans were collected, the Muslims were forced to eat pork and their language was outlawed. Their villages were broken up into small groups, Rebellions were brutally smashed. The Cham used to be self-employed fishermen or small traders — a thorn in the eye of Pol Pot's "revolutionaries." Even before their power grab in 1975 the persecutions are said to have started in certain areas already controlled by the Communist Party of Kampuchea.

About the fate of the Chinese minority living in Kampuchea, Kiernan has this to say:

> Of the 1975 population of 425,000, only 200,000 Chinese survived the next four years. Ethnic Chinese were nearly all urban dwellers, and they were seen by the Khmer Rouge as archetypal city dwellers (who after

---

[1] Ben Kiernan, *The Pol Pot Regime*, New Haven and London, 2008, p. 55. My emphasis.
[2] Ben Kiernan, ibid., p. 297.

the 1975 evacuation of the cities were labeled 'new people') and therefore potential enemies or prisoners-of-war.[1]

The reason why they were targeted was not because of their ethnicity or race, but because they were urban people, according to Kiernan. Irrespective of this anti-Chinese policy, the Chinese government supported the regime nevertheless.

True Communists would never have allowed such things. Looking back to the October Revolution of 1917, one of the first things Lenin's new government did was to issue a decree protecting the minorities of Russia which had been suppressed under czarism for centuries. On November 3, 1917, only days after the Revolution, the *Declaration of the Rights of the Russian Peoples* was issued giving them equal rights. In an appeal to the Russian Muslims Lenin told them to manage their lives freely and unhindered from now on.[2] Stalin was People's Commissar for the Nationalities at the time and was mandated to look after the interests of the nationalities and minorities in Russia.

c) The proportions of the crimes
Pol Pot (Brother No. One) shortly before his death in 1998 in an interview:

> I came to carry out the struggle, not to kill people.[3]

He said that he had a clear conscience and portrayed himself as "a misunderstood and vilified figure," according to Alex Alvarez (2001).

Brother No. 2 Nuon Chea, his deputy, who was convicted in 2014 and given a life sentence, almost forty years after the Khmer Rouge had seized power in Cambodia, said in 2013:

> I'd like to sincerely apologize to the public, the victims, the families, and all Cambodian people.[4]

In 2013, the Cambodian Prime Minister, Mr. Hun Sen, took the initiative to pass legislation to prohibit the denial in public of the Cambodian genocide and other war crimes committed by the Khmer Rouge between 1975 and 1979. The biggest opposition party, however, rejected the bill.

The new Cambodian government that came to power after the Vietnamese army had defeated Pol Pot's forces in late 1978 and bringing down the regime, immediately thereafter passed 'Decree Law No. 1' allowing for Pol Pot and Ieng Sary to be put on trial for the crime of genocide. Both were tried in absentia and found guilty of genocide. The United States, however, refused to hold trial for Pol Pot until 1997. He was never put on trial unlike some of his closest collaborators, among them Ieng Sary and Nuon Chea.

---

[1] Ben Kiernan, *The Survival of Cambodia's Ethnic Minorities*, September, 1990, in: *Cultural Survival Quarterly Magazine*, Cambridge/MA/USA, September, 1990, p. 2.
[2] *Große Sowjet-Enzyklopädie* (Great Soviet Encyclopedia), Vol. 1, Berlin, 1952, p. 671.
[3] en.wikipedia.org/wik/Cambodian_genocide#cite_note-FOOTNOTEChan2004256165.
[4] Ibid.

Mr. Duch, the infamous chief warden of the S-21 prison where up to 17,000 political prisoners are said to have been killed, admitted in an interview with Nate Thayer his guilt for the crimes carried out at Tuol Sleng prison under his supervision. But only in 2010 a court passed a guilty verdict against him giving him a prison sentence of 35 years, which was later changed into a life sentence. At that time, Duch was already an old man who had lived his life. Tuol Sleng is now a war crimes museum, documenting the atrocities of the so-called communist regime.

What are some of the main researchers telling us about the proportions of the crimes?

Ben Kiernan, an Australian scholar working for Yale University, is of the opinion that Between 1.67 and 1.87 people died equaling 21 to 24 percent of the Cambodian population of 1975 (almost 8 million at the time).

Marek Slivinsky from France says that slightly fewer than 2 million died at the hands of the Khmer Rouge.

Michael Vickery says that 'only' 740,000 (under 10 percent of the Cambodian population) had died during that time. But he put the total population only at around 7 million which seems questionable.

And the successor government of the Khmer Rouge installed by the Vietnamese in January 1979 and led by the pro-Vietnamese Communist Heng Samrin, a high army commander who had started an unsuccessful rebellion against Pol Pot in 1978, put the number even much higher: at 3.3 million deaths. But this figure seems to be exaggerated.

So the figures vary considerably. But it cannot be denied that even according to the most moderate estimates, almost one million people were killed when Pol Pot and the people belonging to the Standing Committee of the Communist Party of Kampuchea (consisting of around 20 members) ruled the country, and we should not forget that the total number of the Cambodian population at that time was only about ten million, maybe less.

d) Who Supported the Regime?

Only two months after Pol Pot's coming to power, he and his foreign minister, Ieng Sary, went to Beijing to meet with Mao Zedong. The meeting took place on 21 June 1975. In his conversation   Mao regretted that China's state had become a "capitalist state without capitalists." Here is an excerpt from their conversation:

Beijing, 21 June 1975

Mao Zedong: During the transition from the democratic revolution to adopting a socialist path there exist two possibilities: one is socialism, the other is capitalism. Our situation is now like this. 50 years from now, or 100 years from now, the struggle between two lines will exist. Even 10,000 years from now the struggle between two lines will exist. When communism is realized, the struggle between two lines will still be there. Otherwise you are not a Marxist. This is unity existing among opposites... Our state now is, as Lenin said, a capitalist state without capitalists. The state protects capitalist rights, our wages are not equal. Under the slogan of equality, a system of inequality has been introduced. There will exist a struggle between two lines, the struggle between two lines, the struggle between the advanced and the backward, even when communism is realized. Today we cannot explain it completely...[1]

Maybe, the "great Marxist philosopher" wanted the Khmer Rouge leaders to do a better job than he himself had done in China and to introduce "socialism" on the spot. Three months later, the Pol Pot regime received the biggest credit China had ever granted to a foreign country: a loan in the amount of one billion.[2]

Mao talking to Foreign Minister Ieng Sary (right) and Pol Pot (center), 1975

In Beijing Mao not only promised generous financial but also military aid to the regime.

How close and intimate the relationship between Mao Zedong's China and Democratic Kampuchea was to become is testified by the fact that when Mao had died on 9 September 1976, a five-day period of mourning was announced in Kampuchea. Returning from an overseas trip, Ieng Sary gave a speech on 18 September in which he praised "Marxism-Leninism-Mao Zedong Thought".[3]

---

[1] http://digitalarchive.wilsoncenter.org/document/111267.
[2] *China Quarterly*, No. 64, December 1975, p. 797, also in: Ben Kiernan, *How Pol Pot Came to Power*, New Haven and London, p. 416.
[3] Ben Kiernan, *The Pol Pot Regime*, ibid., p. 330.

Even after the extent of the horrors of Pol Pot's war crimes had become known to the whole world, China did not regret having supported the genocidal regime: Yang Yanyi of the *Asian Department in the Foreign Ministry of China* in December 2000 defended aiding the Khmer Rouge, saying:

> Our assistance and support during that certain historical period was to support Cambodia's effort to safeguard its sovereignty and national independence. We never support the wrong policies of other countries.[1]

Nine years later, the Chinese Foreign Ministry spokeswoman, Jiang Yu, said this in defense of China's former support for the genocidal Pol Pot regime:

> For a long time China has...had normal and friendly relations with previous Cambodian governments, including that of Democratic Kampuchea. As everyone knows, the government of Democratic Kampuchea had a legal seat at the United Nations and had established broad foreign relations with more than 70 countries.[2]

After the downfall of the regime, Pol Pot continued his campaign to win back power in Cambodia allying himself with two other resistance groups: the National Liberation Front of the Khmer and a monarchist group called FUNCIPEC. In the *Süd-Asien Handbuch* by the Germans Dahm and Ptak we read:

> Under pressure form abroad, these three groups formed a coalition government for a Democratic Kampuchea in exile, supported militarily, financially, and diplomatically by China, the United States and the ASEAN member countries. Up to a certain degree it also received support from certain other Western countries.[3]

The ousted regime even retained its former seat in the United Nations for some time.

So China continued to support its former ally even after the regime's downfall and despite the fact that thousands of ethnic Chinese from Cambodian towns had perished under its rule. Ben Kiernan:

> China's interests in Democratic Kampuchea had little to do with the living conditions of Cambodians or the country's ethnic Chinese.[4]

During the time of the Pol Pot regime China sent 15,000 advisers and technicians to Cambodia to assist it in its industrialization effort, but also in helping it to train its military. They used to work in factories, but also throughout the country, particularly at the ports, as Ben Kiernan tells us:

---

[1] English Wikipedia: en.wikipedia.org/wiki/Cambodian_genocide.
[2] Ibid.
[3] Bernhard Dahm und Roderick Ptak, *Südost-Asien Handbuch,* München, 1999, p. 256.
[4] Ben Kiernan, *The Pol Pot Regime,* ibid., p. 384.

But there were also other allies of the genocidal regime: North Korea's Kim Il Sung, the 'Great Leader' of the country, decorated Pol Pot with the award *Hero of the Democratic People's Republic of Korea* in 1977, when persecutions, deportations, witch hunts and pogroms of Cambodian minorities were in full swing. And also in the same year...

Kim Il-sung sent Khieu Samphan a personal message of congratulations on Democratic Kampuchea's rapid revolutionary achievements, asserting that though the Korean revolution advanced at the speed of a "winged horse," the Cambodian one flew "faster than the wind".[1]

Khieu Samphan, alias Hem, was not a nonentity but the Head of the Office of the Communist Party of Kampuchea from 1977 onward and also President of the State Presidium, later jailed on charges of crimes against humanity and war crimes.

Chinese military advisers in Cambodia helping to train Pol Pot's army against the Vietnamese enemy.

As soon as the Khmer Rouge started their war against Vietnam — the diplomatic relations were ended unilaterally by the Pol Pot regime on 31 December of 1977 — the United States, then under President Jimmy Carter, saw a welcome opportunity to take revenge on the Vietnamese who had defeated and humiliated the US military in 1975 and had sent them packing. Carter's national security adviser, the Polish born Zbigniew Brzezinski, visited China in May 1978 and...

---

[1] Ibid., p. 378.

...taking the first step toward a US political alignment with Democratic Kampuchea that would see Brzezinski fostering international support for Pol Pot in 1979.[1]

Half a year later, the United States officially established diplomatic relations with China.

But as we have heard from the spokesperson of the Chinese Foreign Ministry, the Pol Pot regime had many other friends as well: More than 70 nations traded with the regime notwithstanding its dismal human rights record — an issue only too often raised when it came to the Soviet Union and the way they treated their dissidents.

CONCLUSIONS

1. Pol Pot's Four-Year Plan, which exists as a document, has nothing in common with a scientific Marxist plan for the building of socialism in an under-developed, semi-feudal and rural country. Its explicit aim was to build some sort of "socialism now!," a system of complete collectivism, eating halls and people's communes modeled after Mao Zedong's experiments in China in the late 1950s and early 1960s ("Great Leap Forward") which caused a nationwide crisis almost never known in China before, killing at least 30 million people as a result of malnutrition and physical exhaustion. Like Mao Zedong's Great Leap Forward, Pol Pot's "Super Great Leap Forward" failed and was bound to fail, causing a similar catastrophe. Opposition to this human experiment was met by brutal repression and persecution on behalf of Cambodia's "socialism." Both experiments lasted only about three and a half years and did nothing to promote economic and social progress in the respective countries. As a matter of fact, they turned the clock back and therefore must be called criminal and reactionary.

2. The experiences made by other socialist countries, which were many at the time, especially those made in the Soviet Union under Stalin, were thrown to the wind. Socialism à la Pol Pot was to be built immediately, without any transitional periods. Pol Pot was not a Marxist, but a self-confessed Maoist who had spent some months in China in the 1960s where he was educated in Mao Zedong Thought. He is quoted as saying that "the issue of lines and struggle raised by Chairman Mao is an important strategic issue. We'll follow your words in the future. I've read and learned various works by Chairman Mao since I was young, especially the theory of 'people's war.' Your works have guided our entire Party."[2]

3. His Super Great Leap Forward was a cynical human experiment costing the lives of hundreds of thousands of Cambodians. The set target of three tons of

---

[1] Ibid., p. 385.

[2] *Phoenix News Media*, April 10, 2008, quoted in the English Wikipedia, see: en.wikipedia.org/ Cambodian_genocide#cite_note-FOOTNOTEChan2004256165.

rice per hectare had never been achieved in Cambodian history before. The "new people," who had been evacuated from the cities under the pretext of imminent US bombardments in April 1975 and also in the fall of the same year, were sent to cooperatives and rice-fields to fulfill a grandiose and unscientific plan to accumulate the capital for the building of the light industry and after that of the heavy industry. But the history of socialism teaches us that this does not and cannot work. Heavy industry must be given priority over light industry and agriculture in the first stage of socialism, especially in backward rural countries without a solid industrial base. Agriculture can only be developed thoroughly later when enough modern machines (tractors, harvesters...) have been made available to till the land and to make living in the countryside attractive, rendering forced collectivization unnecessary.

4. Pol Pot did great harm to the idea of communism and provided valuable ammunition for all those who equate communism with a police state, supervision, shortages, hunger and the lack of basic freedoms. The international bourgeoisie, the globalist elites based in Washington and London, benefited greatly from this catastrophe and reaped the ideological fruits of this human tragedy. The fact that Pol Pot was protected by the US government till the last days of his life is very telling. He has never been charged of war crimes due to this protection. So, in a sense, he was a useful asset of the imperialists. It is also very telling that the British BBC calls Pol Pot a "Marxist leader" whereby the distinction between Maoism and Marxism is deliberately (or unconsciously) blurred to discredit Marxism by using Pol Pot's genocide against Marxism.[1]

5. The Pol Pot regime did not just make "some mistakes" as certain self-proclaimed Marxists still claim. It was a criminal, murderous and genocidal regime of a racist and fascist type.

Sources:

Chandler, David P. *Voices from S-21*, London, 1999

Chandler, David P., Kiernan, Ben, Boua, Chanthou, *Pol Pot Plans the Future*, New Haven, 1988

China Quarterly, No. 64, December 1975

Cold War International History Project (Wilson Center), Virtual Archive

Dahm, Bernhard und Ptak, Roderick, *Südost-Asien-Handbuch. Geschichte, Gesellschaft, Politik, Wirtschaft, Kultur*, München, 1999

Geschichte der Kommunistischen Partei der Sowjetunion (Bolschewiki), 'Kurzer Lehrgang,' Berlin 1945

Geschichte der Partei der Arbeit Albaniens, Tirana 1971

Große Sowjet-Enzyklopädie, Vol. 1, Berlin 1952

Kiernan, Ben, *How Pol Pot Came to Power*, New Haven and London, 2004

---

[1] www.bbc.com/news/world-asia-pacific-10684399.

_____*The Pol Pot Regime. Race, Power, and Genocide in Cambodia under the Khmer Rouge, 1975–1979*, New Haven and London, 2008

_____*The Survival of Cambodia's Ethnic Minorities*, at: https://www.culturalsurvival.org/publications

Lorenz, Lothar, *Volksrepublik Albanien, Leseund Arbeitsbuch*, Gießen 1974

Marxistisch-leninistischer Studienkreis, *Der Kampf Joseph Stalins und des Kominform gegen den Tito-Revisionismus*, Wien, 1979

Neue Welt, Halbmonatszeitschrift, 8. Jahrgang, Nr. 11, Juni 1953

Politische Ökonomie, Lehrbuch, Berlin 1955

Kim DePaul et al, *Children of Cambodia's Killing Fields, Memoirs of Survivors*, New Haven, 1997

Stalin, J. W., *Werke (works)*, Vol. 12, Berlin, 1954

English Wikipedia on the Cambodian Genocide

Photos from the public domain.

8. Ouk Villa: A Bitter Life, Memories of a Survivor of Pol Pot's Genocide

Introduction (G. Schnehen)

The ideological foundation of what was practiced in Cambodia between 1975 and 1979 when the Pol Pot regime ruled the country with an iron fist, killing at least a million innocent people, was Maoism, not Marxism. This ideology was based on Mao Zedong's 'ideas' which already had been put into practice in China in the late 1950s and early 1960s under Mao Zedong's rule with devastating consequences (more than 30 million people are said to have died during the "Great Leap Forward" in 1958 through to 1961). To my knowledge these 'ideas' have never been fully exposed as anti-Marxist. On the contrary: Even today, Mao Zedong Thought is still considered a variant of Marxism but not as its archenemy. In reality though, Maoism has nothing in common with Marxism which has always been a platform of the struggles of the working classes to free themselves from the shackles of the capitalist society and its ruling classes and elites. Marxism, as developed by Marx and Engels, is an ideology of humanism, of liberation, of freedom and people's democracy, not one of totalitarianism, enslavement and suppression. It is a blueprint for building a new, a better and friendlier society without exploitation, without oppression by a few super-rich oligarchs, their huge corporations and their financial institutions, without constant financial, social, political, economic crises, and endless wars for the benefit of a handful of arms producers and their banks.

Maoism, however, is a thoroughly anti-Marxist and totalitarian ideology which was developed in Yenan/North China by Mao Zedong and his ideologues (among them especially Chen Boda) in the early forties, then called 'Marxism of Reality,' with the aim of discrediting the emerging socialist system of the Soviet Union. The objective was to erect an authoritarian regime under the leadership of one man by the name of Mao Zedong and to transform China into a totalitarian society of "people's communes" without any individual freedoms. Mass indoctrination campaigns were used to instill Mao Zedong's followers and adherents of the Communist Party of China with his 'ideas' and to purge the party from pro-Soviet and pro-Socialist elements, among them Wang Ming, Bo Gu, and many others who were Marxist freedom fighters and who favored broad based anti-fascist popular fronts to fight imperialism and international fascism and to assist the Soviet Union in its life-and-death struggle against the Nazi fascists and the Japanese militarists. But also lots of independent thinking intellectuals were persecuted in Yenan, among them the writer Wang Shiwei, who was imprisoned and later shot for his courageous criticism of Mao Zedong and his cronies.

By making use of the personality cult around Mao Zedong his ideas were developed into some sort of religion, into a sectarian cult, to detract attention from its anti-Marxist essence. Originally, Mao Zedong Thought was intentionally propagated as a "new stage of Marxism-Leninism" and later even as the "highest stage of Marxism-Leninism." At that time Marxism was held in high esteem by large parts of the oppressed Chinese proletariat and also among many landless peasants in China being exploited by a few rich families and a strata of big tenant farmers. So the authority Marxism enjoyed in China in the twenties and thirties due to the Russian October Revolution was skillfully used by Mao Zedong and his ideologues to change its character and to transform it into something completely different: into a leadership cult, a mixture of nationalism, chauvinism, anarchism, and extreme collectivism for the benefit of a few self-appointed leaders and their sponsors. Proletarian internationalism was replaced by Great Han-Chauvinism, the class struggle against the Chinese big bourgeoisie was substituted by welcoming this class and by giving their leaders a substantial say in building state capitalism in the "People's Republic of China" — later openly admitted by Mao Zedong.

Pol Pot, a fanatic follower and adherent of Mao Zedong Thought from his years in Paris and from his months in China in the mid-1960s onward, where he had been a student, was given support by Mao Zedong and his entourage after having seized power in Cambodia in the spring of 1975, following the overthrow of the pro-American Lon Nol puppet regime installed in 1970. Up until then the biggest financial credit in the history of the People's Republic of China was given to him to change Cambodia from top to bottom and to develop a special type of "socialism" based on Mao Zedong Thought from one day to the next. The number three in the Cambodian Communist Party, Ieng Sary, and Pol Pot himself, visited

Mao Zedong in Beijing in June 1975, two months after the victory of the Khmer Rouge, and they were both warmly welcomed by the aging Chinese leader.

By applying Mao Zedong Thought to Cambodia, the Pol Pot regime established a system which led to a human catastrophe as the same ideas had previously led to a similar disaster in China itself in the late 1950s (Great Leap Forward). Hundreds of thousands of people perished, died from starvation or were killed in re-education camps or in the infamous Tuol prison led by Duch, Pol Pot's butcher number one. Those killed had refused to let themselves being re-educated or even staged rebellions.

After the capitulation of the pro-American Lon Nol regime and the ending of the US bombardments following the defeat of the US against Vietnam, the ordinary Cambodians only had one wish: to live in peace without being exposed to daily carpet bombings by B-52 bombers and to build a new future for themselves. What they got instead was new terror even on a larger scale, never before experienced in their whole history. Under the pretext of "imminent US bombardments" the city dwellers of Phnom Penh and other Cambodian cities and towns were swiftly "evacuated for three days" as they were told, and sent to far-away regions to work in rural cooperatives under the watchful eye of the unit leaders of "Angka" — the "Organization" — as the Communist Party of Kampuchea was called. All their belongings either had to be sold to buy some food during the marches or were confiscated by Angka's soldiers. In the cooperatives they had to work under a strict labor regime to help fulfill the first four-year plan.

Even though the Vietnamese liberation army, also called Vietcong, had driven out the US Army from South-East Asia entirely from which also Cambodia and especially the Khmer Rouge benefited greatly, Vietnam and the Vietnamese were soon seen as the number one enemy. Even the Vietnamese Khmer minority living in Cambodia, the Khmer Krom, was treated as second-class citizens with no rights. Even at that stage the new regime proved that it had nothing in common with Marxist ideas, but Mao Zedong supported it nevertheless, telling Pol Pot in June 1975 that he regretted that he himself had not been able to build such a "socialist society" in China, which, according to him, unfortunately, was still "state capitalist without capitalists".

Even after the downfall of the Pol Pot regime due to Vietnam's military intervention in late 1978 after a series of raids by Khmer Rouge militias into Vietnamese territory, Pol Pot continued his struggle from his bases near the Thai border being supported militarily by the US. Many crocodile tears were shed over the killing fields found in the aftermath of the regime's downfall, also and particularly by the US mainstream media. But despite these tears, the Pol Pot regime was still recognized as the sole representative at the United Nations by the US government.

Just one month after the Vietnamese victory over the Pol Pot regime, Maoist China, now led by Hua Kuo-feng and Deng Xiaoping, sent more than 500,000 soldiers into North Vietnam. Only after a few weeks, in mid-March of 1979, the Chinese military suffered a devastating defeat at the hands of the Vietnamese liberation army: Tens of thousands of Chinese soldiers were captured and then guarded by female soldiers to add to their embarrassment. China was forced to retreat from the captured Vietnamese cities.

So there was a close partnership among three players in Cambodia: the US, the Pol Pot regime, and Maoist and post-Maoist China. They all are responsible for what happened to the people of Cambodia during the time of Pol Pot's sinister rule over almost ten million Cambodians. According to moderate estimates, at least ten percent of the Cambodian population died at the hands of the Maoist regime which deserves to be called a genocide — a genocide against the own people. Some of the perpetrators at the top of the hierarchy have never been prosecuted by the "international community." Only in 2007, thirty years after the events, some of the chief perpetrators were arrested, among them Ieng Sary, Pol Pot's foreign secretary. Pol Pot, who enjoyed American protection until 1997, died in 1998, without ever having been tried by a court of law, be it national or international. In his last interview he said that he had a clear conscience. The victims of the Cambodian genocide still demand justice. Will they ever get it?

But what about Maoism which greatly contributed to this genocide as the ideological tool of the killers? When will true Marxists stand up and condemn Mao Zedong Thought which was intentionally forced upon a whole population as it had been enforced over the Chinese population previously? Even today, the Chinese government under Xi Jingping declares Mao and Maoism as part of the Chinese national legacy which should be honored side by side with Confucianism. To this day, Mao's picture can still be seen over Tiananmen Square in Beijing or on the bills of the Chinese currency, the yuan.

What Ouk Villa, one of the survivors of the Cambodian holocaust, tells us in the memoir given below[1] should be a warning to all of us, to all freedom-loving people: never ever give tyranny a chance, even if it comes along in a "progressive" and "red" cloak.

Ouk Villas Recollections, from: Children of Cambodia's Killing Fields (compiled by Dith Pran, edited by Kim DePaul)

On April 17, 1975, the Khmer Republic formally surrendered to the Khmer Rouge and the country was renamed Democratic Kampuchea. My family and other Cambodian families were evacuated from our native

---

[1] *Children of Cambodia's Killing Fields*, edited by Kim DePaul and compiled by Dith Pran, Yale University, 1997, pp. 115–121

homes to the far-off countryside and other rural areas that we never knew existed.

The first day we were in the new village we were warmly welcomed with a greeting ceremony that included a feast. I was nine then. After the welcome we were given an old thatched hut with a rotten roof. My father had to fix it and replace some walls. Later we were despised and called the "new" people, and our possessions were taken away for collective use. That same year, people were divided into three types, including the new and old. The old group hat lived in Khmer Rouge-controlled areas before the country's "liberation" and were "full rights" people. Then there were Khmer Rouge cadres.

We had no private property because everything belonged to Angka and all laws and orders were carried out in the name of Angka. Angka established high-level co-operatives throughout the country with communal eating. No one complained about it and no one spoke badly of Angka. We could speak only in a whisper or in private because we were fearful of being overheard. If they heard us, we would disappear for "reeducation." We were extremely scared of reeducation. It was the only word that everyone knew.

In late 1975 my family was separated. My two sisters were sent to the mobile youth group far away from us. They were forced to work day and night, but they weren't fed enough and they dressed in rags. As for me, I was sent to the child group center, which was about a kilometer from my family. I had to carry manure to the rice fields, and I was badly treated because I was accused of being lazy. From that time on I was not under the care of my parents anymore but was under the control of the unit leaders. We lived in a big house and had to sleep in rows of six, lined up head to toe.

All children had to get up early in the morning or they were kicked and pulled by the unit leaders. We never received any education because schools, money, markets, books, postal services, and religions were banned. The living conditions of the new people grew more desperate and seemed more physically and mentally arduous than the conditions of slaves in the Middle Ages.

We were taught only about hard work and faithfulness to the government. Later we were also taught to call our parents "comrades" and to spy on them.

One night I woke up and looked around to see if everyone was asleep. I walked on tiptoe and climbed down from the house. I ran through the rice fields and the bushes. A couple of times I fell down, and I got many scratches all over my body. Suddenly I saw three men who were tied up and being led by a militiaman to another small bush. From a distance I saw the militiaman force the men to kneel down on the edge of a big pit. A minute later the men were clubbed to death with a hoe. I could see this clearly in the moonlit night. I was terribly frightened and waited for the militiaman to go away.

I scurried to where my parents were. They were fearful of me being noticed and followed by the unit leaders. The next morning, while I was sitting near the window in front of the house, three unit leaders, dressed in black with silk neckerchiefs, approached our hut and said, "Let us bring comrade Villa back to the center." "He is ready to go," said my father. I was shivering with fear, hiding in the house. My father asked me to come out. "Let him follow us," said the big one with a rough voice. Luckily, I was not tied, but I was badly treated and warned. I was very lucky, because any children who escaped or avoided going to the center were tied up and beaten.

Early in 1976 a serious situation arose. My father was separated from my mother and sent to an all-male worksite. My mother was sent to another collective farm to dig canals. As for me, I had to sleep near the cattle. There were strange animal sounds at night, and the wind blowing through the trees scared me.

One night an odd noise woke me up. I was very frightened. What was it? It was a long voice that I had never heard before. It came nearer and nearer. Oh, God! It was under the hut. I screamed and called to my father for help. Everybody jumped up and asked me what was going on. I told them what I had heard. The strange noise came again. I asked them to listen to it. They told me that it was the howl of a wolf, but I didn't know what a wolf was, so I sat shivering with fear and fully awake. Several days later I began to be accustomed to the noises and could sleep well.

While I was looking for crickets and grasshoppers to roast one morning, I saw three militiamen lead six people to the edge of an excavation site. The victims were clubbed on their napes with a hoe and they fell into the grave. They weren't dead yet. They were just unconscious in a pool of blood. The militiamen covered the mass grave with soil and some grass. If they had seen me, I would have been killed as well.

In 1977 my mother, my sister, and I were sent to the village again, but not my father. My mother tried to ask other people about him. They told us the devastating news that he had been sent to be reeducated and was not expected to return home. My mother cried and mourned because it meant that he was killed. He was accused of being involved in an anti-Khmer group, and the head of the village also had found out that he had been a professor in the Lon Nol regime.

There was no doubt that all the people were enemies of and obstacles to the Khmer Rouge government. After my father's death we were spied on all the time and if they had seen or heard any of us complain, we would have been arrested and killed. At night we couldn't talk or walk outside. We had to live in silence.

Early in 1978 my family was separated again. My mother was sent to the widows group, and my sisters were sent to a malarial region where thousands of children died from malaria or from famine and malnutrition. The children had to rely mostly on ineffective traditional herbal remedies.

One day my sisters came from the mobile group. Their faces were haggard, their eyes looked hollow, and their skin was blue. My sisters told our mother how difficult things had been. She hugged them and said nothing, but she shed her tears. I didn't know much about the bitterness of life, but I felt very sad. My two sisters could stay with us only one night. They were starving. We didn't have any food at home. Everything belonged to Angka.

I decided to do something that I didn't want to do. In the morning, before dawn, I got up around four o'clock and went to the collective kitchen to get some tapioca. It was quiet and the cooks were sound asleep. Near the corner of the kitchen there were three big pans of tapioca, which was used for mixing the gruel. Without waiting, I hurriedly picked up some and packed it in both ends of my blanket and silently went home.

When I got there my mother was so fearful of me being caught. "You would have been killed if you had been arrested, my son. Don't do that again." "Yes, Mom. Never again." I had become a thief because of my sisters' starvation.

In mid-1978 we heard gunfire from the east. Many people escaped from the gunshots. We were worried. After late 1978 children were allowed to return home. My two sisters came back and we lived together, but we were still sad because we missed our father.

A few days later we were ready to pack our belongings and escape from the gunfire. We were evacuated from the village to a mountain called Phnom Thom, which means Big Mountain. We had do walk day and night. I carried my youngest brother on my back. My sisters carried packs of torn clothing on their heads. My mother carried a bucket of rice on her head. The rice was given to her in the confusion of the war. We stopped only for a short time to rest for meals. At night we slept in the open field. When we set off again, mostly during the night, we walked hand in hand, and sometimes my mother tied a rope to my waist and then to my sisters' waists and she led us together so we wouldn't get lost. I fell down a lot because I kept walking and falling asleep. The string pulled my sisters down, too.

At last we arrived at the side of the mountain. Early one morning, while we were having dinner, we heard gunshots. All around us shells were falling on the ground and exploding. It sounded like hell. A few moments later, we were bombed and fired at. We screamed and my mother prayed to God for help. Why were we being bombed? Why were they shelling us? Have they come to liberate us or kill us? A few seconds later we learned that we were on the front line of the battlefield.

The gunshots finally calmed down, but a lot of people were killed. The ground was covered with blood from the bodies that lay there. Some were dead and some were still alive. Victims lay motionless in pain an agony. Many people mourned over their relatives. Some had been crying and screaming because they couldn't find their children. Fortunately, no one in my family had been killed.

My family and others hurried to get out of there. We arrived at another mountain called Give It Up Mountain. It was very steep and tall. If we could climb over it we could reach Thailand, but we couldn't carry heavy things or children. Some people were forced to climb without their children or belongings. Lots of people fell down and died because they didn't have enough strength to climb. They didn't return to their villages because they were afraid of the Vietnamese soldiers. We had been taught that the Vietnamese would slit our throats if they caught us. But my family and many others decided not to climb the mountain. "I can't live without my children," said my mother. "We must go back to our village. If we die, we'll die together." So we decided to return to the village.

We met thousands of Vietnamese soldiers on our way home. We were very frightened and shocked to see them. They couldn't speak Khmer, but they were very kind and friendly. They gave us rice, sugar, and yellow noodles and let us go to the village safely.

The village was quiet and our hut was burned down, so we built another one the size of a chicken house. It is very hard for a woman with six children to start a new life with her bare hands. We worked hard in the fields and had to help our mother plant potatoes and rice.

On January 7, 1979, the Khmer Rouge government in Phnom Penh was dismantled. The Khmer Rouge left thousands widowed, orphaned, and disabled. Sorrow and a profound hatred of the criminal genocidal regime and man's inhumanity to man are deep in our hearts. The sound of the victims' cries of pain and agony are still in our minds. They are asking for justice and are demanding condemnation of the Khmer Rouge butchers.

The Khmer Rouge never stopped committing their atrocities and criminal actions. They are still fighting, killing and destroying roads and bridges. This shows that the Khmer Rouge want another genocide to happen in Cambodia. Never again must we let the Khmer Rouge return to power!

9. Maoist China Invades Vietnam — Le Duan's Report to The Communist Party of Vietnam

1. The facts[1]

After a whole series of border incidents, on February 17 (1979 — Ed.) Chinese troops invaded Vietnam and occupied some towns in the border region. Having suffered heavy losses, they started to retreat on March 5th, and on March 16th it was reported that Vietnamese territory had been completely cleared. Negotiations to resolve the border dispute, which started on April 18 and ended on May 18, came to nothing. On June 28, a new round of negotiations started in Beijing.

The decision to start the invasion was taken by the Chinese leaders immediately after Deng Xiaoping's return from a visit to the United States.[2]

The Chinese invasion was sharply criticized by the Soviet bloc, India, and Albania, while Southeast Asian and Western states combined an appeal to the Chinese troops to retreat with similar appeals to the Vietnamese troops to also retreat from Cambodia...The Chinese invasion was condemned by all East European communist countries, except Romania and Yugoslavia, but also by Mongolia and Cuba as well as by the pro-communist governments of Afghanistan, Angola, and Mozambique. In a statement by the Cambodian government of February 18, the "reactionary

---

[1] From: *Keesing's Record of World Events*, entry dated Oct. 1979, *Chinese Invasion of Vietnam*, at: http://keesings.gvpi.net/keesings/Ipext.dII/KRWE/krwe-8261/krwe-82854/krwe-828...

[2] Ibid., p. 1.

Beijing authorities" are accused of "monstrous and despicable crimes." A declaration by the Laotian government of the same day, however, was worded with more restraint and only called for a retreat of the Chinese forces as well as for the restoration of a normal situation at the border...The Yugoslav press was a lot more explicit and claimed that the Chinese invasion had been partly provoked by the Vietnamese invasion of Cambodia... In Albania, Petro Dode (Chairman of the State Planning Commission) condemned the "military aggression of China against the brotherland Vietnam" in strong terms...[1]

Captured Chinese soldiers after China's invasion of Vietnam in February 1979 guarded by female Vietnamese soldiers

2. Plot of the Reactionary Chinese Clique Against Vietnam, Comments by Comrade B, Chairman of the Communist Party of Vietnam)[2]

Generally speaking, after we had defeated the Americans, there was no imperialist that would dare to fight us again. The only persons who thought they could still fight us and dared to fight us were the Chinese reactionaries. But the Chinese people did not want it like that at all. I do not know how much longer some of these Chinese reactionaries will continue to exist, however, as long as they do, they will strike us as they have just recently done (meaning in early 1979). If war comes from the north, then the northern central provinces of Nghe An, Ha Tinh and Thanh

---

[1] Ibid., p. 2

[2] Namely Le Duan; speech given in 1979) http://digitalarchive.wilsoncenter.org/document/112982. Original language: Vietnamese. The translator, Christopher Goscha, teaches at the rAmerican University and at the International School of Paris. He also is a deputy director of 'Groupe d'Etudes sur le Viet Nam contemporain, Sciences politique' in Paris. His comments are in brackets. Abridged text.

Hoa will become the bases for the entire country. They are unparalleled as the most efficient, the best and strongest bases. For if the Deltas in the north continued as an uninterrupted stretch, then then the situation would be very complicated. Not at all a simple matter. If it had not been for the Vietnamese, there would not have been anyone to fight the USA, because at the time the Vietnamese were fighting the USA, the rest of the world was afraid of the USA...

Vietnam's leader, Le Duan, 1966

Although the Chinese helped North Korea, it was only with the aim of protecting their own northern flank. After the fighting had finished in Korea and when the pressure was on Vietnam, he (Zhou Enlai, Mao's foreign minister, as the text seems to suggest — GS) said that if the Vietnamese continued to fight they would have to fend for themselves. He would any longer and pressured us to stop fighting.

When we had signed the Geneva Accords, it was precisely Zhou Enlai who divided our country into two parts. After our country had been divided into the northern and southern zones in this way, he once again pressured us into doing anything in regard to southern Vietnam. They forbade us from rising up (against the US-backed Republic of Vietnam). But they could do nothing to deter us.

When we were in the south and had made preparations to wage guerrilla warfare immediately after the signing of the Geneva Accords, Mao Zedong told our Party Congress that we had to force the Lao to transfer immediately their two liberated provinces to (the) Vientiane government. Otherwise the Americans would destroy them, a very dangerous situation (in the Chinese view)! Vietnam had to work at once with the Americans (concerning this matter). Mao forced us in this way and we had to do it.

Then, after these two (Lao) provinces had been turned over to Vientiane (the capital of Laos), the (Lao) reactionaries immediately arrested Souphanouvong (President of Laos, 1975-86). The Lao had two battalions which were surrounded at the time. Moreover, they were not yet combat ready. Later, one battalion was able to escape (encirclement). At that time, I gave it as my opinion that the Lao must be permitted to wage guerrilla warfare. I invited the Chinese to come and discuss this matter with us. I told them, "Comrades, if you go ahead pressuring the Lao in this way, then their forces will completely disintegrate. They must now be permitted to conduct guerrilla warfare."

Zhang Wentian, who was previously the Secretary General (of the Chinese Communist Party) and used the pen name Luc Phu, answered me...

"Yes, comrades, what you say is right. Let us allow that Lao battalion to take up guerrilla warfare."

I immediately asked Zhang Wentian: "Comrades, if you allow the Lao to take up guerrilla war, then there is nothing to fear about launching guerrilla war in south Vietnam. What is that frightens you so much so that you still block such action?"

He (Zhang Wentian) said: "There is nothing to be afraid of!"

That was what Zhang Wentian said. However, Ho Wei, the Chinese ambassador to Vietnam at that time, (and) who was seated there, was listening to what was being said. He immediately cabled back to China (reporting what had been said between Le Duan and Zhang Wentian). Mao replied at once: "Vietnam cannot do that (taking up guerrilla war in the south). Vietnam must lie in wait for a protracted period of time!" We were so poor. How could we fight the Americans if we did not have China as a rearguard base? (Thus), we had to listen to them, correct?

However, we did not agree. We secretly went ahead in developing our forces. When (Ngo Dinh) Diem dragged his guillotine machine throughout much of southern Vietnam, we issued the order to form mass forces to oppose the established order and to take power (from the Diem government). We did not care (about the Chinese). When the uprising to seize power had begun, we went to China to meet with Zhou Enlai and Deng Xiaoping. Deng Xiaoping told me: "Comrade, now that your mistake has become an accomplished fact, you should only fight at the level of one platoon downward."

That was the kind of pressure they exerted on us.

I said (to the Chinese): "Yes, yes! I will do that. I will only fight at the level of one platoon downwards." After we had fought and China realized that we could fight efficiently, Mao suddenly had a new line of thinking. He said that as the Americans were fighting us, we would bring in (Chinese) troops to help us build roads. His essential aim was to find out about the situation in our country so that later he could strike us, and thereby expand into Southeast Asia. There was no other reason. We were aware of this matter, but had to allow it (the entry of Chinese troops). But that was OK. They decided to send in their soldiers. I only asked that they send personnel, but these troops came with guns and ammunition. I also had to countenance this.

Later, he (Mao Zedong) forced us to permit 20,000 troops to come and build a road from Nghe Tinh into Nam Bo (the Vietnamese term for southern Vietnam). I refused. They kept proposing, but I would not budge. They pressured me into permitting them to come, but I did not accept it. They kept on pressuring, but I did not agree. I provide with these examples, comrades, so that you can see their long-standing plot to steal our country, and how wicked their plot is.

After the Americans had introduced several hundred thousand troops into southern Vietnam, we launched a general offensive in 1968 to force them to deescalate. In order to defeat the US, one had to know how to bring them to deescalate gradually. That was our strategy. We were fighting a big enemy, one with a population of 200 million people and who dominated the world. If we could not bring them to deescalate step-by-step, then we would have floundered and would have been unable to destroy the enemy. We had to fight to sap their will in order to force them to come to the negotiating table with us, yet without allowing them to introduce more troops.

When it came to the time when they wanted to negotiate with us, Ho Wei wrote a letter to us saying: "You cannot sit down to negotiate with the US. You must bring US troops into northern Vietnam to fight them." He pressured us in this way, making us extremely puzzled. This was not at all a simple matter. It was very tiresome every time these situations arose (with the Chinese).

We decided that it could not be done that way (referring to Ho Wei's advice not to negotiate with the US). We had to sit back down in Paris. We had to bring them (the US) to deescalate in order to defeat them. During that time, China made the announcement (to the US): "If you don't attack me, I won't attack you. However many troops you want to bring into Vietnam, it's up to you."

China, of its own accord, did this and pressured us in this way.

They (the Chinese) vigorously traded with the Americans and compelled us to serve as a bargaining chip in this way. When the Americans realized that they had lost, they immediately used China (to facilitate) their withdrawal (from southern Vietnam). Nixon and Kissinger went to China in order to discuss this matter. Before Nixon went to China, to solve the Vietnamese problem in such a way as to serve US interests and to lessen the US defeat, as well as to simultaneously allow him to entice China over the US (side) even more, Zhou Enlai came to visit me. Zhou told me: "At this time, Nixon is coming to visit me principally to discuss the Vietnamese problem, thus I must come to meet you, comrade, in order to discuss (it with you).

I answered: "Comrade, you can say whatever you like, but I still don't follow. Comrade, you are Chinese; I am Vietnamese. Vietnam is mine (my nation); not yours at all. You have no right to speak (about Vietnam's affairs), and you have no right to discuss (with the Americans)."

Today, comrades, I will personally tell you something which I have not even told our Politburo, for, comrade, you have brought up a serious matter, and hence I must speak:

In 1954, when we won victory at Dien Bien Phu, I was in Hau Nghia (province). Bac Ho (Ho Chi Minh) cabled to tell me that I had to go to southern Vietnam to regroup (the forces there) and to speak to the southern Vietnamese compatriots (about this matter). I traveled by wagon to the south. Along the way, compatriots came out to greet me, for they thought we had won victory. It was so painful! Looking at my southern compatriots, I cried. Because after this, the US would come and massacre (the population) in a terrible way.

Upon reaching the south, I immediately cabled Bac Ho to ask to remain (in the south) and not to return to the north, so that I could fight for another ten years or more. To Zhou Enlai:

"Comrade, you caused me hardship such as this (meaning Zhou Enlais role in the division of Vietnam at Geneva in 1954). Did you know that, comrade?"

Zhou said: "I apologize before you, comrade. I was wrong about that."After Nixon had already gone to China, he once again came to Vietnam in order to ask me about a number of problems concerning the fighting in southern Vietnam.

However, I immediately told Zhou Enlai: "Nixon has met with you already, comrade. Soon they (the US) will attack me even harder." I am not at all afraid. Both sides (the US and China) had negotiated with each other in order to fight me harder. He did as yet reject this as unfounded, and only said that

"I will send additional guns and ammunition to you, comrades."

Then he said (concerning fears of a secret US-Chinese plot): "There was no such thing." However, the two had discussed how to hit us harder, including B-52 bombing raids and the blocking of Haiphong (harbor). This was clearly the case.

If the Soviet Union and China had not been at odds with each other, then the US could not have struck us as fiercely as they did. As the two were in conflict, the Americans were unhampered. Although Vietnam was able to have a unity and solidarity both with China and the USSR, to achieve this was very complicated, for at that time we had to rely on China for many things. At that time, China annually provided assistance of 500,000 tons of foodstuffs, as well as guns, ammunition, money, not to mention dollar aid. The Soviet Union also helped in this way. If we could not do that, things would have been very dangerous. Every year I had to go to China twice to talk to them about southern Vietnam. As for the Soviets, I did not say anything at all. I only spoke in general terms. When dealing with the Chinese, I had to say that both were fighting the US. Alone I went. I had to attend to this matter. I had to go there and talk with them many times in this way, with the main intention to build closer relations between the two sides. It was precisely at this time that China pressured us to move away from the USSR, forbidding us from going with the USSR any longer.

They made it very tense. Deng Xiaoping, together with Kang Sheng, came and told me: "Comrade, I will assist you with several billion every year. You cannot accept anything from the Soviet Union."

I could not allow this. I said: "No, we must have solidarity and unity with the whole camp."

In 1963, when Khrushchev erred, the Chinese immediately issued a 25-point declaration and invited our Party to come and give our opinion. Brother Truong Chinh and I went together with a number of other brothers. In discussions, they listened to us for ten or so points, but when it came to the point of "there is no abandonment of the socialist camp," they did not listen...Deng Xiaoping said: "I am in charge of my own document. I seek your opinion but I do not accept this point of yours."

Before we were to leave, Mao met with Brother Truong Chinh and myself. Mao sat down to chat with us, and in the end announced: "Comrades, I would like you to know this. I will be president of 500 million land-hungry peasants, and I will bring an army to strike downwards into Southeast Asia."

Also seated there, Deng Xiaoping added:

"It is mainly because the poor peasants are in such dire straits!"

Once we were outside, I told Brother Truong Chinh: "There you have it, the plot to take our country and Southeast Asia. It is clear now." They dared to announce it in such a way. They thought we would not understand. It is true that not a minute goes by that they do not think of fighting Vietnam!

I will say more to you comrades so that you may see more of the military importance of this matter.

Mao asked me: "In Laos, how many square kilometers are there?" I answered: "About 200,000." "What is its population?" "About three million." "That's not very much! I'll bring my people there, indeed!"

Mao asked: "How many square kilometers are there in Thailand?" "About 500,000." "And how many people?" "About 40 million." "My God, Szechwan province of China has 500,000, but has 90 million people. I'll take some more of my people there, too!"

As for Vietnam they did not dare to speak about moving in people this way. However, he told me: "Comrade, isn't it true that your people have fought and defeated the Yuan army?" I said: "Correct." "Isn't it true, comrade, that you defeated the Qing army?" I said: "Correct." He said: "And the Ming army as well?" I said: "Yes, and you, too. I have beaten you as well. Did you know that?" I spoke with Mao Zedong in that way. He said: "Yes, yes!" He wanted to take Laos, all of Thailand as well as wanting to take all of Southeast Asia. Bringing people to live there. It was complicated.

In the past we had made intense preparations; it is not that we were unprepared. If we hadn't made preparations, the recent situation would have been very dangerous. It was not a simple matter. Ten years ago, I summoned together our brothers in the military to meet with me. I told them that the Soviet Union and the US were at odds with each other. As for China, they had joined hands with the US imperialists. In this tense situation, you must study this problem immediately. I was afraid that the military did not understand me, so I told them that there was no other way to understand the matter. But they found it very difficult to understand. It was not easy at all. But I could not speak in any other way. And I did not allow others to grab me.

When I went to the Soviet Union, the Soviets were also tough with me about China. The Soviet Union had convened a conference of 80 (communist) parties in support of Vietnam, but Vietnam did not attend this conference, for it was not simply aimed at helping Vietnam, but it was also designed to condemn China. Thus Vietnam did not go. The Soviets said: "Have you now abandoned internationalism or what? Why have you done this?" I said: "I have not abandoned internationalism at all. I have never done this. However, to be internationalist, the Americans must be defeated first. And if one wants to defeat the Americans, then there must be unity and solidarity with China. If I had gone to this conference, then the Chinese would have created very severe difficulties for us. Comrades, please understand me."

In China there were many different and contending opinions. Zhou Enlai agreed on forming a front with the Soviet Union in order to oppose the Americans. Once I went to the USSR to participate in a national day celebration, I was able to read a Chinese cable sent to the Soviet Union saying that "whenever someone attacks the USSR, then the Chinese will stand by your side." This was because there was a treaty of friendship between the USSR and China dating from earlier times (February 1950). Sitting next to Zhou Enlai, I asked him: "In this cable recently sent to the USSR, you have agreed, comrade, to establish a front with the Soviet Union, but why won't you form a front to oppose the US?" Zhou Enlai said: "We can. I share that view. Comrades, I will form a front with you." Peng Zhen, who was also seated there, added: "This opinion is extremely correct!" But when the matter was discussed in Shanghai, Mao said it was not possible, cancel it. You see how complicated it was.

Although Zhou Enlai held a number of those opinions, he nonetheless agreed on building a front and he helped Vietnam a lot. It was thanks to him that I could understand (much of what was going on in China). Otherwise it would have been very dangerous. He told me: "I'm doing my best to survive here, to use Li Chang to accumulate and provide assistance for you, comrades." My understanding is that without Zhou Enlai this would not have been possible at all. I am indebted to him.

However, it is not correct to say that other Chinese leaders shared Zhou Enlai's view at all. They differed in many ways. It must be said that the most uncompromising person, the one with the Great Han mentality, and the one who wanted to take Southeast Asia, was mainly Mao. All policies were in his hands.

The same applies to the current leaders of China. We do not know how things will turn out in the future, however, they have already attacked us. In the past, Deng Xiaoping did two things which have now been reversed. That is, when we won in southern Vietnam, there were many in China who were unhappy. However, Deng Xiaoping nonetheless congratulated us. As a result of this, he was immediately considered a revisionist by the others.

When I went to China for the last time, I was the leader of a delegation, and I met with the Chinese delegation led by Deng Xiaoping. In speaking of territorial problems, including discussion of several islands, I said: "Our two nations are near each other. There are several areas of our territory which have not been clearly defined. Both sides should establish bodies to consider the matter. Comrades, please agree with me. He (Deng) agreed, but after doing so he was immediately considered a revisionist by the other group of leaders.

But now he is crazy, because he wants to show that he is not a revisionist, therefore he has struck Vietnam even harder. He let them go ahead in attacking Vietnam. After defeating the Americans we kept in place over one million troops, leading Soviet comrades asked us: "Comrades, whom to you intend to fight that you keep such a large army?" I said: "Later, comrades, you will understand." The only reason we had kept such a standing army was because of China. If there had not been (such a threat), then this would have been unnecessary. Having been attacked recently on two fronts, it would have been very dangerous if we had not maintained a large army.

In the wake of WWII, everyone held the international gendarme to be American imperialism. They could take over and bully all the world. Everyone, including the big powers, were afraid of the US. It was only Vietnam that was not afraid of the US.

I understand this matter for my line of work has taught me it. The first person to fear (the Americans) was Mao Zedong. He told me, that is, the Vietnamese and Lao, that: "You must immediately turn over the two liberated provinces of Laos to the Vientiane government. If you do not do so, then the US will use it as a pretext to launch an attack. That is a great danger."

As for Vietnam, we said:

"We have to fight the Americans in order to liberate southern Vietnam."

He (Mao) said:

"You cannot do that. Southern Vietnam must lie in wait for a long period, for one lifetime, 5–10 or even 20 lifetimes from now. You cannot fight the Americans. Fighting the US is dangerous."

Mao Zedong was scared of the US to that extent...

But Vietnam was not scared. Vietnam went ahead and fought. If Vietnam had not fought the US, then southern Vietnam would not have been liberated. A country which is not liberated will remain a dependent one. No one is independent if only one-half of the country is free. It was not until 1975 that our country finally achieved its full independence. With independence would come freedom. Freedom should be freedom for the whole of the Vietnamese nation...

Engels had already spoken on people's war. Later the Soviet Union, China, ourselves also spoke on this matter. However, these three countries differ a lot on the content. It is not true that just because you have millions of people you can do whatever you like. China also spoke on people's war, however, they held that "when the enemy advances, we must retreat." In other words, defense is the main feature, and war is divided into three stages with the countryside to surround the cities, while the main forces remain in the forests and mountains only...The Chinese were on the defensive and very weak. Even with 400 million people pitted against a Japanese army of 300,000 to 400,000 troops, the Chinese still could not defeat them.

I have to repeat it like that, for before China had sent advisers to us some of our Vietnamese brothers did not understand. They thought the Chinese were very capable. But they are not so skilled, and thus we did not follow the Chinese advice.

In 1952, I left northern Vietnam for China, because I was sick and needed treatment. This was my first time abroad. I put questions to them and saw many very strange things. There were areas occupied by the Japanese troops, each with a population of 50 million people, but which had not a single guerrilla fighter...

When I returned from China, I met Uncle Ho. He asked me: "This was your first time to go abroad, isn't it right?" "Yes, I went abroad for the first time." "What did you see?" "I saw two things: Vietnam is very brave and they are not brave at all."

I understood that from that day on. We were entirely different from them. Courage is inherent in the Vietnamese person, and thus we have never had a defensive strategy. Every inhabitant fights.

Recently, they have brought several hundred thousand troops to invade our country. For the most part, we have used our militia and regional troops to attack them. We were not on the defensive, and thus they suffered a setback. They were not able to wipe out a single Vietnamese platoon, while we wiped out several of their regiments and several dozen of their battalions. That is because of our offensive strategy.

The American imperialists fought us in a protracted war. They were so powerful, yet they lost. But there was a special element, that is the acute contradictions between the Chinese and the Soviets. Because of this they have attacked us hard like this.

...Vietnam fought the Americans, and fought them very fiercely, but we know that the US was an extremely large country, more than capable of amassing 10 million troops and bringing all of its considerably powerful weapons in to fight us. Therefore we had to fight over long period of time in order to bring them to deescalation. We were the ones who could do this; the Chinese could not. When the American army attacked Quong Tre, the Politburo ordered troops to be brought in to fight at once. We were not afraid. After that I went to China to meet Zhou Enlai. He told me: "It is probably unparalleled, unique. In life there is only one chance, not two. No one has ever dared to do what you, comrades, have done."

Zhou Enlai was the Chief of the General Staff. He dared to speak, he was more frank. He told me: "If I had known before the ways which you, comrades, employ, we would not have needed the Long March." What was the Long March for? At the beginning of the march there were 300,000 troops; and at the end of the Long March there were only 30,000 remaining. 270,000 people were lost. It was truly idiotic to have done it this way. I speak as such so that you, comrades, know how much we are ahead of them. In the near future, if we are to fight against China, we will certainly win...However, the truth is that if a different country were to fight against China, it is not clear that they would win like this.

..If China and the USSR had been united with each other, then it is not certain that the US would have dared to fight us. If the two had been united and joined together to help us, it is not certain that the US would have dared to have fought us in the way in which they did. They would have balked from the very beginning. They would have balked in the same way during the Kennedy period. Vietnam, China, and the USSR all helped Laos and the US immediately signed a treaty with Laos. They did not dare to send American troops to Laos, they let the Lao Party participate in the government right away. They did not dare to attack Laos anymore.

Later, as the two countries (the USSR and China) were at odds with each other, the Americans were informed (by the Chinese) that they could go ahead and attack Vietnam without any fear. Don't be afraid. Zhou Enlai and Mao Zedong told the Americans: "If you don't attack me, then I won't attack you. You can bring in as many troops into southern Vietnam as you like. It's up to you."

...We are bordering on a very strong nation, one with expansionist intentions which, if they are to be implemented, must start with an invasion of Vietnam. Thus, we have to shoulder yet another, different historical role. However, we have never shirked from our historical tasks. Previously, Vietnam did carry out its tasks, and this time Vietnam is determined not to allow them to expand. Vietnam preserves its own independence, and by doing so is also safeguarding the independence of Southeast Asian nations. Vietnam is resolved not to allow the Chinese to carry out their expansionist scheme. The recent battle was one round only. Presently, they are still making preparations in many fields. However, whatever the level of their preparations, Vietnam will still win...

Waging war is no leisurely walk in the woods. Sending one million troops to wage war against a foreign country involves countless difficulties. Just recently they brought in 500,000 to 600,000 troops to fight us, yet they had no adequate transport equipment to supply food to their troops. China is presently preparing 3.5 million troops, but they have to leave half of them on the Sino-Soviet border to deter the Soviets. For that reason, if they bring one or two million troops to fight us, we will not be afraid of anything. We have just engaged 600,000 troops, and, if, in the near future, we have to fight two million, it will not be a problem at all. We are not afraid.

We are not afraid because we already know the way to fight. If they bring in one million troops, they will only gain a foothold in the north. Descending into the mid-lands, the deltas, and into Hanoi and even further downwards would be difficult. Comrades, as you know, Hitler's clique struck fiercely in this way, yet when they arrived in Leningrad they could not enter. With the cities, the people, and defense works, it is impossible to carry out effective attacks against each and every inhabitant. Even fighting for two, three, or four years they will still not be able to enter. Every village there (in the north) is like this. Our guidelines are: Each district is a fortress, each province a battlefield. We will fight and they will not be able to enter at all.

However, it is never enough just to fight an enemy at the front line. One must have a strong direct rearguard. After the recent fighting ended, we assessed that, in the near future, we must add several million more people to the northern front. But as the enemy comes from the north, the direct rear for the whole country must be Thanh Hoa, Nghe An, Ha Tinh...The direct rear to protect the capital must be Thanh Hoa and Nghe Tinh. We have enough people. We can fight them in many ways...We can use two to three army corps to inflict a strong blow on them that will make them stagger, while we continue to hold our land. To this end, each soldier must be a real soldier and each squad a real squad.

Having now fought one battle already, we should not be subjective. Subjectivism and underestimation of the enemy are incorrect, but a lack of self-confidence is also wrong. We are not subjective, we do not underestimate the enemy. But we are also confident and firmly believe in our victory. We should have both these things.

The Chinese now have a plot to attack us in order to expand southwards. But in the present era nothing can be done and then wrapped up tidily. China has just fought Vietnam for a few days, yet the whole world has shouted: "Leave Vietnam alone!" The present era is not like the olden times. In those days, it was only us and them. Now the whole world is fastened closely together. The human species has not yet entered the socialist phase at all; instead this is a time where everyone wants independence and freedom. Even on small islands, people want independence and freedom. All of humankind is presently like this. This is very different than it was in olden times. In those days, people were not yet very aware of these things. Thus the sentence of Uncle Ho: "There is nothing more precious than independence and freedom" is an idea of the present era. To lay hands on Vietnam is to lay hands on humanity and infringe on independence and freedom...Vietnam is a nation that symbolizes independence and freedom.

When it came to fighting the US, our brothers in the Politburo had to discuss together this matter to consider whether we dared to fight the US or not. All were agreed to fight. The Politburo expressed its resolve:

In order to fight the Americans, we must not fear the USA. All were of the same mind. As all agreed to fight the US, to have no fear of the USA, we must also not fear the USSR. All agreed. We must not fear China. All agreed. If we don't fear these things, we can fight the US. This was how we did things in our Politburo at that time.

Although the Politburo met and held discussions like this and everyone was of the same mind, there was later one person who told a comrade what I said. That comrade rose to question the Politburo, asking for what reason does Anh Ba once again say that if we want to fight the Americans then we should not fear the Chinese? Why does he have to put it this way again?

At that time, Brother Nguyen Chi Tanh, who thus far was suspected of being sympathetic to the Chinese, stood up and said: "Respected Politburo and respected Uncle Ho, the statement of Anh Ba was correct. It must be said that way, for they give us trouble on many matters. They blocked us here, then forced our hands there. They do not let us fight..."

While we were fighting in southern Vietnam, Deng Xiaoping stipulated that I could only fight at the level of one platoon downward, and must not fight at a higher level. He said: "In the south, since you have made the mistake of starting the fighting already, you should only fight at the level of one platoon downward, not at a higher level."

That is how they brought pressure to bear on us. We are not afraid of anyone. We are not afraid because we are in the right. We do not fear even our elder brother. We also do not fear our friends. Of course, we do not fear our enemies. We have fought them already. We are human beings; we are not afraid of anyone. We are independent. All the world knows we are independent.

We must have a strong army, because our nation is under threat and being bullied...It cannot be otherwise. If not, then it will become extremely dangerous, but our country is poor.

We have a strong army, but that does not in any way weaken us. The Chinese have several policies towards us: To invade and to occupy our country; to seek to weaken us economically and to make our living conditions difficult. For these reasons, in opposing China we must, first of all, not only fight, but also make ourselves stronger. To this end, in my view, our army should not be a force that wastes the resources of the state, but should also be a strong productive force. When the enemies come, they grab their guns at once. When no enemy is coming, then they will produce grandly. They will be the best and highest symbol in production, producing more than anyone else. Of course, that is not a new story...

At present, our army shoulders a historical task: to defend our independence and freedom, while simultaneously protecting the peace and independence of the whole world. If the expansionist policy of the reactionary

Chinese clique cannot be implemented any longer, that would be in the interest of the whole world. Vietnam can do this. Vietnam has 50 million people already. Vietnam has Lao and Cambodian friends and has secure terrain. Vietnam has our camp and all of mankind on its side. It is clear that we can do this.

...Do our comrades know anyone in our Party, among our people, who suspects that we will lose to China? No one, of course. But we must maintain our friendly relations. We do not want national hatred. I repeat: I say this because I have never felt hatred for China. I do not feel this way. It is they who fight us. Today, I also want you comrades to know that in this world, the one who has defended China is myself! That is true. Why so? Because during the June 1960 conference in Bucharest, 60 parties rose to oppose China, but it was only I (and the Albanian delegation) who defended China. Our Vietnamese people is like that. I will go ahead and repeat this: However badly they behave, we know that their people are our friends. As for our side, we have no evil feelings towards China. Yet the plot of several Chinese leaders is a different matter. We refer to them as a clique only. We do not refer to their nation. We did not say the Chinese people are bad towards us. We say that it is the reactionary Beijing clique. I again say it is strictly like this.

Thus, let us keep the situation under firm control, remain ready for combat, and never relax in our vigilance. It is the same with respect to China. I am confident that in 50 years, or even in 100 years, socialism may succeed; and then we will not have this problem any longer. But it will take such a long time. Therefore, we must prepare and stand ready in all respects.

At present, no one certainly has doubts anymore. But five years ago I was sure there were no comrades who doubted that China could strike us. But there were. That was the case because comrades had no knowledge about this matter. But that was not the case with us (with the leadership). We knew that China had been attacking us for some ten years or more. Therefore, we were not surprised."

Note (G. Schnehen):
Le Duan's suspicion that Mao Zedong was the nationalistic hardliner within the Chinese leadership as far as its attitude towards Vietnam was concerned, is confirmed by what Otto Braun wrote in his *Chinesische Aufzeichnungen* (Chinese Records). Braun had been sent to China by the Communist International ("Comintern") in the early thirties as an adviser to the Communist Party of China and later accompanied the People's Liberation Army on its Long March (1934–1936). He had daily encounters with Mao Zedong at the time and saw how the leadership of the Communist Party of China was gradually seized by Mao and

his followers, especially due to the support he enjoyed among a large part of the military personnel. Braun is citing from the interview Mao gave the American journalist Edgar Snow in 1936 where he states that...

> [I]t was 'the immediate task of China not just to defend its sovereignty on this side of the Wall but to recapture all the lost territories'. I learned from the same source that he had named Indochina, also Vietnam, Laos, and Cambodia as well as the Mongolian People's Republic as members of a 'Chinese Federation'. And, finally in 1964, he openly laid claim to the Soviet Far East.

Braun's conclusion (in the early 1970s):

Thus it is possible to trace back the first ideological and political signs of Mao's current great power chauvinism...[1]

---

[1] Otto Braun, *Chinesische Aufzeichnungen*, Berlin 1973, p. 358 (Chinese Records).

10. Mao Zedong's Early Plot Against the Communist Party of China — Three Unknown Documents[1]

Introduction and comments by G. Schnehen

Pyotr Parfenovich Vladimirov was born in 1905. His first job was a fitter's apprentice at the Voronezh farm implements plant. Later he worked as a fitter at the locomotive repair works in Tihoretsk. In 1927 he joined the All-Union Communist Party of the Bolsheviks. In 1931 he was called up for military service. Back from the Red Army, he entered the Narimanov Institute of Oriental Studies in Moscow, which he finished with honors.

From May 1938 until the middle of 1940, P. P. Vladimirov was a TASS correspondent in China. From April until August 1941, he was in China again on an assignment from TASS, the Soviet newsagency.

In May 1942, he was sent to Yenan (Special Area) as a liaison officer of the Comintern at the Headquarters of the Central Committee of the Chinese Communist Party and doubled as a military correspondent for TASS. He remained there till November 1945.

In 1946, he took a job at the Ministry for Foreign Affairs of the Soviet Union.

From 1948 until 1951, he was Soviet consul general in Shanghai and in 1952 was appointed Soviet ambassador to Burma (today Myanmar). He died in Moscow on September 1953 as the result of a severe illness.

---

[1] Source: Peter Vladimirov, *The Vladimirov Diaries, Yenan, China: 1942–1945*, New York, 1975

In his diaries Vladimirov recorded both his personal impressions and extracts from official correspondence. He did that because of being shadowed by Kang Sheng, head of the punitive bodies of the Special Area and close collaborator of Mao Zedong. The notebooks and diaries, therefore, were the only convenient and secure place for keeping copies of translations, documents of the Executive Committee of the Comintern, articles, reports, business telegrams, etc.

The documents expose Mao Zedong as an enemy of the Communist Party of China. He sabotaged instructions of the Central Committee, set up his own circle of people with himself as the 'Chairman' and was therefore stripped of his post as a commander in the Chinese Liberation Army. However, he neither accepted his sacking nor his successor as commander and then organized a plot against leading cadres of the local party committee of Kiangsi together with his close friend Liu Shaoqi, who did the dirty work for him, capturing leading officials of the party, torturing them and having some of them killed. They were falsely accused of being "Anti-Bolsheviks" and agents of the "AB Alliance," the party of the Chinese landlords and big farmers. The plot failed due to the fact that the 174th Regiment of the Chinese Communist Party accidentally found the detainees and liberated them. But only Liu Shaoqi was expelled from the party, although he had carried out Mao's instructions. Later Liu was readmitted and became one of Mao's closest collaborators who popularized his "ideas" in Yenan. During the Cultural Revolution, however, Liu was dropped by Mao Zedong, caught by Mao's Red Guards, humiliated in public as a "counterrevolutionary" and then arrested. He died in captivity.

November 10, 1943[1]

> Very important documents came into my possession.
>
> The first document is the Letter from the Central Front Committee to the Assistance Committee, of December 5, 1930.
>
> The second — Emergency Circular Message of the Provincial Executive Committee No. 9, of December 15, 1930.
>
> The third — letter to the CCP (Communist Party of China — ed.) Central Committee from Liu Ti, commissar of the 172nd Regiment, XX. Corps, of January 11, 1931.

In the second document — the one we concentrate on here — written by leading comrades of the Chinese Communist Party, who knew Mao Zedong well, we also get some information about Mao Zedong's person, but primarily about his plan to destroy leading cadres of the provincial CP leadership of Kiangsi and to set up his own group within the party with himself as 'Chairman' — a plan which later materialized in the special area of Yenan (pp. 169–174 ibid.):

> Kiangsi Provincial Committee

---

[1] Ibid., pp. 167ff.

Yunnan, December 15, 1930

...Thus Mao Zedong has long since nurtured his plan against the Bolshevik organization of Kiangsi. He is seeking to destroy all responsible workers and, acting with his right-opportunist line, to liquidate the revolutionary struggle and then, his dreams come true, to become the emperor of the party. Such are the reasons behind the developments in Futien.

1. Mao Zedong as a person.

As everyone knows, Mao Zedong is a very sly and treacherous man with an extreme sense of individualism. His head is full of vain thoughts. His way of influencing his comrades is through orders and threats and a system of repressions. When he takes a decision on party questions, he seldom discusses them at meetings and is always concerned with obtaining approval just of his own views.

Mao Zedong is particularly weak when it comes to an action. He adopts a right-opportunist line and tends to anarchism and "khvostism" (ultra-left radicalism — GS). He doubts every operation and is very unstable, especially in connection with the present stage of the bitter class struggle, which he tries to avoid and run away from, sparing no effort to extinguish it.

Mao Zedong has long been against the Central Committee. He sabotaged instructions of the previous committee many times when he chose to, using insignificant practical difficulties as a pretext. He read and distributed among the lower party organizations only a few of the Central Committee's instructions. He did not reckon with the workers sent down from the center and raised every obstacle in their way. For example, the Central Committee had sent Tsai Shenhsi to the IV. Corps to rectify the mistakes of the fallacious guerrilla tactics. Later Tsai Shenhsi was supposed to have assumed the post of commander of the III. Corps.

Mao Zedong not only ignored the Central Committee's advice but even organized baiting of Comrade Tsai Shenhsi and prevented him from taking the post of corps commander.

The Central Committee has repeatedly sent in letters demanding that Mao Zedong be transferred to another post, but he pays no heed to anybody.

Shunning no political trick, Mao Zedong constantly attacked his comrades.

In his work with the cadres, he wholly relied on factional methods and, using relations of companionship and personal ties, was raising a group which served him as an obedient political instrument.

Mao Zedong has not proved himself as a revolutionary leader in any of his past activities, and not even as a rank-and-file proletarian Bolshevik and fighter.

From head to toe Mao Zedong is a right opportunist, carrier of vain ideas, and an enemy of the party organization. He is an embodiment of the idea of evasion of battle and liquidation of the revolutionary class struggle. The party of Bolsheviks will not hesitate and will expel him from its ranks.

2. Details of the developments of December 7.

A few days before the events, Mao Zedong detailed Liu Shao-qi with a company of men of the XII. Corps from Hua-nien-po. The conspirators set out for Futien in a hurry and arrived there at noon on December 7, 1930.

At 3 PM in Futien Liu Shao-qi stationed his men at the entrance to the building of the Provincial Committee, announcing that he was looking for a place to spend the night.

Liu Shao-qi went to the Executive Committee and asked for Tseng Shan and Chen Chen-jen. At that time comrades Jen Hsin-ta and Pai Fang were talking.

The Traitor Liu Shao-qi saw that his accomplices Tseng Shan and Chen Chen-jen had left the room and immediately followed them. By that time Comrade Tuan Lien-pi returned.

Then the traitor Liu broke into the building of the Provincial Executive Committee (where the provincial party leadership of the Chinese Communist Party was seated — GS) with some of his soldiers and tied Tuan Lien-pi and Pai Fang first of all. Comrade Liu Wen-ching and Comrade Jen Hsin-ta were arrested right there. A little later comrades Hsieh Han-chang, Chi Wen-pang, Ma Ming, and others were arrested. When they asked what the matter was, Liu Shao-qi and his accomplices Tseng Shan and Chen Chen-jen only threatened them with revolvers.

The traitor Liu commanded the soldiers and did the searching. Tseng and Chen helped him. Then the traitors ordered the company to surround the building. The soldiers started an overall search. All documents were destroyed and the valuables appropriated. This lasted for several hours.

By night another nine people, operators of the communications system of the Provincial Executive Committee, had been arrested. At night the comrades were put to horrible torture. They were cruelly beaten right before Liu Shao-qi, Tseng Shan, and Chen Chen-jen, who were asking such questions as: "Do you admit your membership in the AB alliance? (The AB alliance was a coalition of big landlords and farmers fighting the Communist Party at the time. So the local CP leadership was accused of being "agents of the landlords" to have a pretext for their action — GS). When did you enter it? How is it organized and what are its tactics? Who are its responsible workers? Tell us the whole truth!"

The comrades denied the charges. They were tortured with burning kerosene wicks. Then the interrogation was resumed. If the prisoners were stubborn, the torture became diversified. They had no choice but to plead guilty. Their nails were broken and their bodies were covered with burns. They could neither stir nor speak.

Such was the situation on the first day.

On the second day, December 8, the traitor Liu Shao-qi and the others, on the basis of verbal admissions wrenched from the tortured comrades, arrested another ten people from the provincial government, the political guards, the Finance department, youth organizations, and the Provincial Executive Committee. They were also tortured with burning kerosene-dipped wicks. And they all "admitted" their guilt — not to do so would mean death from torture. Liu, Tseng, and Chen supervised the interrogations. The screams of the prisoners never stopped. The most monstrous tortures were devised.

The wives of comrades Pai Feng, Ma Ming, and Chou Mien were arrested at the same time. They were undressed and beaten up, their hands were pierced with a sharp tool, their bodies and private parts were burned with the flaming wicks, their breasts were cut away with pen knives. The butchers went to such extremes, mere mention of which curdles the blood.

The prisoners, both those who had been interrogated and those who had not been, were kept separately, tied hand and foot. They dared not speak or move. The guards were standing over them with bayoneted rifles at the ready. The second a voice was heard, the bayonets would go into action. The prisoners were fed on offal.

Such was the situation on the second day.

On the third day another punitive platoon arrived. Wang Huai and many other comrades from the Executive Committee of Western Kiangsi were arrested. After breakfast the soldiers marched away twenty-five people to be executed, many of whom had not even been questioned.

The traitor Liu Shao-qi set out for Tungku with the prisoners of the XX. Corps, including Hsieh Han-chang. The rest of the prisoners were taken away to the mountains where torturing continued in the villages.

Such was the situation on the third day.

In Tungku the prisoners were tortured again. The comrades were tied with ropes. Only once were they given food. Savage tortures were applied at those interrogations. First a name would be given and they would demand that the particular person be acknowledged as "counter-revolutionary" and the prisoners' "accomplice." In this way all the provincial officials were named...

Each one of the prisoners would be tortured for two or three hours before the questioning even started. The executioners were going to leave the following morning. So they executed a large group of comrades in the evening.

However, at this point the 174th Regiment of our XX Corps arrived unexpectedly. The men surrounded the building and released the prisoners.

The XX. Corps exposed the members of the punitive expedition in Tungku and launched an uprising. The traitor Liu was seized. The officials of the XX Corps and Hsieh Han-chang were also released. They were the ones to have related the happenings in Futien.

The men of the 174th Regiment were enraged when they learned the story. Comrade Liu Ti led them to Futien. In Futien they surrounded the building where the prisoners were kept, disarmed the punitive detachment, and seized the principal reactionaries. The traitor Tseng Shan fled.

Such was the situation on the fourth day.

We have told only briefly about the events of a few days. Other monstrous, indescribable facts are numerous.

3. Until we get the Central Committee's sanction, we do not allow openly proclaiming the slogans of overthrowing Mao Zedong.

Obviously, Mao Zedong is a bad man, a criminal in the class struggle, an enemy of the Bolshevik Party. It is necessary to mobilize all party members to overthrow him without ceremony.

But it is not only the question of Mao Zedong's personality. It is a vital question bearing on the prospects of the Chinese Revolution and concerned with the international revolutionary movement. That is why we must be very careful before making any decision. The crime must not be left unpunished. The Kiangsi party organization must launch a determined struggle against Mao Zedong from Bolshevik positions.

However, the party organization of Kiangsi must not settle the question on its own. It is our duty to inform the Central Committee of Mao Zedong's scheme to destroy the leading cadres of Kiangsi and its party organization, and it is up to the Central Committee to pass its decision...

Having received the documents, Vladimirov then translated them into Russian and made a careful analysis. He came to the following conclusions:[1]

In 1930, Mao Zedong was in the office of the chairman of the Central Front Committee (this was a leading position within the Communist Party of China, but he was not General Secretary of the Party at the time. That was Bo Gu elected by the delegates of the 6th Party Congress of the CP of China in 1928. Mao Zedong was absent — GS). Apparently this is where he "borrowed" his post as "chairman" for the Communist Party of China. In the autumn of the same year Mao Zedong was sharply criticized

---

[1] Ibid., pp. 167f.

for extremes in military and agrarian matters at a plenary meeting of the Western Kiangsi Party Committee. The same meeting expelled Liu Shaoqi, his associate, from the party.

Informed of the decisions of the Western Kiangsi Party Committee, the Central Committee of the Communist Party of China in Shanghai resolved to recall Mao Zedong and appointed Comrade Hsiang Chung-fa to replace him.

Mao Zedong concealed the decision of the Central Committee of the Communist Party from the Front Committee, deluded its members by accusing the Western Kiangsi Party Committee of an alliance with the big farmers and landlords, and on his own initiative set up the "Assistance Committee" with the intention of destroying the party cadres of Western Kiangsi. On December 5, 1930 he began to act...

To take revenge on the Western Kiangsi Party which had succeeded in getting rid of Mao Zedong from a leading party position at the center, he wrote a letter to his accomplice Liu Shao-qi also now belonging to the newly created "Assistance Committee." Mao wrote the letter on behalf of the Central Front Committee to which he however no longer belonged, from which he had already been expelled. Liu was told that evil landlords and big farmers had penetrated the party in the Western Kiangsi district, members of the so-called AB group. There were many "criminals" and "traitors" to be found there, and they should be arrested immediately and thoroughly investigated. Liu was given a free hand to deal with the matter thoroughly which he did, as we have seen.

So Mao Zedong organized a plot to get rid of the comrades of the Western Kiangsi committee of the Communist Party in order to set up his own organization there instead. The letter was also preserved as a document. It is the first document Vladimirov refers to:[1]

To Comrade Liu Shao-qi to be referred to the provincial Assistance Committee.

The extremely serious uprising of landlords and kulaks (big farmers — GS) who have penetrated the party has already spread far. You must suppress it with determination...According to Lung Chao-ching, the chairman of the Provincial Komsomol Committee, Tuan Lien-pi, chief of the Agitation and Propaganda Department, Yuan Chao-huan, and the chief of the Organizational Department Chiang Ko-huang are now in Tung-tien. They should all be immediately arrested and thoroughly investigated. Li Po-fang is an even more dangerous criminal!

We hope that you have already arrested them! Besides, use them to discover even more important criminals!

---

[1] Ibid., p. 168.

Two Red Army men were sent in the evening with a letter informing about the interrogation of Ting Shu-chi, an important criminal. He hasn't given a sincere testimony yet.

You must not limit yourself to following the instructions of this letter. Tomorrow more of the prisoners will be interrogated. Let the two Red Army men who will deliver the letter stay with you so as to send them back with the post in two or three days' time. If you are in need of delivering an emergency report, send it with the postman. Have him put the papers in an inside pocket with an ordinary letter on top so that the AB group (a reactionary group of kulaks and landlords) is not able to read your reports.

In the last document one of the accused, a comrade by the name of Liu Ti, the commissar of the 172nd Regiment of the XX. Corps, wrote a complaint to the Central Committee, telling them how he was suspected and treated by Liu Shao-qi and how he achieved of arresting him. He also mentioned how badly other prisoners of Mao Zedong and his accomplice were treated.

I heard Liu Shao-qi questioning Shang Chi-lung, chief of the political science sector of the Political Department. He was beating him so brutally that the sky itself heard the screams and the earth shuddered...[1]

In the end, he succeeded in arresting Liu Shao-qi and his accomplices and liberated the comrades that had been taken prisoner. In the early forties, Liu Shao-qi was readmitted to the party in Yenan and soon became one of Mao's chief agitators to spread his "ideas" among ordinary party members. Mao Zedong's erstwhile torturer later became President of the People's Republic in China (1959). He died in prison in November 1969 during Mao's Cultural Revolution, having fallen from Mao's grace. He was accused of being a "counter-revolutionary".

---

[1] Ibid., p. 176.

11. The Poisoning Of Wang Ming By Mao Zedong

Introduction by G. Schnehen

Wang Ming, former member of the Central Committee of the Politburo of the Communist Party of China and also a member of the Communist International's Executive Committee, Mao Zedong's number one rival, tells us the story about Mao's attempts to poison him in the special area of Yenan in the early forties. His story is corroborated by two other sources: by Peter Vladimirov, the Soviet TASS correspondence for military affairs and also special envoy of the Communist International ("Comintern") and also by the Chinese historian Jung Chang in her biography of Mao Zedong. In the Wikipedia on Wang Ming we read however that the poisoning was just an "allegation" made by him and that his health issues were probably due to the "great stress" he experienced at that time in Yenan. Here again the Wikipedia proves to be completely unreliable, even taking sides with Maoist historiography.

In his diaries he confirms that Wang Ming was poisoned by Mao Zedong's private physician Jin Maoyan something he himself admitted when a special commission of a dozen doctors had reached the same conclusions. Only by chance Wang survived the attack on his life, but remained handicapped nearly all his life due to the poisoning. Only in 1950 was he permitted to leave China for the Soviet Union where he was treated in a Moscow hospital. After his return to China the witch-hunt against him continued and further attempts on his life were made to get rid of him.

Wang Ming and his wife Meng Qingshu who saved his life after Mao tried to poison him with mercury (1943)

Mao Zedong succeeded in putting the blame on Dr. Jin Maoyao who was never held responsible for the attempted murder. Later in Beijing, Jin Maoyao still belonged to the group of Mao's personal physicians (until 1954) and was even given the post of a hospital director in Beijing.

1st source: Wang Ming's own report[1]

It started at the time of the active preparation for the *Campaign to Correct the Work Style*. The following happened:

In the late hours of 3 October 1941 Mao Zedong brought me a telegram written by Comrade Dimitrov (The Bulgarian Georgi Dimitrov was leader of the Communist International at the time — GS). It contained fifteen questions for the Central Committee of the Communist Party of China. Among other things, it was asked what kind of measures the Chinese Party had in mind in view of the fascist offensive of Germany against the USSR in order to activate the combat operations at the Chinese-Japanese front to deprive Japan, the ally of Germany in the East, of the possibility to open up a second front and to invade the USSR. Mao Zedong asked me to think about the telegram adding: "Tomorrow we'll discuss how to respond."

---

[1] Wang Ming, *50 Jahre KP Chinas und der Verrat Mao Zedongs*, Berlin, 1981, pp. 48ff. (50 years of CP China and the treason of Mao Zedong).

On October 4 and 5 we had an unusually sharp and principled discussion. I insisted that we ought to activate the anti-Japanese combat operations in China to make Japan desist from supporting the German aggressors during their offensive against the USSR. Mao Zedong did not agree with me, but didn't give any reasons. Again and again my arguments pushed him into a corner. He looked at me with open eyes, in vain looking for arguments. When I accused him of anti-Sovietism and being in favor of an alliance with Japan, he started shouting and clamoring, banging his hand on the table. But he was unable to say something reasonable. On October 6 and 7 he invited Ren Rishi and Wang Jiaxing to join us; on October Kang Sheng and Chen Yun. He expected support from them. But all of them kept quiet, thus telling us that they supported Dimitrov's proposals and mine as well.

This made Mao Zedong very upset. To put an end to this unfavorable and dangerous situation and to get rid of his main political rival who did not support his anti-Soviet and pro-Japanese line of national betrayal and who was also against his forthcoming campaign to "rectify the work style" and his attempts to falsify the history of the Party, Mao Zedong decided to liquidate me. On October 14 he put pressure on me to visit the hospital. He told Li Fuchun, the director of the chief office of the Central Committee, to tell Dr. Jin Maoyao (as it turned out later) to slowly poison me by giving me mercury injections. It was only due to the special care and help which I got from many comrades and doctors, especially from Li Dengming (deputy chairman of the government of the border area of Shaanxi-Gansu-Ningxia) who specializes in Chinese medicine and who is a very experienced physician, and also from Li Yun-shi, a very conscientious and caring doctor, that I was called back to life having almost passed away at one point. But my inner organs had already been seriously affected by the illness causing me to stay in bed for four years. Even during the following decades I was suffering a lot from it. The illness became chronic and fits occurred from time to time making me suffer a lot.

For years on end Mao Zedong traded all sorts of stories to cover up his crime, and he also claimed that I was just "feigning illness" in order not having to take part in his "campaign to rectify the work style." So I have to touch on it briefly.

Let me start by telling you about the poisoning which undermined my health.

I've told you before that from 4 to 9 October I had an argument with Mao Zedong in his house about Dimitrov's telegram. From 4 October 1941 I had a meal with him at least once a day. On 8 October severe stomach pain started, I lost a lot of blood and I also experienced heart failure and strong dizziness. The doctors who examined me came to the conclusion that the symptoms were typical of a poisoning. On 9 October my condition was already serious, but Mao Zedong had me dragged to a meeting by his personal assistant Ye Zilong when I was still in bed. The next day I was incapable of getting up.

Under the pretext that the conference hall and the office of the Central Committee had to "be built urgently," Mao Zedong ordered Li Fuchun to start the work without delay. Some dozen meters away from my apartment workers started rock blasting day and night. The deafening noise did not stop for a minute. I didn't get a rest and my condition worsened. I asked Li Fuchun to stop the work for two days or to continue them somewhere else. He told me: "It's an order by Chairman Mao. The work must not be interrupted one minute!" On 14 October Li Fuchun and Fu Lianzhang came to me and took me to the Central Hospital in their car. Dr. Jin Maoyao was assigned to treat me.

At the hospital Jin Maoyao gave orders for a treatment that contributed to worsening my condition, and from then on, I was unable to leave the hospital. From March until May 1942 he by and by gave me large doses of mercury preparations. This was at a time when Mao Zedong was openly running his campaign to "rectify the work style" which was directed against the Communist International and the Soviet Union, against the Communist Party of China, against myself and the others he called the "Moscow Group." Often I fell unconscious. I only escaped death due to the attention and vigilance of Meng Qingshu, my wife, who kept vigil at my bedside in the hospital. Unfortunately, at that time she had no knowledge of medicine and pharmacology. But as she realized how badly my organism reacted to the drugs prescribed, she told me not to take them anymore and threw them away. Later, she disposed of those prescriptions she found suspicious, told the doctors not to give her any drugs anymore and asked to urgently send doctors with knowledge in Chinese and European medicine.

On 13 August I returned home to Yangjialin. But Jin Maoyao was still in charge to "cure" me. He became specially active when, in February of 1943, Dimitrov's telegram reached us. There he wrote: "We're making preparations to take you to Moscow in a plane."

Here I have to tell you that one month earlier I had sent my only telegram to Moscow. On January 8, 1943, some comrades had paid me a visit — two Soviet military correspondents. I asked them if they could send a telegram to Comrade Dimitrov via their radio station. They agreed. At that time my condition was very bad. I thought this would be my last chance to fulfill my internationalist duty. I asked the comrades to tell the leaders of the Communist International that during the past five years since my return to Yenan late in November of 1937 Mao Zedong had committed a great number of fundamental political errors and crimes and that he had been conducting the campaign to "rectify the work style" for more than a year now which, basically, was an anti-Leninist, anti-communist, anti-

Soviet and anti-Party campaign. Finally, I asked if there was a chance to take me in a plane to Moscow for treatment to enable me to inform the leadership of the Communist International about Mao Zedong's crimes.

Comrade Dimitrov's reply telegram and especially the flight for Moscow offered to me caused great anxiety with Mao Zedong. That's why he immediately told Jin Maoyao to take new measures to kill me. On 12 February 1943, on instructions from Mao Zedong, he prescribed me to take a large dose of an aqueous solution of calomel consisting of an addition of sodium bicarbonate and magnesium sulfate which can change calomel into corrosive sublimate, and on 19 February he also prescribed me a highly concentrated ten percent Tanin solution as an enema. These two medical prescriptions were designed to get rid of me immediately. Having doubts, Meng Qingshu gave these prescriptions other doctors for examination, and they confirmed the highly toxic effect of these substances and told her that the medicine should under no circumstances be taken. Then she officially turned to the Central Committee of the Party and also to other physicians and accused Jin Maoyao of criminal behavior. Fearing public opinion, Mao Zedong had to give his consent to summon other doctors from Yenan Hospital, from Norman Bethune Hospital as well as from a medical institute for consultations.

The group met for the first time on June 30, 1943 and only finished their consultations on July 30. The physicians took a close look at the prescriptions issued by Jin Maoyao, the diary of the nurses and their notes and also listened to the testimony of the pharmacist, and only after that compiled a "medical report on the diagnosis of the illness and the previous medical treatment of Comrade Wang Ming" and on "provisional proposals for further treatment." About the fact that Dr. Jin Maoyao had prescribed Wang Ming a large dose of toxic substances the medical report had this to say:

"Having taking the medicine, Comrade Wang Ming showed symptoms of vomiting, dizziness, severe pain in the liver, an enlargement of the spleen, pain in the heart area and low temperature...The following fact cannot be denied: Only speaking about calomel (mercury chloride — GS) which has already been taken, the total dose is actually very large, having caused a poisoning (...) and has had harmful effects on the heart, the liver, the spleen, the kidneys, the colon, the stomach, the oral cavity, on teeth, nerves and other organs."

"Calomel is not water soluble," it also says in the medical report. "However, Jin, the attending physician, prescribed Wang Ming to take a water soluble solution of calomel...If you mix calomel with sodium bicarbonate, sodium sulfate, magnesium sulfate, bromine preparations, etc., then it can change into corrosive sublimate or else into soluble mercury salt, which can be absorbed even more easily and can be even more poisonous.

Jin, however, told Wang Ming to take calomel together with the incompatible components. Although the incompatible preparations and calomel were not part of the prescription, he now and again advised Wang Ming to take the medicines from both prescriptions at the same time. Having swallowed calomel, symptoms of a mercury poisoning soon emerged in the patient. Nevertheless, the attending physician kept on prescribing to take the medicine, etc.

I cannot deal in great detail with the exact circumstances of my poisoning and the damage to my health in the period between October 1941 and June 1943 and with the different methods which were being used at the time. This would take up too much space here. However, I have the following documents in my possession which can throw some light on the issue:

1. The medical report of the doctors' committee and other documents by the same body which had a meeting in Yenan lasting from June 30 till July 30, 1943 (...). Out of the 15 physicians who were members of the committee 11 signed the report, among them Jin Maoyao himself and the doctor defending him (Ma Heide or George Hatem, an American doctor). Due to the testimonies and the material evidence they had no choice.

Among the four who refused to sign the declaration were: Qu Zhen, a countryman of Jiang Qing (Mao Zedong's wife — GS) from Shangdong who had been trained in fascist Germany. During the entire medical consultations he had tried to defend Jin Maoyao, and when it came to signing the document, he got out of the way at the last moment. Besides, there was Hou Jianqun, Jin's colleague who had studied with him at the medical faculty of Shangdong Qilu University which belonged to the Americans and who had worked together with him at the Xiehe Hospital which likewise belonged to them. He was Lina's godfather, Mao Zedong's and Jiang Qing's daughter, and was head of the pediatric department of the Central Hospital where his wife used to be a head nurse. Jing Qing often left her daughter in her care. The two others, Zhu Zhonli and A. J. Orlov, could not come.

When the report was ready, the signing dragged on for another two days, as Jin Maoyao denied the charges and Ma Heide and Qu Zhen was trying to come to his defense.

Most doctors, among them the Soviet physician Orlov, obtained the drugs from the pharmacy, the way Jin Maoyao had prescribed them for me for the aqueous solution of calomel together with the incompatible substances and then produced the solution. After that they asked Ma Haide, who had claimed that Jin Maoyao's prescription would not cause any poisoning at all, to drink it. But Ma Heide flatly refused to do so. After a few hours, the solution preserved in a glass bottle, took on a green color and then all of a sudden there was a bang and the cork was ejected. Ma Heide's face became ashen for fear, and from then on he no longer defended

Jin Maoyao. Qu Zhen was afraid that he as well could be asked to drink the solution and then left the place in a hurry. Only Jin Maoyao still brazenly denied everything. But when Meng Qingshu presented the prescription which he had issued on 12 February 1943 for general inspection, he ran towards her, fell on his knees and then said, in tears: "I thank you so much, Comrade Meng Qingshu, for not getting this prescription filled and for not giving Comrade Wang Ming the drugs. Thereby you not only saved his life but also mine." After that eleven out of the twelve doctors present put their signature under the report, with Hou Jianqun being the only exception.

After the medical report had been signed, Jin Maoyao came to me, dropped on his knees in front of my bed and started wailing in tears: "Comrade Wang Ming, I owe you a great debt. I have poisoned you. Whenever I prescribed you a poison my heart was heavy."

"Why did you do that?" I asked him.

"Li Fuchun told me. He said you were a dogmatic, a man who had turned against Chairman Mao and that's why it was decided to get rid of you. I was the attending doctor and was assigned to carry out the order. I said I was a very religious man, and the Central Committee of the Party had decided to accept me as a candidate of the Party — how could I do such a thing? But Li Fuchun said: 'This is an unusual undertaking, and as soon as you have been instructed to do that, you have to do it. You are already a member of the Party and therefore you have the duty to submit to the Party's decisions!' ..."

This very moment two members of the military entered the room. One of them shouted at Jin Maoyao: "We have been looking for you everywhere and now you are here! Why are you kneeling over there, why are you wailing and mumbling something? Come on, let's go to Zaoyuan (Mao Zedong's house), you're a criminal and have no right to talk to other people!" They grabbed him by the collar and led him away.

2. Several prescriptions issued by Jin Maoyao to poison me.

Among them are some which were found in the pharmacy of the Central Hospital at the time and those we still have in our possession. The remaining prescriptions were either "not kept" or had not been issued, for some of the drugs Jin Maoyao brought from home.

3. Protocols about the tests of the daily quantities of urine to establish the mercury content which were taken in July 1943 during the medical consultation in Yenan; those taken between December 1950 and October 1952 as well as those taken at the Beijing Hospital; protocols of other analyses and various other documents.

The Yenan medical consultation uncovered facts about my systematic poisoning. After the medical consultation had ended, pediatrician Dr. Li Yunshi, who is a very conscientious and attentive person, took over my treatment. On the basis of a completely new diagnosis — mercury poisoning — she introduced the appropriate treatment and tried hard to restore my health. Thus, the hope emerged that the danger of death could be overcome and a turn for the better was on the horizon.

Besides, the following important reasons helped me to stay alive, although I was close to death several times:

a. In spite of all the suffering, despite the danger and the illness, which was due to the repeated attempts of poisoning, in spite of all the prophecies made by Jin Maoyao and others that my death was close, Meng Qingshu and I never gave up hope. We asked experts of Chinese and European medicine for help and advice, and we ourselves started dealing with medical issues.

b. As much as Mao Zedong slandered me during the "campaign to rectify the work style," I was still convinced I was right in ideological, political and organizational matters. I believed in the correctness of Lenin's ideas, in the line of the 4th Session of the Central Committee following the VI. Party Congress of the Communist Party of China, in the policy of the anti-Japanese united front, the policy of proletarian internationalism, and I was convinced that Mao Zedong's campaign was reactionary and wrong and that he was also falsifying the history of the Communist Party of China.

c. In spite of Mao Zedong's attempts to isolate me by all means possible, the majority of leaders and party officials either openly approved of my attitude or assured me in private of their sympathy and support. Directly it showed in that I had frequent visitors, and indirectly in that the majority of party officials was against Mao Zedong's campaign which he himself openly admitted in April of 1944 in a conversation. Thereby they not just showed that they cared but also that they were in favor of Leninism and the line of the Communist International.

Although many party official could not visit me for fear of persecution or incarceration, there were still a great number who regularly came to the hospital or to my home in the hardest time — during the "campaign to rectify the work style" and during the "rescue operation." Among them were eight members and two candidates of the politburo. At that time, the politburo consisted of ten members and four candidates.

Among them were also some responsible comrades who had come to us from the liberated or the Kuomintang areas. To deceive the public, even Mao Zedong paid me a visit when I was severely ill. Comrades from party organs, for whose work I was responsible, also came round. At the time I was in charge of the following activities: I was the person nominated by the Central Committee of the Communist of China being responsible for matters of the anti-Japanese united front; I was chairman of the Committee for the Party press and also instructor of the politburo for the work of the office of the CC for North-West China, including the border area Shansi-Gansu-Ningxia; I was chairman of the Commission of the CC for South China, for the provinces of Hunan, Jiangxi, Fujian, Guangdong, and Guangxi and of the Commission for South-West China, i.e, for the provinces of Sichuan, Guizhou, Yunnan, and Xikang; I was chairman of the Commission of the CC for North-East China and also secretary of the Communist Party group in the national consultative conference.

Many times I was visited by Lin Boqu (Lin Zuhan), Xie Juezai, Chen Zhengren, Ren Zuomin and other comrades who were members of the office of the CC of the Party for North-West China and the border area Shansi-Gansu-Ningxia and who were closely connected with me through their work.

The most frequent visitor was of course Ke Qingshi, the deputy chairman of the department for the united front, and we often exchanged our thoughts about Mao Zedong's "campaign to rectify the work style".

But there were also visitors of a different kind. Very often Li Fuchun came round who had been charged by Mao Zedong to poison my health or to damage it, but as a head of the office of the Central Committee which was responsible for the institutions of the CC and for the medical facilities he could not fail to render me all sorts of services. He visited me to talk about questions of my treatment or my present condition, however, I was not very keen to do that...

In the late forties and the early 1950s Mao Zedong again made several attempts to bring about my death quickly. I shall mention only a few briefly:

1. On 25 June, 1948, Dr. Huang Shuze, the attending physician in the Central Hospital of Zhuhao prescribed me Lysol instead of medicinal soap for intestinal flushing, the application of which could have led to my death (Lysol is a disinfectant — GS). Only thanks to the watchful eye of my wife I again succeeded in preventing tragic consequences. The hospital manager, Mr. Zhou Zezhao and other physicians as well, were kept informed about the incident.

Referring to the incident, the Office for Health Affairs at the Central Committee of the Party distributed a newsletter on July 7 claiming that the pharmacist had made "a mistake when compiling the drugs. By dispensing Lysol instead of medicinal soap, he has contributed to worsening the illness even more which constituted grave negligence..." Obviously, this new attempt to bring about my death was intended to be covered up — an attempt which, apparently, had been ordered from high above.

2. On October 25, 1950 at 11:00 AM, the chief of the head office of the Central Committee of the Party, Yang Shangkun, came to me and said:

"At 9:00 AM Liu Shaoqi sent for me telling me that this night Mao had told him that Wang Ming should leave for the Soviet Union even this afternoon. The train he is to take will go to the Manchuria border station

(Manshouli). He instructed me to complete all formalities as soon as possible. What I now have to do is this: Call the Foreign Office so that passports for the whole family can be issued and then hand them over to him immediately. He is allowed to take with him whomever he wishes. Only passport photos are still needed. The Ministry of Railways has already been instructed to attach a company car to the regular train. The train will depart for Manchuria today evening at 6:00 PM. Till then not much time is left. He should get ready for the trip..."

I asked him: "There are reports that our army of volunteers is going to enter Korean territory across the big Yalujiang Bridge around midnight to counter the US aggression, to help Korea and to start combat operations, and General MacArthur has already given orders to the American air force to cover the entire railway line from Shanghaiguan to Manchuria with massive bombardments to destroy the supply lines from Beijing and the USSR to Manchuria the moment the Chinese volunteers enter Korea. Is this news correct?"

"Yes, it's correct," replied Yang Shangkun.

"So when we have reached Manchurian territory tomorrow morning, we will be in the midst of these massive bombardments. Is that so?" I inquired.

"Yes, but you should decide for yourself if you want to travel today or not," he replied. "Should you wish not to leave, please let me know. In that case, I shall inform the Ministry of the Railways accordingly."

Meng Qingshu and I of course immediately understood why Mao Zedong had suddenly decided to send us away even today. Liu Shao-qi had allowed the exit for the USSR long before, but for more than half a year we had been waiting for the fixing of the departure date. So we discussed what to do and in the end decided to travel despite the risk, as we did not know whether we would have succeeded in leaving the country otherwise. Not just for the treatment I wanted to go to Moscow, I also wanted to see the Soviet Union again which had been victorious during the Great Patriotic War and which I had not seen for 13 years.

At the reception which five administrative and legal institutions had organized for us, several comrades advised us not to risk our lives. However, we boarded the train at half past five and off we went.

We reached the station of Manchuria without any incidents. Then we changed to the Soviet train and in the end reached the longed-awaited Moscow...

In the winter of 1952, Liu Shao-qi said to me in Moscow: "You have been spared the bombing raid, because Truman didn't want a war with China. He had strongly advised MacArthur not to bomb Chinese territory..."

3. We returned to Beijing in December 1953. From April 1954 to January 1956 I had seven severe fits of acute cholecystitis and hepatitis. They appeared in April/May for the first time. Huang Shuze, Fu Lianzhang and the others feared to admit that I was suffering from a liver and gall bladder disease as this could have revived the story of the poisoning. For five days I was confined to bed and, on the following day, I had to be admitted to the Beijing Hospital. The doctors diagnosed acute cholecystitis, but Huang Shuze did not want to know and said: "The patient is also suffering from peritonitis."

Meanwhile Huang Shuze had been promoted to Deputy Head of Health Care at the Central Committee of the Communist Party, and now the Beijing Hospital had become his subordinate. Of course, the doctors did not dare to refuse him obedience. He insisted to immediately remove the gall bladder. On the fourth day of my stay in hospital, nine days after the fits had begun, my condition became critical. The morning of that day Meng Qingshu asked our two sons to come to the hospital to say goodbye to me. At the same time, she herself started to treat me with tried and tested medicines. For three days she was fighting for my life, and after some time my condition started to improve gradually, the pain subsided, the temperature dropped and I was able to eat something. But the doctors insisted on putting me on the operation table. We were strictly against that as I hadn't had anything to eat for six days in a row. My body weight of almost 60 kilograms was down to 40 now and there was the risk that my organism would not have endured the operation. On repeated request, I was given two blood transfusions of a total of 500 milligrams. At the same time, we also contacted experts of Chinese medicine and used their medication. This led to a normalization of the situation. However, the physicians still insisted on an operation. When we resisted that, they forced us to sign a document about our refusal.

4. In the summer of 1955 my condition worsened so that I had to be taken to Beijing Hospital again. The surgeon, Dr. Shoa, gave me a physiological saline infusion and also a glucose solution. This happened with a speed of 60 drops per minute. He himself later admitted it, but he added that the head of surgery, Dr. Wang, had told him to do that. A few minutes after the infusion had started, Dr. Shao went outside. I got such a chill that six hot water bottles and three cotton blankets were of no help. I went pale, the sweat ran down my face in streams, my heart vibrated, and I was overcome by a terrible weakness. Meng Qingshu asked the nurse to immediately pull out the cannula. But she refused to do so and said:

"Dr. Shao has instructed me not to interrupt the infusion in his absence. I'm going look for him."

When the nurse had left the room, Meng Qingshu pulled out the cannula at once, stopped the infusion and immediately gave me camphor to stimulate the activity of the heart. Only then did I gradually regain my composure. But the heart failure remained. After some time, the nurse and Dr. Shao returned. He was very displeased when he realized that the infusion had been interrupted and said that we should have awaited his appearance and only then we should have taken a decision.

Professor J. M. Voloshin, a specialist from the Soviet Union, who at that time used to work in the surgical department of the Beijing Hospital, told us when he heard about it: "In view of the condition of Comrade Wang Ming's body, it would have been appropriate to give an infusion with only 20 to 30 drops per minute. How can you administer 60 drops?! If there is a new infusion, the speed in the tube must be watched carefully."

He said that Comrade Meng Qingshu was right, or Comrade Wang Ming's heart could have failed. We are very indebted to Comrade Voloshin! He was our loyal advisor. He also always rejected the suggestion made by Huang Shuze to immediately operate on me. He said: "Not only does Comrade Wang Ming suffer from cholecystitis (gall bladder inflammation — GS), his internal organs are all sick. His life is hanging by a threat anyway. How can you want to operate on him?"

He always gave us this advice: "Never say yes to an operation! At your current state a surgical intervention could be devastating, Comrade Wang Ming!"

When Liu Shao-qi gave permission to return to the USSR for treatment, he was keen on accelerating our departure and, contrary to what other people said, he always tried to prove that my heart would be able to endure the flight.

Apart from the facts mentioned, there were also other events and facts showing that Mao Zedong stirred up hatred against me and kept on following me.

2nd source: Peter Vladimirov's Yenan diaries[1]

In his Yenan diaries Peter P. Vladimirov closely followed the events taking place in the special area occupied by the Chinese Communist Party after the "Long March." Here we find more than a dozen entries on Mao Zedong's attempts to poison Wang Ming through Dr. Jin Maoyao, his personal physician, and we also learn something about his motives:

October 26, 1942

Wang Ming is in very poor health. His wife is worried. Wang Ming is under observation of the Chinese doctors who attend to the leading figures of the CCP Central Committee.

---

[1] Peter Vladimirov, *The Vladimirov Diaries*, ibid., pp. 72ff.

January 8, 1943

His disease has taken a new dangerous turn. Wang Ming's life is at stake now. His liver and kidneys are failing him. He complains of agonizing headaches and a general weakness.

At a meeting of leading medical specialists the question was raised of the need to wire Chiang Kai-shek for a plane for the patient. The Chairman of the CCP Central Committee (Mao Zedong — GS) crossed out the text of the doctors' telegram and sent his own instead: asking Chungking (the then Chinese capital where the Kuomintang government headed by Chiang Kai-shek was based — GS) to send an experienced therapist to Yenan for consultation — and nothing more![1]

January 14, 1943

The scheming around Wang Ming continues among Mao Tse-tung's entourage. Mao Tse-tung for the second time refused to send a telegram to Chiang Kai-shek despite doctors' insistence on the immediate evacuation of the patient...

Wang Ming has been terrorized by Kang Sheng (Mao Zedong's head of the secret service — GS) and fears our visits. Through Orlov (the chief Soviet doctor in the area — GS) he conveyed to me his request to help him go to the Soviet Union for treatment, so that he could escape Mao Tse-tung's vengeance.[2]

April 3, 1943

Mao Tse-tung is trying, by hook and by crook, the departure of Wang Ming...It is impossible to get to Wang Ming except through persons trusted by the Chairman of the CCP Central Committee.[3]

April 6, 1943

Mao Tse-tung and Kang Sheng are sure that we know what is behind the "case of the prescription" that is premeditated poisoning of Wang Ming...This compelled them to give up the idea of murdering Wang Ming: Chinese doctors can be bullied, but what about us? Chiang Ching's visits (Mao's wife — GS), importunate talks about the prescription, and the intensified shadowing of us corroborate this conclusion...[4]

April 15, 1943

At the insistent request of Rosa Vladimirovna I went to see Wang Ming. He feels very bad. What's wearing him down is not so much his physical

[1] Ibid., p. 91.
[2] Ibid., p. 92.
[3] Ibid., p. 110.
[4] Ibid., pp. 110f.

ailment as moral suffering...Wang Ming told me bitterly about Kang Sheng's behavior in Moscow...[1]

November 29, 1943

While Wang Ming is bedridden and isolated completely from the external world through the efforts of Kang Sheng, the developments are becoming ever more grim for the entire political course that he headed. One sitting of the Politburo is analyzing the mistakes of the "Moscow Group." Wang Ming is accused of all mortal sins...It is at the sittings of the Politburo and not just any place that he is labeled "Kuomintang accomplice[2] and counterrevolutionary." They use the meanest pretext to prove Wang Ming's "counter-revolutionism"...[3]

December 23, 1943

Mao Tse-tung has "covered" Wang Ming with different "proofs" of his guilt before the party...But Mao Tse-tung's aim is not only to smear Wang Ming. He is set on breaking his spirit. It is important to make Wang Ming admit the "correctness of his course" by word of mouth.[4]

August 29, 1944

Not to yield his positions on the major issue, the necessity of struggle against the "Moscow group," headed by Wang Ming, the CCP Central Committee Chairman (Mao Zedong — GS) gave instructions to write a play condemning Wang Ming. But still it is not like poisoning him with a mercury preparation or isolating him in a cave without any qualified medical aid. It is quite an acceptable variant of the "Muscovites" in the new conditions. It is not merely the condemnation but the continuation of struggle, too! Mao Tse-tung is true to himself. His hatred for the "Muscovites" has taken a new form which is in the spirit of the times, and outwardly is perfectly harmless. The play has already been concocted. It is entitled *Comrade, You Follow the Wrong Road.*[5]

February 26, 1945

Wang Ming is not called otherwise than a "right-wing opportunist element." This definition is taken as a matter of fact...The Mao Tse-tung leadership has gradually convinced all that Wang Ming "has been

---

[1] Ibid., pp. 112f. Kang Sheng spent two years at the Communist International in Moscow together with Wang Ming who, at that time, was a member of the Executive Committee of the Communist International, being the Chinese representative there. During his whole stay in the USSR (1935-37) Kang always pretended to be his loyal follower.

[2] Kang Sheng also used this label for Wang Shiwei, a translator of Marx and Lenin in Yenan and a writer who openly criticized leading officials in Yenan but especially their authoritarian attitudes and corrupt lifestyles, cp. Dai Qing, *Wang Shiwei and "Wild Lilies,"* London and New York, 2015.

[3] Ibid., p. 180.

[4] Ibid., pp. 184f.

[5] Ibid., pp. 245f.

implanting alien elements in the party ever since 1931-34." ... Even Wang Ming's former associates have begun to discredit him again...[1]

April 2, 1945

"Wang Ming wanted to make himself a petty ruler in the party. He kowtowed to Chiang Kai-shek. He is an opportunist," etc. This is what everybody is sure of. And this means that all that Wang Ming has stood for has been discredited...The internationalists inside the Chinese Communist Party are vilified for trying to introduce the principles of "Western Marxism," which are allegedly alien to China. All the difficulties and troubles of the Communist Party are being blamed on the "dogmatists," for they have failed to take into consideration the national peculiarities of the country...[2]

3rd source: Jung Chang[3]

After the German invasion of the Soviet Union on June 22, 1941, Stalin demanded from Mao Zedong and the Chinese Communists to take resolute action against the Japanese army to assist the Soviet Union in its struggle against fascism, as Japan, at that time, was an ally of Nazi Germany and threatened to invade the USSR from the east. Mao Zedong declined the request but Wang Ming, who was still an influential member in the politburo of the Chinese Communist Party at the time, was in favor of fighting the Japanese militarists. Mao Zedong had not become the undisputed 'Chairman' of the Communist Party of China yet. Then the Communist International based in Moscow intervened and asked Mao Zedong to clarify his position. Wang Ming supported the telegram containing some serious questions for Mao Zedong and suggested an open debate on Mao's war policies which he declined...Jung Chang and her co-author Jon Halliday on the power struggle between Wang Ming and Mao Zedong:

> Meanwhile, just after he had challenged Mao in October 1941, Wang Ming collapsed from a sudden illness, and was hospitalized. He claimed he had been poisoned by Mao — which may or may not be true on this occasion. What is certain is that Mao attempted to have him poisoned the following March, when Wang Ming was just about to be discharged from hospital. Wang Ming remained defiant: "I will not bow my head even if all others are fawning," he vowed...
>
> The agent for Mao's poisoning operation was a doctor called Jin Mao-yue, who had originally come to Yenan as part of a Nationalist medical team, at the height of the cooperation between the Nationalists and the CCP. He was a qualified gynecologist and obstetrician, and so the Communists kept

---

[1] Ibid., p. 358.
[2] Ibid., p. 380.
[3] Jung Chang, Jon Halliday, *Mao – The Unknown Story*, London, 2007, pp. 308-315.

him in Yenan. When Wang Ming was admitted to the hospital, Jin was assigned as his chief doctor. That he had poisoned Wang Ming was established by an official inquiry involving Yenan's leading doctors in mid-1943. Its findings, which we obtained, remain a well-kept secret. (The present Chinese rulers do not want to put Mao Zedong in a bad light — GS).

As of the beginning of March 1942, Wang Ming was described as "ready to be discharged." Dr. Jin had been trying to keep him in hospital by advocating a whole string of operations — 'having his teeth taken out, piles excised and tonsils removed'. These operations were dropped after another doctor objected. The inquiry found that the operations for both the tonsils and the piles (which were 'large') 'would have been dangerous.'

But just as Wang Ming was about to leave hospital on June 13, Dr. Jin gave him some pills, after which Wang Ming collapsed. The inquiry recorded that: "On 13 March, after taking one pill, Wang Ming felt a headache. On 14 March, he took two and starting vomiting, his liver was in severe pain, his spleen was swollen, there was pain in the area of his heart.' After more pills from Dr. Jin, Wang Ming was diagnosed as having acute cholecystitis (of the gall bladder) and...hepatomegaly (enlarged liver)".

The inquiry never found out what the pills were, as there was no prescription. Under questioning, Dr. Jin gave 'very vague answers' about the type of drug, and the amount. But the inquiry established that after taking the pills, Wang Ming showed 'symptoms of poisoning'.

Dr. Jin then prescribed further pills: large doses of calomel and soda — two medicines which, when taken in combination, produce poison in the form of corrosive mercury chloride. The inquiry found that these prescriptions were 'enough to kill several people,' and concluded: "It is a fact that he was poisoned."

Wang Ming would have died if he had taken all Dr. Jin's poisonous prescriptions. But he grew suspicious and stopped. In June, Dr. Jin halted his murderous treatment. The reason was that a new and very senior Russian liaison man, Pyotr Vladimirov, had just arrived in Yenan. Vladimirov, who held the rank of general, had worked in northwest China, spoke fluent Chinese, and knew some of the CCP leaders personally. His reports went to Stalin. He also brought with him a GRU surgeon, Andrei Orlov, who also held the rank of general, plus an extra radio operator.

On 16 July, shortly after Vladimirov and Orlov arrived, Moscow was informed, for the first time, that Wang Ming 'after nine months of treatment is at death's door'. At this stage it seems Wang Ming did not tell the Russians that he suspected he was being poisoned. Not only was he in Mao's hands, but he had no proof. He first tried to drive a wedge between Stalin and Mao by telling Vladimirov that Mao had no intention of helping Russia out militarily. Wang Ming says, Vladimirov recorded on 18 July, "that if Japan attacks (Russia)...the Soviet Union ought not to count on the CCP".

Vladimirov quickly became very critical of Mao. "Spies watch our step," he noted. "These last few days (Kang Sheng) has been foisting upon me a teacher of Russian whom I am supposed to accept as a pupil. I have never seen a Chinese girl of such striking beauty. The girl doesn't give us a day's peace..."

Within weeks, Vladimirov had fired the cook who he was convinced was 'a Kang Sheng informer'.

At the beginning of 1943, Wang Ming's condition took a sharp turn for the worse. Doctors, who now had the Russian surgeon Orlov in their ranks, recommended treatment in the Nationalist area of Russia. Mao refused to let Wang Ming go.

To save his life and get himself to Moscow, Wang Ming knew he had to make Stalin feel that he was politically useful. On 8 January, he dictated a long cable to Vladimirov, addressed to Stalin by name. According to his own account, it detailed Mao's 'many crimes,' which he called 'anti-Soviet and anti-Party'. At the end, he 'inquired if it was possible to send a plane for me and have me treated in Moscow, where I would also give the Comintern leadership particulars about Mao's crimes.

Wang Ming's message, much watered down by Vladimirov, reached Comintern chief Dimitrov on 1 February. Mao obviously found out that Wang Ming had got a dangerous message out to Russia, as he immediately cabled Dimitrov with counter-accusations against Wang Ming. Still, Dimitrov promised Wang Ming: 'We'll have you flown to Moscow.'

At this point Dr. Jin made another attempt on Wang Ming's life. On 12 February, right after Dimitrov's message, Jin prescribed the deadly combination of calomel and soda again. A week later, he prescribed tannic acid as an enema at a strength that would have been fatal. This time, Wang Ming not only did not follow the prescriptions, he kept them carefully.

Mao clearly felt a sense of acute urgency, as he now made a startling move. On 20 March, in total secrecy, he convened the Politburo — minus Wang Ming — and got himself made supreme leader of the Party, becoming chairman of both the Politburo and the Secretariat. The resolution gave Mao absolute power, and actually spelled out: 'On all issues...the Chairman has the power to make final decisions.' Wang Ming was dropped from the core group, the Secretariat.

This was the first time that Mao became Party No. 1 on paper, as well as in fact. And yet this was a deeply surreptitious affair, which was kept entirely secret from his own Party, and from Moscow — and was to stay secret throughout Mao's life, probably known to no more than a handful of people.

Wang Ming may have got wind of Mao's maneuver, as he now, for the first time, exposed the poisoning attempt to the Russians. On 22 March he showed Orlov one of Dr. Jin's prescriptions, which Vladimirov cabled to Moscow. Moscow wired back immediately, saying that the prescription 'causes slow poisoning' and 'in grave cases — death'. Wang Ming then showed the prescription to Yenan medical chief Dr. Nelson Fu, and this led to an inquiry, which found beyond doubt that Wang Ming had been poisoned.

But Mao, the ace schemer, turned the inquiry to his advantage. Whilst the inquiry did establish that attempts had been made on Wang Ming's life, Mao used the fact that it was still sitting as an excuse to stall Wang Ming's trip.

And for Mao, scapegoats were always at hand — in this case Dr. Jin. On 28 March, Mme Mao "came to see me quite unexpectedly," Vladimirov noted. "She talked at length about 'the unreliability of Doctor Jin' who she said is probably a Nationalist agent..."

Fifty-six years later, in a drab concrete building in dusty Peking, the only surviving member of the medical panel of fifteen that drew up the official findings in Yenan, Dr. Y, a physically energetic and mentally alert 87-year-old, gave us a tape-recorded interview.

Once the decision was taken to carry out a medical inquiry, Dr. Y was assigned to establish whether Wang Ming had indeed been poisoned. He 'stayed with Wang Ming for a month, sleeping in his study,' heating up his urine each day and then dipping a sliver of gold into it and examining it under a microscope. It proved to contain mercury: 'He was being poisoned slowly,' Dr. Y reported to his medical superior. But nothing was done for weeks. The medical inquiry finally opened on 30 June, more than three months after the poisoning was exposed. The findings, drawn up on 20 July, stated that Wang Ming had definitely been poisoned by Dr. Jin, and were signed by Jin himself. After his signature, he wrote in brackets: "Will make separate statements about several of the points."

But he never did. In the middle of one meeting, in front of his colleagues, he threw himself at the feet of Wang Ming's wife, weeping. Dr. Y was present. He told us that Dr. Jin "went down on his knees, begged for forgiveness, saying that he was wrong".

He admitted mistakes. Of course, he wouldn't admit it was deliberate. In fact, Dr. Jin had been carrying a pocket medical manual, which stated specifically that it was taboo to use calomel in combination with soda, and he had underlined these words. Dr. Y had actually confronted him on this: "Look, it's written here: taboo prescription, great harm. You have even underlined it."

Jin was silent.

Far from getting into trouble, however, Jin was protected by being taken to the haunt of the security apparatus, Date Garden, where he lived with the security elite. He continued to be one of the doctors for Mao and other leaders, which would have been inconceivable if Mao had had the slightest doubt about either his competence or his trustworthiness.[1]

The inquiry did not mention Mao, of course, but the Russians had no doubt: "Wang Ming was being poisoned and...Mao Tse-tung and Kang Sheng were involved."

Mao's key accomplice in preventing Wang Ming from making it to Moscow was, one again, Chou En-lai, his liaison in Chongqing (where the Nationalist government of Chiang Kai-shek was seated at the time — GS). Chiang Kai-shek's permission was needed for Russian planes to come to Yenan so Mao hypocritically asked Chou to obtain permission from Chiang for a Russian plane to come and collect Wang Ming, while making it clear to Chou that he did not want Wang Ming to leave. Chou duly told the Russians that: "the Nationalists would not allow Comrade Wang Ming to leave Yenan."In fact, Lin Biao, who was in Chongqing at the time, told Soviet ambassador Panyushkin that Chou never raised the issue with the Nationalists, because of 'instructions from Yenan'...

On 19 August, a Russian plane left for Yenan to collect Wang Ming, and An-ying (Mao's son who was studying in Moscow at the time — GS) was supposed to be on it. But that day he was called in to see Dimitrov. When the plane arrived in Yenan, there was no An-ying on board. This was Moscow saying to Mao that it wanted Wang Ming first before releasing his son.

But Mao held on to Wang Ming. Vladimirov: "Doctors were...told to say Wang Ming...couldn't stand the strain of the flight... The crew kept delaying the flight as long as they could, but Mao got his way."

Another Soviet plane came on 20 October and stayed four days, before leaving with some Russian intelligence men — but again not Wang Ming.

"On seeing Dr. Orlov," Vladimirov recorded, "Wang Ming burst into tears...he is... still unable to walk...his friends have abandoned him...He is all alone in the full sense of the word..."It was two years now since his health crisis had begun, and a good nineteen months since the start of the poisoning. In those long and agonizing days, his wife looked after him devotedly, presenting a strong calm face to him. But occasionally she would lock the door and try to release her anguish. Her son told us that as a young boy he once caught her rolling and kicking on the earthen floor,

---

[1] The footnote says: "Dr. Jin remained particularly close to Mme Mao, on whom he had performed an induced abortion and oviduct ligation in summer 1942. When the Communists took power, he became head of the Peking Hospital, which catered for Party leaders and their families...," ibid., p. 313.

muffling her sobbing and screaming with a towel. The son was too young to comprehend, but the traumatic scene was etched into his memory.

In Yenan, Dr Y. said:

"many people knew that Wang Ming had been poisoned by mercury, and that someone was trying to murder him...Word got around."

And not only among senior officials, but also among ordinary Party members who had connections to medical staff. So many people suspected the truth that Mao felt he had to flush out the undercurrent suspicion and kill it off. That meant getting the Wang Mings to make a public denial.

On 1 November, a week after the second Russian plane had left, Mao convened a large meeting for senior officials. He himself sat on the platform. Wang Ming was kept away. The star witness was a veteran commander who was trotted out from detention to say that over a year before, Mrs. Wang Ming had told him her husband was being poisoned — and had strongly hinted that Mao was responsible. Mrs. Wang Ming then made a vehement denial on stage. On 15 November she wrote to Mao and the Politburo, vowing that she and her husband had not even harbored such a thought, and felt nothing but gratitude to Mao. The poisoning case was formally closed.

Source material:

1. Wang Ming, *50 Jahre KP Chinas und der Verrat Mao Tse-tungs*, Berlin 1981 (50 years of the CP of China and the treason of Mao Zedong);

2. Peter Vladimirov, *The Vladimirov Diaries*, New York 1975;

3. Jung Chang, Jon Halliday, *Mao. The Unknown Story*, London 2007.

12. The Gao Gang Affair: Mao Zedong Liquidates the Marxist Faction, 1953–1955

Introduction (G. Schnehen)

If one takes for granted what Maoists have been saying for decades about the 'Great Proletarian Cultural Revolution'— a campaign launched by Mao Zedong in early 1966 — then the purpose of this 'revolution' supposedly was to save Chinese socialism from the restoration of capitalism. That's why all Maoists support it, but by doing so, they turn a blind eye to the ugly side of this event, to the many crimes committed in the name of Marxism-Leninism and on behalf of the 'great helmsman' Mao Zedong.

It is assumed that there was Chinese socialism at the time and that Mao Zedong, the 'great revolutionary,' just wanted to save socialism by mobilizing the masses, above all the young people. He had good intentions as he was a socialist through and through and only wanted to serve his people and to defend them against the evil 'capitalist roaders,' who had surreptitiously wormed their way into the Communist Party — among them his old comrade-in-arms, Liu Shao-qi and Deng Xiaoping.

There was socialism in China then and Mao Zedong was a socialist — these are the two basic tenets upheld by Maoists causing them to defend the Cultural Revolution and to downplay its excesses. The mean justifies the end: Mao wanted to prevent socialism from being turned into capitalism by bourgeois 'counter-revolutionaries,' and if some people used violence, they may be forgiven. The end justifies the means.

Chinese Communist leader Gao Gang (1905-1955), who died in one of Mao's prisons.

If one puts these two assumptions into doubt, one risks being labeled a 'revisionist,' a 'bourgeois intellectual' or someone who has evil intentions.

But are these two basic assumptions true? It is surely necessary to work with clearly defined terms, something Maoists always shy away from. How do Marxists describe 'socialism'?

Socialism is described as a social system. It differs from other social systems (such as feudalism, capitalism, etc.) in that the working class (in modern states the majority of the population, the wage and salary earners) exercises political power (not the bourgeoisie as in capitalism, not the aristocracy as in feudalism). It controls the state, which is the state of the working class. Number two: It differs from other social systems in that the exploitation of labor of man by man is abolished and outlawed. No-one is allowed to reap the fruits of labor of someone else and everybody has to work to make a living. Idlers are unwelcome and need to be productive to benefit the whole society. And number three: Social production is planned so as to benefit the whole society, not just an exploitative minority or some few rich families and their big corporations. Planning follows certain well-established rules and laws which every regime that wants to build socialism must abide by.

In socialism the basic economic law of capitalism is no longer in place — the necessity to make the highest possible profit, to reap a super profit; instead, a new law ruling the economy has come into being: the law to ensure the maximum satisfaction of the material and cultural needs of the whole society by always ensuring the perfection of socialist production on the basis of the most highly developed technology.[1]

What are 'socialists'? Socialists are people who stand up for such a new society which can only be built after a successful socialist revolution serving the interests of the working class and its allies. Building socialism can only be successful if these socialists at the top of a new society have a thorough knowledge about how to build socialism systematically and know the basic laws governing the building of socialism. If they don't have this knowledge, building socialism will come to nothing, will end up in chaos and capitalism will have an easy comeback. We know this from experience.

This is a Marxist definition, of course, the one I prefer. Maybe there are other valid definitions. But Mao Zedong claimed to be a 'Marxist-Leninist' who allegedly wanted to build socialism or communism, so he should have defined the term in a similar fashion.

Back to the initial question: Was China socialist when Mao Zedong was at the top of the Chinese state?

Of course, China could only have been 'socialist' if a socialist revolution had taken place in advance. A national-democratic revolution is not sufficient. What is the difference between the two?

In a national-democratic revolution a formerly oppressed country declares itself independent. To back up its newly-won independence by economic measures it then may nationalize all or at least the most important foreign companies and corporations and declare that, from now on, the foreign capital belongs to the new state. If the foreigners used to possess large amounts of land and real estate, it will also be expropriated and taken over. Likewise the real estate of domestic feudal lords is transformed into state property. However, the capitalist system, if there had been, will not be touched and will stay in place, i.e., the national bourgeoisie is welcome and is invited to share state power with the new rulers. So the bourgeoisie is not ousted from its state positions.

This is a national-democratic revolution or anti-colonial revolution — the concrete types of which may differ from one country to another. But basically these are the main characteristics.

In a socialist revolution not just the national independence of a certain country is reestablished, but, mostly shortly afterwards, the national-democratic revolution is followed by another revolution: the expropriation of the national

---

[1] Cp. J. V. Stalin, *Ökonomische Probleme des Sozialismus in der UdSSR*, Berlin 1953, p. 41; economic problems of socialism in the USSR.

bourgeoisie and the nationalization of its capital, leaving the working class solely in charge of state power. This provides favorable conditions for the planning of the whole economy in the interests of the working people and their allies. The working class controls the state alone and carries out further reforms, which does not mean that it is without allies: in underdeveloped countries the peasantry is its chief ally but also the intelligentsia, however, they do not share state power with them. Allies are needed to isolate the old exploiting classes and to make sure that their attempts to win back power come to nothing.

This basically is a socialist revolution that happened in Russia in late 1917. In Russia there had been a democratic revolution before, in February 1917, and then the next step followed some months later in October 1917 when Lenin and his Bolshevik party organized the socialist October Revolution — almost without bloodshed.

What was the situation like in China? Was there a socialist revolution?

On October 1st, 1949, the new China declared its independence after a four-year civil war, lasting from 1945 until 1949. The People's Republic of China was created. Was this a national-democratic or a socialist revolution, paving the way for Chinese socialism?

With the defeat of the nationalist Kuomintang under Chang Kai-shek, who fled to Taiwan in the fall of 1949 after his troops had been defeated by the those of the Communist Party of China, the path for a national-democratic revolution had been cleared. What exactly did the new regime do shortly after reaching Beijing and declaring victory? The number two in the political hierarchy, Liu Shao-qi, a close friend of Mao Zedong and his comrade-in-arms for more than 20 years, tells us. In his political report to the 8th Congress of the CP of China held in September 1956 he said:

> The People's Government confiscated all enterprises operated by bureaucratic capital...These enterprises, including the Japanese, German, and Italian concerns in China taken over by the Kuomintang government following the victory of the War of Resistance to Japanese Aggression, were turned into...state-owned enterprises.[1]

> So the new People's Government led by the Communist Party of China took over already nationalized property belonging to foreigners and, in addition to that, also nationalized the enterprises of four rich Chinese families who were called 'war criminals'. The remaining capital was not touched. Thus, nationalizations were limited to foreign capital and a few wealthy Chinese oligarchs. That was it. The powerful Chinese national

---

[1] Liu Shaoqi, *Political Report of the Central Committee of the CP of China to the 8th National Congress of the Party*, September 1956, p. 12, cited by William B. Bland, *Class Struggles in China*, London, 1997, p. 38.

bourgeoisie was not expropriated and retained its economic status — at least for the time being.

In the years of 1950–1952 the national-democratic revolution was taken a step further: the real estate of the core of the large Chinese landowner class was also nationalized. A land reform was initiated on behalf of small peasants and "The local landlord gentry was destroyed."[1]

However, the rich peasants and even the small landlords (half-feudal landlords) were not expropriated; they retained their economic positions as did the national bourgeoisie. Mao Zedong sent a telegram to a regional party group dated 12 March 1930, saying:

> The essence of this tactical approach in the land reform movement consists in... not only leaving the large capitalist farmers but also the half-feudal farmers untouched and to postpone the matter for a few years. Please consider if this approach wouldn't be more favorable.[2]

The land reform redistributing vast amounts of land in favor of small peasants was completed by 1952 but land belonging to rich peasants was protected according to Article 6 of the new land act. By completing the land reform, the national-democratic revolution came to an end in China in 1952.

What conclusion can be drawn from this?

The Chinese Revolution was a national-democratic revolution. It was incomplete because vast amounts of land remained in the hands of large capitalist farmers and half-feudal landlords. But it surely was an anti-imperialist revolution due to the fact that practically all foreign capitalists, who had been operating in China for decades, were expropriated, thus safeguarding China's sovereignty for the time being.

Can this revolution be called a 'socialist revolution' as well?

No, it can't. As we have seen, in a socialist revolution the national bourgeoisie is also expropriated after the national-democratic revolution has ended. A new state apparatus is created, and this new state apparatus is the state of the working people acting on its behalf. The working class does not share power with the representatives of the national bourgeoisie or any other class, as was the case in China. (Also see the Chinese flag with its four stars representing the working class, the national bourgeoisie, the intelligentsia, and the peasantry). The socialist state has allies, of course, but these allies — among them the peasantry — are not allowed to share power at the state level.

---

[1] Franz Schurmann, *Peasants*, in: Franz Schurmann & Orville Schell, eds., *Communist China: Revolutionary Reconstruction and International Confrontation: 1946-1966*, Harmondsworth, 1977, p. 170, quoted by: William B. Bland, ibid., p. 39.

[2] Mao Tse-tung, *Ausgewählte Werke*, Vol. 5 (Selected Works), Peking 1978, p. 21.

Lenin wrote his 'April theses' after the arrival in Russia in April 1917 in which he outlined his plans for organizing the socialist revolution. He wrote: "We will not stop halfway!" meaning: we will not be satisfied with a national-democratic revolution, we will proceed further to organize a socialist revolution paving the way for a new state machine and also for a new economic system. Once in power, we will then also expropriate the national bourgeoisie and the rich peasants as well and transfer their capital to the poor by creating people's and collective property nationwide.

So there was no socialist state in China at the time and there had not been a socialist revolution either. But in both cases revolutions had taken place, huge social upheavals never known before, leading most people to believe that both revolutions were more or less identical in nature. But they were not! For this reason, Stalin once called the Chinese revolution a "fake revolution" and Mao Zedong a "margarine Communist" (some sort of fake Communist) — butter being the original, margarine the watered down version. For Stalin a Communist was someone fighting for socialism not just for some sort of "democracy," leaving the state machine more or less in the hands of the old exploiters and proprietors.

Very often an equal sign is placed between the two revolutions, the Russian and the Chinese one, and what is more: another one is set between Stalin and Lenin on the one hand and Mao Zedong on the other. In each case we need to take a closer look at these two upheavals, especially at the Chinese one and also to the main protagonists to get the broad picture. What some people tell us about this "socialist" revolution is not important, we need to analyze it ourselves, and we also need to look at what kind of measures were taken shortly after the old semi-feudal Chinese regime had been toppled, as revolutions are not made on a single day. They are made and completed over a long period of time.

There is another misconception: Many analysts do not deal with what goes on inside a certain party. They call the Chinese party "Communist" and that's it. The label says it all. So supposedly, all members of this party were genuine Communists fighting for socialism in unison. To get a more realistic view of what happened inside the Chinese Communist party, it is necessary to look behind the curtain, to recognize that there were different factions and groupings with different concepts and views as to how to proceed to or to achieve "socialism" or "communism." Even the term "communism" is vague. If you have ten people in a room calling themselves "communist," you will get ten different answers as to what communism looks like or should look like. And the various factions may stand for different class interests: There may be one fighting for the interests of the national bourgeoisie, another one fighting for the working class, a third for the peasantry and a forth for the intelligentsia. For Marxists, the main criterion for a socialist is his or her commitment to take the interests of the working people at heart. So we also need to know if there were such people in the Chinese Communist Party and who they were. We need to know especially if Mao Zedong was someone who was fighting for the interests of the working class or maybe he wasn't. Maybe he was just fighting for himself, for his own interests and glory, to preserve power and to remain "Chairman" in the CP of China. But when he launched the "Cultural Revolution" in May 1966 most people thought that he wanted to prevent "Chinese socialism" from being destroyed or undermined by evil and vicious "capitalist roaders".

But was this really so?

1. The dispute about the transition to socialism

Up to now, we have seen that in October 1949, when the People's Republic of China was founded, this event was not a socialist but a national-democratic revolution which may also be called 'anti-imperialist' or 'anti-colonial'. Immediately afterwards, the belongings of the imperialist nations which had suppressed China for decades on end, among them Germany, Japan, Great Britain and others, were confiscated and declared state property. Politically speaking, a system of 'New Democracy' was established led by the Communist Party of China. It was an alliance of four different classes, including the peasantry, the national bourgeoisie, the working class and also the Chinese intelligentsia. Within the Communist Party, as later turned out, there were representatives of at least three of these classes: Liu Shao-qi represented the national bourgeoisie of China, supported by Mao Zedong and Zhou Enlai; Gao Gang represented the working class, and other people, especially some military leaders like Peng Dehui the Chinese peasantry. A Democratic Party, representing the intelligentsia, was allowed to take part in the leadership as well.

We have seen that the national-democratic revolution was incomplete, as rich peasants and even some feudal lords were also allowed to take part in the Revolution. Their property rights were respected.

We have not seen a socialist revolution like the one in Russia in late 1917. A socialist revolution leads to the establishment of the power of the working class, which has also been called 'dictatorship of the proletariat'. After the successful launching of a socialist revolution, the national bourgeoisie is also expropriated and its capital transferred to the workers' state. The working class rules alone; it does not share power with other classes. It has allies, principally the peasantry (in underdeveloped countries), but these allies are not represented in the new state apparatus. They remain outside.

How then can the miracle be explained that China became socialist after 1949, without having gone through a genuine socialist revolution? Mao Zedong claimed that a socialist revolution is not required, as socialism can also be built by transferring the capital held by the national bourgeoisie to the new state on a step-by-step basis, thus creating 'state capitalism,' which basically was the same as socialism. Later, in a conversation with Pol Pot, he denied that, however, and regretted having created only state capitalism in China.

Never the less, officially the new Chinese state was socialist because one only needed to reeducate the former capitalists to make some of them become proletarians. But if you abide by Marxist principles, this is not possible. Marxists are of the opinion that there can be no peaceful transition from capitalism towards socialism and that there has never been such a transition in history.

Here is how Lenin saw it (1905):

> [F]rom the democratic revolution we shall immediately begin to pass over ... in proportion to our strength, to the strength of the class conscious and organized proletariat...to the socialist revolution. We stand for uninterrupted revolution, we will not halt half-way.[1]

Stalin, Lenin's comrade-in-arms, agreed. He saw the difference between a bourgeois or democratic revolution and a socialist revolution this way:

> The bourgeois revolution limits itself to substituting one group of exploiters for another in the seat of power, and therefore has no need to destroy the old state machine, whereas the proletarian revolution removes all groups of exploiters from power and places in power the leader of all the toilers and exploited, the class of the proletarians and therefore it cannot avoid destroying the old state machine by the new one.[2]

Lenin stressed the need to immediately pass over to the socialist revolution because he clearly recognized that a bourgeois democratic revolution is unable to create socialism. A regime of a 'New Democracy,' including the national bourgeoisie, is not in a position to go over to socialism due to the fact that this class will do everything in its power to prevent this from happening. no social class will voluntarily consent to its complete dispossession and removal from power. History shows this.

Let's take the German example, after the end of the First World War. The November Revolution was launched all over Germany in 1919. The old German bourgeoisie massacred 20,000 workers in Berlin alone, to present the revolutionaries from establishing a socialist regime there. Karl Liebknecht, one of the socialist leaders, had already proclaimed the German Socialist Republic from a balcony in the center of the city. Shortly afterwards he was murdered. This is how a national bourgeoisie usually reacts if its position as a ruling class comes under attack. They even resort to open terrorism and fascism if need be.

Back to China in 1949:

---

[1] Collected Works, Vol. VIII, pp. 186-87, Russian edition, quoted by J. Stalin, *Problems of Leninism*, New York, 1934, pp. 14f.
[2] Ibid., pp. 16f.

To launch a socialist revolution would have meant to end the system of 'New Democracy,' to put the four-class alliance aside and to establish a proletarian state, and then, after a while, to dispossess the national bourgeoisie. This would, of course, haven provoked violent resistance on the part of the Chinese bourgeoisie. But the Chinese Communist Party had at its disposal a strong army that had already defeated the Kuomintang under Chiang Kai-shek and sent him to Taiwan.

So why not use the Chinese Liberation Army to chase away the representatives of the bourgeoisie instead of becoming friendly with them and inviting them to share power as Mao Zedong did? If he had been a true proletarian leader and revolutionary, as he always claimed to be, he would have done just that. He would have followed Lenin's path. But, although endlessly claiming to be a staunch Marxist-Leninist he had completely different ideas about building socialism.

These 'ideas' later developed into 'Mao Zedong Thought,' praised by Maoists to this day.

In 1953, when the national-democratic revolution had been completed, Mao developed some theses soon to be used in a speech to representatives of private Chinese industry and private traders on the subject of how to reach socialism without putting off the national bourgeoisie.

The text says:

> The transformation from capitalism into socialism must pass through the intermediate stage of state capitalism...

> 2. The experiences made in these more than three years allow us to say with certainty that the socialist transformation of private industry and private trade and commerce via state capitalism is a rather sound policy and method.[1]

Should Chinese capitalists have been fearful of a violent second revolution like the one in Russia in October 1917 under Lenin? Were they to be removed from their positions in the state apparatus?

Mao Zedong:

> 4. State capitalism can also be practiced in the case of private trade...

> 7. Private industry and private trade with their approximately 3.8 million workers and commercial clerks are a valuable asset of our state and are of great importance for our economy as well as for the people's standard of living...[2]

Then he made a plea for re-education:

---

[1] Mao Tse-tung, *Ausgewählte Werke (Selected Works, German)*, Vol. V, Beijing, 1978, p. 123; Mao Zedong's theses for a speech to industrialists and traders, 1953.
[2] Ibid., p. 124.

Some workers are proceeding too fast and don't want the capitalists to be allowed to earn profits anymore. We have to reeducate them and also the capitalists and to help them to gradually (but as quickly as possible) adapt to the political guidelines of the state saying that China's private industry and commerce mainly serve the national economy and the standard of living of the people. Besides, it is to help the capitalists to make profits, thus leading them on the path towards state capitalism. The following table shows the distribution of profits in state capitalist enterprises: ... dividend for capitalists: 20.5%.[1]

Having promised them to get a fixed amount of the profits, he also wanted to give them another incentive to become real 'socialist state capitalists':

9. It is necessary to continue to educate the capitalists to become patriots. For this purpose one should systematically recruit a number of far-sighted capitalists who are prepared to approach the Communist Party and the People's Government to enable them to convince the majority of capitalists.

10. The introduction of state capitalism not only presupposes that the necessities and possibilities are considered (see the common program) but also to ask the capitalists to take part on a voluntary basis, as this is a matter of cooperation and collaboration not tolerating any coercion...[2]

What conclusions can be drawn from this?

Mao Zedong and his entourage attempted to ride a middle course with the national bourgeoisie. He refrained from fighting the big capitalists, instead he offered them a fixed rate of profit in the state capitalist enterprises and the top jobs in the state bureaucracy, as there was a lack of qualified personnel with a working class background.

In his political report to the 8th Party Congress in September 1956, Liu Shaoqi, Mao's ally at the time, said:

For some time, representatives of the national bourgeoisie and their parties have been participating in the work of our state organs.[3]

It is striking that, at this time, Mao identifies state capitalism with socialism. The newly created state capitalist system, highly involving the national bourgeoisie in the running of the state enterprises as well as in the state apparatus, is simply baptized "socialism." It reminds one of what the British Labor Party did after WWII, when a number of big private British companies, being in the red,

---

[1] Ibid.

[2] Ibid., p. 125.

[3] William B. Bland, *Class Struggles in China*, London, 1997, p. 50, quoting from Liu Shaoqi's Political Report.

were nationalized (later to be denationalized) — something that was also called "socialism" — "British socialism" that is.

No surprise that later the majority of the Chinese national bourgeoisie consented to this type of strange "socialist" system and gave permission to be called "comrades" and "socialists," as a fixed dividend was guaranteed to them and, what is more, the risk of going bankrupt was taken away from them by the new state.

By the way, a similar system was also created in Communist North Korea under Kim Il-sung.

Officially, though, a "return" to capitalism was totally out of the question! Far from it! Mao Zedong used different phrases in a speech he had already given one month before meeting the national bourgeoisie, this time addressed to his own Party comrades:

> Should the transition period lead to socialism or to capitalism? The General Line (formulated by Mao Zedong himself — GS) of our Party prescribes the transition to socialism. This transition requires a relatively long period of struggle...On whom should we rely? On the working class or on the bourgeoisie? The resolution passed by the Second Plenum of the 8th Central Committee has long since made clear: "We have to wholeheartedly rely on the working class."...Briefly, we must be modest, ready to learn, be persistent and adhere to our collective leadership in order to complete the socialist transformation and lead socialism to victory.[1]

> Depending on his audience, he skillfully chose the appropriate terms so as not to provoke discontent or resistance. Now the Party should rely on the working class and there would be a "struggle"! Of course, Mao Zedong was in favor of "socialism" when addressing this kind of audience. One month later, however, he would again rule out such a struggle when talking to the national bourgeoisie. They didn't need to be afraid of his socialism. Double talk.

To sum up:

In China 1949 and afterwards, the national bourgeoisie was welcome in a system of pseudo-socialism, retained its right to make profits (20.5 percent of the profits of enterprises); they were assured top positions within the state enterprises, and the risk of going bankrupt was taken away from them — reason enough to become "socialists" and "comrades," reason enough to adopt state capitalism ("New Democracy") and "to leave capitalism behind." they remained the dominant class in China under the supervision of the Communist Party where they could become members. The system was intentionally called "socialist" to

---

[1] Mao Tse-tung, Vol. V, ibid., p. 115, p. 122.

deceive the toilers in the Communist Party, the ordinary, hard-working members. And what is more: they had their people at the top echelons of the Party apparatus: Liu Shao-qi, Zhou Enlai, Deng Xiaoping, and, not to forget, Mao Zedong himself.

But there was only one problem for Mao: the Marxist faction within the Communist Party and the many Soviet advisers and experts in the country who had been sent by Stalin after the foundation of the People's Republic on October 1, 1949.

2. The first five-year plan (1953–57)

In view of the fact that there was also a faction of the working class in the CP of China, led by Gao Gang, it does not come as a surprise that Mao's general line of state capitalism and his cuddle course with the Chinese bourgeoisie met some fierce resistance.

Many ordinary members of the Communist Party who were sympathetic to real socialism and Leninism had fought all their lives for the "cause," many of them were hardly literate, had not learned a trade, so the Party was everything for them, their only "profession" and also their home. Some were sent to the Soviet Union in the thirties and were trained there in matters of Marxism-Leninism, and, once being back, were regarded with suspicion by the Party leadership and often called the "Moscowites" as Peter Vladimirow tells us in his diaries. They must have known that the Soviets had followed a completely different line when building socialism. They also must have known the *Short Course*, a brief outline of the history of the Bolshevik party, and maybe they knew or they felt that Mao Zedong's line was very similar to that supported by Stalin's main adversaries within the Bolshevik party in the thirties, Trotsky and Bukharin. Bukharin for example propagated the idea that the rich farmers, also called "kulaks" in Russia, would peacefully grow into socialism like the Chinese bourgeoisie should and that their enrichment would do no harm to socialism. On the contrary: would even be beneficial for "Chinese socialism".[1]

To plan a national economy as big as China's under those circumstances was practically impossible. If the national bourgeoisie is not deprived of power and the exploitation of the workforce goes unabated, these people will do everything possible to sabotage central planning, as it is not in their vested interest. And if one invites them to become functionaries of the state bureaucracy, they will use their position to turn it into a farce.

Now, Gao Gang, one of the heroes of the Chinese national liberation struggle, who at that time was the party leader in the northeastern region of China, was told by the party center in Beijing to leave his post, to come to Beijing and to

---

[1] *Geschichte der Kommunistischen Partei der Sowjetunion, Bolschewiki, 'Kurzer Lehrgang'*, Berlin 1945, p. 353; History of the Communist Party of the Soviet Union, Bolsheviks, 'Short Course'.

adopt the position of a head of the newly established State Planning Commission. Adhering to party discipline, he accepted the nomination and left his power base behind him. He should bitterly regret that later on.

As one of the few Marxists at the top of the Party, he must have known that central planning at that early stage was next to impossible, also and especially in view of the fact that the bourgeoisie had not been deprived of power and influence in the country.

Let us first consider some of the main preconditions for central planning. There are at least four:

(1) Socialist property. The majority of the means of production need to be state-owned. No competition is allowed among the enterprises anymore. Private-national companies are not sufficient.

(2) A united leadership in the leading party is an absolute must. If there are different factions fighting each other, central planning will come to nothing in the long run. There may be one faction that rejects planning altogether and after winning a power struggle, it might then decide to put an end to the whole project.

(3) A brisk exchange of goods must take place between the city and the countryside. The countryside must be able to supply the cities with goods and, vice versa, the city the countryside. On the basis of a shortage of goods, no centrally planned economy is going to work.

(4) A certain cultural level must have been achieved. Without a well-trained and educated workforce to run the new enterprises, economic planning in the interest of the working class will come to nothing. If there is not such a level, you will have to rely on the old experts, the managers of the former proprietors who serve different class interests and will do everything in their power to sabotage the new regime. Company directors need to have management skills, they need to know something about bookkeeping, cost accounting, they need to know at least the basics of managing an enterprise — but this time in the interest of the working people, not in the interest of the exploiters. To achieve such a level of training, there have to be universities and lots of technical schools and, of course, illiteracy must have been eliminated.

For comparison:

In the USSR eleven years passed from the October Revolution in 1917 to the adoption of the first five-year plan in 1928. There the necessary preconditions were carefully prepared over years to make the plan work which proved to be a huge success — especially the first one for the years 1929-33.

In 1953, three or four years after the national-democratic revolution, all these preconditions were absent in the People's Republic and there was considerable bickering over the principles of planning inside the party leadership. Only in July of 1955 the plan was finalized at the People's National Congress, retroactively incorporating the plans for 1953 and 1954.[1]

However, the Chinese plan broadly followed Soviet planning principles: emphasis was laid on industrialization, a high degree of centralization in economic planning was allowed and the investment priority was accorded to heavy industry, taking the form of

> ...very large complexes concentrated in a few big cities...The Soviet Union provided credit and technical assistance for 156 major projects, in what was perhaps the largest transfer of technology ever carried out by any country.[2]

By and large this first plan became a success story despite all the odds, as Marc Blecher tells us:

> Industrial output grew faster than the very high target of 14.7% per year...Heavy industrial output nearly tripled, while light industry grew by 70%. Railway freight volume more than doubled.[3]

It was probably due to Gao Gang's great work as planning chief and also to the massive presence and assistance by the Soviet union and their many experts especially in the NE of the country, which became the industrial hub of China. This strengthened the position of the Marxist faction at the top of the Communist Party. Soon Gao even gained more followers, among them Rao Shu-shi, the comrade in charge of East China — reason enough to go forward to the socialist stage of the revolutionary process and not to wait any longer.

To prevent this scenario from happening, the leading group within the Communist Party headed by Mao Zedong, Zhou Enlai, Liu Shao-qi and others made preparations for a coup to get rid of the Marxist faction. Conditions were favorable, since meanwhile Stalin had died (March 5, 1953) and Gao had thus lost an important international ally. Prior to that, in 1949, he had made a trip to the Soviet Union and arranged massive financial help for his northeastern region which he immediately got promised.

Even in the mid-thirties, when Gao was successful in defending the Soviet local area in a North China region called Shaanxi against Kuomintang forces led by Chiang Kai-shek, he was very popular and threatened Mao Zedong's leadership role. Only in early 1935, at the Party conference of Tsunyi during the Long March, Mao Zedong, with the help of Deng Xiaoping — even then an influen-

---

[1] Cp. Mark Selden, Ed., *The People's Republic of China: A Documentary History of Revolutionary Change*, New York, 1979, p. 294, quoted by W. B. Bland in: *Class Struggles in China*, ibid., p. 44.
[2] Marc Blecher, *China: Politics, Economics and Society: Iconoclasm and Innovation in a Revolutionary Socialist Society*, London, 1986, p. 54, quoted by W. B. Bland, ibid., p. 45.
[3] Ibid., pp. 56f.

tial political commissar — and some military leaders gained dominant influence within the Politburo at an extended meeting. "Chairman" of the Party he did not become until 20 March 1943 in Yenan at a secretly convened Politburo meeting after his main rival for the Party leadership, Wang Ming, had been poisoned by him and lay in hospital. But his position was not very stable. He had many opponents who resented him. The methods Mao Zedong used to get rid of Gao clearly show that he had little respect for Party rules and human lives and had no wish to give up this chairmanship so easily, and history should prove him right: he remained Party leader until his death in September 1976 uninterruptedly.

3. Mao Zedong's first attempt to get rid of Gao Gang, 1935

Even before the remainder of the army of the Communist Party of China had arrived in the Special Area of Yenan in the North of China in 1936, an area liberated by other units belonging to the Party not belonging to the Long March unit, Mao Zedong made an attempt to get rid of one of the most popular leaders of the Communist resistance forces who could challenge his plea for perpetual leadership: Gao Gang.

Gao had not participated in the Long March himself but was actively involved in the fighting in the North Shansi area tenaciously defended against the troops of Chiang Kai-shek's Kuomintang forces blockading the area. Due to his prowess and courage he and his comrades were considered heroes by the local population writes Peter Vladimirov in his Yenan diary.

But before Mao Zedong's and Deng Xiaoping's troops arrived in Yenan, something very strange had occurred in the liberated area of which Vladimirov speaks in his diary. On 27 April, 1945 he made the following entry:

> Kao Kang (= Gao Gang — GS), and especially Liu Chih-tan, enjoyed the well-earned popularity in this area and were looked up to as popular heroes. In the face of the Kuomintang blockade and the long-standing national strife, they created and strengthened a Soviet base area near the town of Panyen (a short distance from Yenan), in the course of a long guerrilla war.
>
> In October 1935 the advance task force of Mao Tse-tung put Shansi to the sword. All local party and administrative workers were arrested. The commanders and soldiers who stepped in to defend their leaders were savagely murdered.
>
> The massacre continued with the arrival of the main forces headed by Mao Tse-tung. The main force of the Red Army arrived in North Shansi in November 1936.

The punitive actions of the task force and the Army caused strong indignation among the members of the CCP Central Committee. Mao Tse-tung was considered responsible for the reprisals, for there was no doubt in anybody's mind that it was he had given the order...

In this situation the Chairman of the CCP Central Committee (i.e. Mao — Ed.) chose to put the blame on the military commanders who had led the punitive expedition. Kao Kang, Liu Chih-tan, and all the other survivors of the massacre were rehabilitated...(They had been accused of "treason" — Ed.).

The perpetrators of the punitive action had arrested Kao Kang, Liu Chih-tan, and their comrade-in-arms in the winter. As a torture they kept the arrested men out in blistering cold. When Kao Kang, Liu Chih-tan, and other comrades dropped down half dead with fatigue, they were forced back on their feet with blows and kicks and made to run the gauntlet.

Back in the Futien days (when Mao conducted his first punitive action using Liu Shao-qi as his tool — Ed.) Mao Tse-tung's henchmen had made wide use of torture by fire.

This time they did the same. The arrested men were tortured by fire.

All these years Kao Kang has said nothing about what he was forced to go through, that in the course of such torture sessions the flesh on his right thigh had been burned down to the bone.

Mao's typical artifice: to deal mercilessly with leading party workers who show too great a measure of independence and whose authority is too great for comfort and then to disassociate himself from the reprisals and blame them on their technical perpetrators.

The same thing happened after the Futien reprisals and also after the case of Kao Kang and Liu Chih-tan.

The same thing happened after cheng-feng (Mao Zedong's long-lasting rectification campaign in Yenan to quieten down dissent — Ed.), when the whole blame was put on Kang Sheng and some of his associates (Kang Sheng was Mao's loyal executioner in Yenan, his secret service chief — Ed.)."[1]

"The punitive expedition" Vladimirov mentions in his Yenan diary did not consist of a few lone gunmen but was a large army unit to "enforce law and order" in the liberated area in the Shansi region. The aim was:

---

[1] Peter Vladimirov, *The Vladimirov Diaries, Yenan, China: 1942-1945*, New York, 1975, pp. 406f.

to set up a new base for the old one. Mao Zedong hoped that he would be the lord and the master of the new base and that his authority would be unchallenged there.[1]

Thus Mao had to beat a retreat; his first attempt to get rid of the popular Gao Gang and his followers had come to nothing. Later Gao Gang would be classified "anti-party" by the same person who had shown how anti-party he himself was in actual fact.

Now Gao Gang was there again making leadership claims. And there was another special trump card for him: he had Stalin's confidence:

> There is little doubt that Gao had established both warm personal rela-
> tions with Stalin...and smooth working relations with Soviet officials in the
> Northeast, adjacent Soviet territory, and Korea.[2]

In his reminiscences Mao admits that Stalin was very fond of Gao:

> Stalin liked Gao Gang a lot...Each time on August 15 Gao sent Stalin a
> congratulatory note..[3]

After the revolution in 1949, Gao Gang preferred to stay in the NE of China, his power base, where he was the undisputed number one in the hierarchy of the Chinese CP. His position had become so strong that in July of 1949 he was able to go to Moscow to conclude an important trade agreement with the Soviets on his own.[4]

One month later, on 27 August 1949, and even before the proclamation of the People's Republic of China (1 Oct. 1949), he became president of the People's Government of the Northeast.

Later Mao Zedong claimed that apart from being "anti-party," Gao had maintained "illicit contacts with a foreign power," meaning his contacts to the Soviet government So his contacts with Soviet leaders were used to defame him even more. In late 1949, Mao himself was in Moscow on the occasion of Stalin's birthday (21 December) where he stayed for two months. So what about his own contacts with a foreign power?

4. The recall of Gao and Rao to Beijing, 1952

In late 1952, Gao Gang was transferred to Beijing by the leaders of the CPC to head the newly established State Planning Commission. Gao himself had

---

[1] Ibid., p. 406.

[2] Frederick C. Teiwes, *Politics at Mao's Court. Gao Gang and Party Factionalism in the early 1950s*, London and New York, 1990, p. 47.

[3] Stuart Schram, Ed., *Mao Tse-tung Unrehearsed. Talks and Letters: 1956-71*, Harmondsworth, 1975, cited by: W. B. Bland, ibid., p. 51; Schram quoting from Mao Zedong's talks at the conference in Chengdu, March 1958.

[4] Cp. Jacques Guillermaz, *Le Parti communiste au pouvoir. De l'avènement du régime d'éducation socialiste, 1949-1962*, Paris 1979, p. 130.

belonged to the Politburo since 1949, but could apparently do nothing against this decision he must have been unhappy with. He adhered to party discipline and left his power base leaving behind the area with his deputy.

As part of a more general shift of regional leaders to the capital, Gao Gang was transferred to Beijing in late 1952 from his position as a leading Party, government, and military figure in China's Northeast to become head of the State Planning Commission (SPC).[1]

Later he said that the Beijing leaders wanted to "lure the tiger out of his cave" when recalling him. In early 1953, he was assisted by Rao Shushi who was recalled from East China where he had been the regional leader:

In early 1953, Rao Shushi, the leading Party and government official in East China, similarly came to Beijing to head the Central Committee's organization department.[2]

Similar to Gao Gang his comrade Rao Shu-shi also lost his power bases by this decision and now had to make do with the post of a head of the Central Committee's Organization Department. He was not even made a member of the Politburo where the representatives of the Chinese bourgeoisie and those being in favor of an alliance with the national bourgeoisie enjoyed a solid majority (Mao Zedong, Liu Shaoqi, Zhou Enlai and others). [3]

Here is what the hierarchy in the Party looked like in 1952:[4]

1. Mao Zedong: chairman of the Party and the State, chairman of the Politburo;

2. Liu Shao-qi: member of the Politburo, Chairman of the Secretariat of the Politburo, Mao Zedong's Deputy (in 1931 expelled from the Communist Party on account of the Futien massacre, readmitted in Yenan in the forties);

3. Zhou Enlai, Prime Minister, member of the Politburo;

4. Chu De: Chief-of-Staff of the People's Liberation Army, member of the Politburo;

5. Chen Yun, Deputy Prime Minister and member of the Politburo;

6. Kao Kang (Gao Gang), head of the State Planning Commission (SPC), member of the Politburo;

7. Peng Dehuai, Commander of the Chinese Forces in Korea during the Korean War (1951–1953);...

11. Deng Xiaoping, Deputy Prime Minister, not a member of the PB;...

---

[1] Frederick C. Teiwes, ibid., p. 6.
[2] Ibid.
[3] Mao Zedong was in favor of such an alliance, too. In August 1953 he gave a speech to the *National Conference on Financial and Economic Work*, June-August 1953, where he spoke about the alliance between the working class and the national bourgeoisie.
[4] See: *Great Soviet Encyclopedia*, 1952, quoted by Frederick C. Teiwes, ibid., p. 100.

13.Rao Shushi, Head of the Organization Department of the Central Committee, no member of the PB.

There were ten Politburo members altogether. They were: Mao Zedong, Liu Shaoqi, Chou Enlai, Chu De, Chen Yun, Gao Gang, Peng Dehuai, Dong Biwu, Lin Boqu, Peng Chen (1952).

Most of these people were linked to the main social classes in China: the working class, the national bourgeoisie, the peasantry and the intelligentsia. For example: Gao Gang was linked to the Chinese working class, Liu Shaoqi to the national bourgeoisie, etc.

After the recall of Gao and Rao to Beijing in 1952-53, who did not support the official line of an alliance with the Chinese bourgeoisie and a peaceful transition to socialism via state capitalism, these people found themselves in a clearly weak- ened position. Gao was the only Politburo member representing the Chinese working class. He was the only member who had explicitly not given his consent to this line. Rao, his ally, was not even a PB member. He, too, should become a victim of Mao Zedong's vengeance and purges and would later be thrown into prison like Gao, but contrary to him he survived. Their allies — twelve in number — were also purged.

Now being present in Beijing, the two leading Marxists found themselves directly under the supervision of the party bureaucrats and Mao Zedong. Each of their steps would be traced closely and later denounced as "evidence" for having creating an "anti-Party alliance" and a "conspiracy" working in the "underground," as Mao Zedong later put it.

Back in Beijing, the two now made use of their influential positions to promote their own line which contradicted Mao's "General Line." At the various party conferences in the second half of 1953 they both attacked those who were trying to implement Mao Zedong's General Line in his absence. Their chief targets were Liu Shaoqi and Zhou Enlai. But there is no evidence that they operated on the basis of a written agreement or that they coordinated their actions in any way.

Frederick C. Teiwes comments on the state of historical research in China (1990):

> In particular, the 1955 conclusion that Gao and Rao formed an anti- Party "clique" or an "alliance" is no longer used in Party history accounts, and scholars are deeply skeptical that the two men engaged in any explicit coordination of activities. Yet the larger verdict and accompanying biases remain in the published sources of the reform era (= the Deng Xiaoping era — GS).[1]

---

[1] Frederick C. Teiwes, ibid., p. 12.

5. The National Conference on Financial and Economic Work, June-August 1953

The subsequent reproaches made against Gao Gang and Rao Shushi were officially related to an alleged "underground activity" and to "secret backstage deals against the Party" in order to "seize power." But the real reasons were very different from these pretexts. The main reason was that they had different opinions about how to go over to socialism during the transition period. They, above all, disagreed with Mao Zedong's "General Line" to achieve socialism via state capitalism in a close alliance with the national bourgeoisie. So instead of dealing with those pretexts, it is probably more appropriate to deal with what Gao and Rao actually said at the Party conferences held in the second half of 1953 where the course to be chosen towards socialism was to be discussed in great detail.

The first conference, the National Conference on Financial and Economic Work, was held between June 14 and August 12 in Beijing with some interruptions.[1]

There were many items on the agenda: the first five-year-plan, the new tax system, the issue of food supply, price policies, problems concerning capitalist industry and private trade, the construction of the country in general as well as the implementation of Mao Zedong's "general line".

Mao Zedong was present at the conference and spoke about his "general line"; likewise present were his allies, Liu Shao-qi and Zhou Enlai and others[2]. The Marxist opposition represented by Gao and Rao was also there. Gao gave a speech about the economic reconstruction of the country. Mao Zedong was vague on the "transition to socialism" to be achieved within "ten to fifteen years" — "maybe a little longer." He repeated his well-known stance that private trade and industry...

..should be steered in the direction of state capitalism.[3]

During the conference this line was put in concrete terms. The result was *shumaj*, the concrete version of Mao's general line of a gradual transition to socialism. Li Weihan, one of Mao's followers, suggested three methods to achieve this:

(1) *Shougou*: buying up small capitalist enterprises by the new-democratic state;

(2) Processing and ordering of products to monopolize the purchase and marketing of goods of private companies by the state;

(3) State-private ownership of private enterprises taken over by the state.

[1] Ibid., p. 53.
[2] Mao often asked Liu Shaoqi to chair meetings when he was absent, showing that he fully trusted him at that time.
[3] Mao Tse-tung, Vol. V., 1978, ibid., p. 115.

Shougou was rejected during the discussion but the other two points were adopted by majority vote. Frederick C. Teiwes:

> By the end of June the issue was settled. Mao had approved Li's *shumai* approach, Liu Zhou, Zhu De, Chen Yun, Deng Xiaoping and Li Fuchun had all agreed, and Li Weihan was instructed to revise his report for the conference. After the conference, in September, Mao gave a ringing endorsement of peaceful transition in his address to democratic party leaders and national capitalists when he emphasized that transformation must be voluntary, warned against impatient rash advance (*jizao maojin*) and noted that private industry and commerce "in the main serve the nation's economy and the people's livelihood."[1]

The only one at the conference who did not agree to *shumaj* was Gao Gang. We do not know anything about Rao Shu-shi's position, whether he voiced an opinion or not. Thereupon, Mao Zedong asked Li Weihan to contact Gao after the conference and to try and convince him that the official line, being in keeping with his General Line was correct. Li and Gao had known each other in the thirties. Later, Li told Mao what Gao had told him in a private conversation:

> Have you ever read *On the Opposition*...Didn't Bukharin also advocate a peaceful entry into socialism?[2]

Let's dig a little deeper: What exactly did Stalin write at the time about the Soviet opposition around Bukharin, Tomsky, Rykov, and their supporters within the Communist Party of the Soviet Union (1929)? They had indeed developed very similar ideas about the entry into socialism as Mao Zedong had. Bukharin, who had already been sharply criticized by Lenin, took the view that the Communist Party should make far-reaching concessions to the private traders and capitalist farmers, also called "Kulaks." From a speech made by Stalin at a meeting of the Central Committee of the All Union Communist Party of the USSR late in January 1929:

> This group has its special platform which can be seen from their declaration — a special platform it opposes to the policy of the Party. In opposition to the current policy of the Party they demand to slow down the development of our industry...Thirdly — again contrary to the policy of our Party — they want full freedom for private trade and the renunciation of the regulatory role of the state in the field of trade and commerce, claiming the regulatory role of the state makes the development of trade impossible...

---

[1] Frederick C. Teiwes, ibid. p. 61, quoting Mao in: *The Writings of Mao Zedong, 1949-1976*, pp. 383-85.
[2] Ibid., Teiwes quoting Li Weihan, *Recollections and Research*, 1986.

The basic fault of the Bukharin people consists in their belief, in their conviction that our grain problems, and all the other difficulties we are facing, could be solved and the political situation of our country be improved, if we made concessions to the kulaks, if we didn't restrict their exploitative tendencies, if we gave them a free hand, etc...

It is deplorable that the Bukharin people do not understand the mechanics of class war, that they refuse to comprehend that the kulak is the sworn enemy of the toilers, the sworn enemy of our entire social system...[1]

So questions of principle were being discussed at this conference — whether to make concessions to private traders and other capitalist forces or not. Gao Gang rejected this, and he became very outspoken at the conference as well. He did not pull his punches, as Frederick C. Teiwes states in his book on the Gao Gang affair. Unlike him, Mao Zedong did that:

Most significantly, for all his heightened awareness of the unity issue, Mao never confronted Gao Gang...Mao's only approach during the conference had been the indirect one of sending Li Weihan to argue the virtues of the peaceful transformation of the bourgeoisie.[2]

He did not criticize him for his dissension but instead chose to tell Li — one his people — to speak to Gao privately, apparently to find out more about Gao's attitude. After that, Li reported back to his mentor. This was later used against Gao to make him appear "anti-Party." Mao, who felt that this charge was not enough, then added that Gao had also been engaged in "underground work." But all Gao had done was do clearly and openly state his opinion on a crucial question. The person actually being engaged in "underground work" was Mao Zedong himself — one of his favorite methods to smear a popular comrade.

In September/October 1953, another party conference followed, the National Organization Work Conference. There Gao Gang's ally, Rao Shu-shi, came out strongly against Liu Shao-qi who was chairing the meeting in Mao's absence. A comrade called An Ziwen, a supporter of Mao and Liu, suddenly presented a list for a major reshuffle within the Party leadership to strengthen the position of those party officials who were prepared to abide by Mao's General Line.

The idea was to exclude a number of military men who were sympathetic to Gao and Rao from top positions. Rao opposed the move — a stance later used as "proof" that he had been engaged in "anti-Party activities" and that he was a "conspirator." After his "exposure" and dismissal, none other than Deng Xiaoping

---

[1] J. W. Stalin, *Die Bucharin-Gruppe und die rechte Abweichung in unserer Partei*, in: Stalin-Werke (Stalin Works), Vol. 11, Berlin 1954, pp. 285-88 (the Bukharin group and the right deviation in our party).

[2] Frederick C. Teiwes, ibid., p. 76.

was given his post as leader of the organization department of the Central Committee.

In October/November a third conference was held on agricultural policies.

The conference showed that the power struggle at the top of the Chinese Communist Party was becoming more intense. Behind the scenes Mao was collecting incriminating material against Gao, Rao and their followers in the Party, using his cronies, among them Li Weihan, Zhou Enlai, and Deng Yiaoping as informants.

6. The December 24 Enlarged Politburo Meeting

Whenever it came to muzzling or even eliminating critics and dissidents, Mao Zedong convened extended Politburo meetings, inviting close allies from the provinces to take part and to assist him. The first time he used this type of tactic had been during the Long March, when he was given an influential position in the Party at an enlarged meeting of the Central Committee in the provincial town of Tsunyi, in January 1935. Certain generals and political commissars, among them Deng Xiaoping, also were invited to participate to take part in a crucial vote that lifted Mao to the top, even though the Party statutes did not allow this.[1]

Gao Gang had suggested introducing the rotation system to give other Politburo members a chance to chair meetings. Now the standard practice was that Mao's trusted lieutenant, Liu Shao-qi, always chaired these sessions in his absence which happened quite often. But this time he was present and opposed the idea:

> It was at the enlarged Politburo meeting on December 24 that Mao finally confronted Gao Gang...Mao now criticized the rotation proposal, formally decided on Liu's acting role, and revealed Gao and Rao's various sins.[2]

Later Mao quoted himself on what he had said at the meeting:

> I said there were two headquarters in Beijing: One was ... led by me; we blew a positive wind and lit a positive fire; The other was a headquarters commanded by someone else; it blew a sinister wind and lit a sinister fire and was operating underground.[3]

In Mao's Selected Works, Volume 5, a heavily redacted version of what he actually said and wrote can be seen. Mao is quoted as saying this:

---

[1] Cp. Otto Braun, *Chinesische Aufzeichnungen (1932-1939)*, Berlin 1973, p. 144.
[2] Ibid., p. 120.
[3] Ibid., p. 120.

At an enlarged meeting of the Politburo of the Central Committee which was dedicated to the exposure of Gao Gang, I said that there were two headquarters in Beijing. One led by me, blew an earthly wind and lit an earthly fire; The second headquarters was run by others and, operating underground, blew a hell wind and lit a hell fire.[1]

Good fighting Evil, with Mao being the good guy, his opponents being the evil guys.

The Chairman then proposed a draft resolution to give a stern warning to the two Marxists which, allegedly, was carried unanimously.[2]

It seems that Gao Gang was not very impressed by the "stern warning" and "his exposure" he most probably did not consent to: shortly afterwards, he took part in an inauguration ceremony for three more Soviet assisted large industrial projects of the steel industry in the NE, knowing full well that he enjoyed the support of the Soviets.

But some months previously, on March 5, 1953, he had lost his most influential ally in Moscow: Stalin died on that day under mysterious circumstances. Gao was still politically active and did not shun the public light. Still!

7 The 4ᵗʰ Plenum of the Central Committee and the subsequent discussion meetings, February 1954

In the following months after the enlarged Politburo session, a whole series of meetings took place at the highest party level, but subsequently also on a regional and local level — a clear indicator that the whole affair was not over yet. Gao and Rao had not caved in to the pressure put on them, had not exercised self-criticism and had refused to grovel in front of Mao and his followers — reason enough to take further steps to break their backs.

Then came the 4ᵗʰ Plenum of the Central Committee, and once again Mao appointed Liu to preside over the meeting, emphasizing his position as Mao's deputy and as the number two in the Party hierarchy. Mao preferred to stay away and to let his most trusted lieutenants do the dirty work. Along with Zhou Enlai and Deng Xiaoping, Liu Shao-qi was among the most ardent champions of the interests of the Chinese national bourgeoisie. Thus, Mao Zedong who could have taken sides with the Marxist faction to prove that he was a true Marxist and Socialist as he always claimed to be, gave evidence to the fact that he was not defending the interests of the working class in the upcoming class battle with the bourgeoisie, and that he was not a true Marxist-Leninist despite his usual

---

[1] Mao Tse-tung, V., ibid., p. 180
[2] Frederick C. Teiwes, ibid., 126.

"proletarian" rhetoric. Mao Zedong openly sided with the representatives of the national bourgeoisie.

The photo taken of the participants of the meeting inside the conference building shows the more than 70 members of the Central Committee, maybe also the candidates.[1]. In the first row one can see Gao Gang, next to him his adversaries Zhou Enlai, Liu Shao-qi, Zhen Yun and others. Rao can be seen in the second row, fourth from left. Deng Xiaoping was also there.

The main item on the agenda: Gao and Rao's alleged anti-Party activities.

After the official part of the session of the supreme Party body, discussion meetings took place. They were arranged because the two Marxists had not budged and the position of others had still remained unclear:

> With Gao and Gang Rao Shushi refusing to admit serious fault and the roles of others still unclear, discussion meetings (*zuotanhui*) were convened in mid-February in Beijing...[2]

The meeting on Gao was chaired by Zhou Enlai. He gave a long speech making numerous accusations — the first document in which Gao's alleged "errors" and "faults" are mentioned in great detail. It can be assumed that this speech was agreed with Mao in advance who again preferred to stay in the background for the time being. Zhou painstakingly listed all the sins Gao had supposedly committed over a long period of time — nine major ones altogether — to thoroughly destroy Gao's high reputation.

Stalin had now been dead for one year. Had he still been alive, would these Communist leaders, who were taking sides with the Chinese national bourgeoisie, have dared to dismantle one of his chief Chinese allies? But in Moscow a different wind had started to blow: Nikita Khrushchev had come to power assisted by the top echelons of the Soviet Army.

From Zhou Enlai's speech at the discussion meeting[3]:

> 1. He alleged that the mainstays of the Chinese Party were trained in the army, and that the cadres of the white areas were now attempting to seize Party power...he tried to incite and influence high-ranking cadres in the army with his fallacies while preparing to form a group of deputies to the 8th Party Congress in order to seize Party leadership. (The Party Congress took place only in 1956 — GS).
>
> 2. He engaged in sectarian activities and opposed comrades of the central leadership...Gao Gang vilified central leading comrades for being sectarian to cover up his own sectarian activities. He did so...to gain leadership over the Party and the state.
>
> 3. He resorted to lies and fomented discord at every opportunity to sow dissension in the Party...

---

[1] Ibid., photo on p. 123.
[2] Ibid., p. 126.
[3] Ibid., pp. 241ff.

4. He implemented a factional cadre policy, thereby undermining unity inside the Party...Gao Gang's cadre policy is unprincipled and factionalist...

5. He regarded the region under his leadership as personal capital and, in fact, his independent kingdom (an accusation Mao should later repeat — GS)...He never made self-criticisms and would not take criticism from others...

6. Gao Gang distorted many things in the political life of the Center and spread many lies and rumors, attacking others and glorifying himself...

7. He plagiarized others' works to elevate himself and impress and cheat the Center. To seize power, he spent much thought on showing off, not by studying hard but through taking over others' viewpoints...Gao knows next to nothing of Marxism-Leninism, and in action, has actually gone over to the reverse of Marxism-Leninism, but he often bragged about how hard he studied Marxism-Leninism in order to gain influence.

8. On the question of Sino-Soviet relations, he sowed discord and behaved in a way detrimental to Sino-Soviet unity...He also made many remarks that were obviously disruptive to Sino-Soviet unity.

9. He engaged in schemes to seize Party and state power...[1]

Still unsure if these points would be sufficient to convince the participants in the meeting of Gao's sins, Zhou, the No. 3 in the Party hierarchy and also Mao's chief diplomat, then resorted to personal defamation by saying:

In addition to the above activities to split the Party and seize power, according to the latest revelations made by comrades, Gao Gang led a dissolute life completely contrary to the moral standard of a Communist. We must point out that the decadence of his personal life is one manifestation of the corrosive influence of bourgeois thought on our Party, and that we must oppose and resolutely resist such corrosion...

...the decadence of his lifestyle continued unchecked for a long time... The progressive worsening of his dark side turned him, step by step, into a de facto agent of the bourgeoisie within our Party...[2]

Of course, these serious "crimes" must also have canceled out the... partial contributions he had made to the revolution; they prove that his motives in taking part in the revolution were impure. For Gao Gang, bourgeois personal ambition has completely overruled loyalty to serving the people that Communist Party members must preserve.[3]

Having completed his character assassination on Gao, Zhou gave some advice on "re-educating" the sinner. The standard method of the Maoists since Yenan

---

[1] Ibid., source: *Zhonggong Dangshi Jiaoxue Cankao Ziliao*, 20:267-69 (CCP History Teaching Reference Materials). So it seems that this document was used to educate young Communists in China.
[2] Ibid., pp. 243f.
[3] Ibid., p. 244.

in the early forties: supervision by Kang Sheng's secret service and long-time thought control:

> We must put him under supervised education for a long time to come. If Gao is really repentant, then he should submit to the Party's supervised education, genuinely confess and admit his crimes. Without long-term testing, we will never believe that he is ready to reform his extremely individualistic thoughts and actions, which have developed for a long time.[1]

What kind of conclusions did Zhou Enlai draw from the affair? What was the Party supposed to be learning from all this?

> From Gao Gang's case, we should draw the following lesson: all conceit, liberalism, individualism, sectarianism, cliquism, decentralism, localism, and partmentalism must be criticized...The idea of establishing independent kingdoms must be eliminated...[2]

More control was needed to avoid such a scenario from happening again:

> All cadres of the Party, without exception, must be subject to the supervision of the Party organization and the masses of the people.[3]

Later, a Party Control Commission was installed to nip such affairs and dissension in the bud.

Reading Zhou's speech carefully, it is noticeable that the issue at stake, the entry into socialism through state capitalism and in close cooperation with the bourgeoisie, was carefully circumnavigated.

Also noticeable is the Party leadership's great fear of losing control of the situation in the Party. Thus the constant pleas for Party unity and the fight against "sectarianism," against attempts to "throw discord" into the Party and evil "bourgeois individualism." There should be more control and, if necessary, more "education" and "re-education" if deemed necessary. Of course everything on behalf and in the name of the "masses of the people," as Zhou put it.

Zhou's incendiary speech was unanimously adopted by the Politburo on March 1, 1954, when the tribunal against the two Marxists was already over. Mao had reappeared from nowhere to chair the meeting but Gao was no longer to be seen. He had disappeared from the face of the earth. This way Party unity was restored at the top echelon of the Communist Party and Mao still remained the undisputed leader, the Chairman and Great helmsman.

What happened to Gao next? Do we know anything about his fate?

First they did not report anything at all but later it was said that he had committed suicide and had died after the second attempt. This doubtful version has also been accepted by the wikipedia. As committing suicide

---

[1] Ibid.
[2] Ibid., pp. 244f.
[3] Ibid., p. 245.

was regarded as an admission of guilt by the Communist Party of China, this version seems to have been used to further vilify him and also to conceal the truth for good.[1]

In *Who's Who in Communist China*, Vol. one, it says that he was thrown into prison where he supposedly died in 1955. William B. Bland, a British Marxist, confirms:

> ...with regard to the allegation of the revisionists that Kao 'committed suicide,' one may note that, according to a 'Red Guard' pamphlet entitled 'Down with Liu Sha-chi' published in 1967 during the Cultural Revolution: "Kao was 'put to death' not long after the (1955 — GS) conference".[2]

The sessions to condemn and purge Rao Shushi were chaired by Deng Xiaoping — another Mao Zedong favorite.

All in all, seven meetings were organized in February to crush Rao's reputation thoroughly. He, too, had resisted Mao Zedong's "general line" of allying the CP with the national bourgeoisie to achieve socialism gradually and via state capitalism. Again, Mao Zedong refrained from taking part in the meeting, letting Deng Xiaoping do the job for him. On 1 March 1954, shortly after the meetings had ended, Deng gave a long report to the Central Committee on the results of the "discussions," some sort of summary. Altogether 26 comrades took part in the sessions, which was just a tiny minority of the Central Committee. On the final day, when the "discussions" were over, 66 participants however suddenly appeared on the scene having been transferred from the regions to listen to Deng's report. Deng, who directly benefited from the purge, as he was allowed to become a Politburo member after Rao's dismissal, had this to say about his "extremely individualistic, careerist and bourgeois" former comrade-in-arms. (Of course, he avoided touching on the real issue at stake: the transition to socialism side by side with the Chinese bourgeoisie):

> According to the facts as verified by the discussions, Comrade Rao Shushi has been shown to be an extremely individualistic bourgeois careerist. His personal ambitions were constantly on the ascendant. His most glaring crime was his and Gao Gang's activities in 1953 to split the Party.
>
> The discussions examined the question of how Comrade Rao Shushi undermined the prestige of the central leadership and disrupted Party unity in 1953 from the time of the National Conference on Organization Work. During this period, Rao Shushi's activities completely exposed him as a sinister careerist and that, in fact, he had already formed an anti-Party alliance with Gao Gang.

---

[1] Cp.: *Who's is Who in Communist China*, Vol. 1, Hong Kong, 1969, p. 330, quoted by W. B. Bland, ibid., p. 53.
[2] William B. Bland, ibid., p. 55.

After he was appointed director of the central organization department in February 1953, to achieve his infamous aim of climbing step by step to a higher position, Rao, starting out from his own ugly thoughts of sectarian power struggle, began to distort political life within the central leadership. He erroneously estimated that certain comrades were on their way out and certain others were on their way up. Based on these ridiculous speculations, he energetically stirred up dissension inside the Party...

...He was determined, by hook or by crook, to damage the prestige of the Party Center, oppose central leading comrades, participate in Gao Gang's anti-Party activities, and engage in political speculation to achieve his futile ambition of climbing to a higher position after he succeeded and in an effort to consolidate and develop his despicable goal of personal power... Rao Shushi, in following the anti-Party activities of Gao Gang, is actually demonstrating the attempt of the bourgeoisie to corrupt, subvert, and split the Party...

Deng Xiaoping, Chen Yi, Tan Zhenjin

March 1, 1954[1]

The following pages of Deng's report repeat these accusations over and over again (he was a careerist, a bourgeois individual, he tried to split the Party, to climb to the very top, he wanted to create chaos to achieve his bourgeois ambitions, his activities were outright sectarian, he resorted to methods also used by the exploiting classes of the old society, he invented lies to dupe the center, he had an unsavory personal style, he was a rumor monger, a master of the power play, he had a dishonest attitude, his nature was ugly, etc, etc.).[2]

Similar to Zhou Enlai, Deng is also of the opinion that conclusions must be drawn from these "anti-Party activities" that had severely threatened the unity of the Party and the Center. It was necessary to improve criticism and self-criticism, to be vigilant, and the Party needed to sharpen its "proletarian senses." No enemy should think he could undermine the unity of the Party, every cadre should have a "Communist outlook," should receive a thorough "Marxist-Leninist education" to enable the Party to fulfill its historic mission in the period of transition, etc.

Rao, however, was treated slightly more lenient than Gao. In another report by the East China Bureau on these expanded meetings of the 4th Plenum of the Central Committee it says:

Gao and Rao come from the same mold. Their difference is in the extent of their crimes and the different forms their activities manifested. We must criticize Gao Gang and Rao Shushi together as agents of the bourgeoisie for

---

[1] Frederick C. Teiwes, ibid., pp. 246f. Approved by the Politburo on 15 March, 1954.
[2] Cp. ibid., pp. 248-52.

us to be able to understand the resolution of the Fourth Plenum, heighten our vigilance, and enhance our ability to expose hypocrites and schemers...[1]

Rao was put behind bars but, unlike Gao, he managed to survive the purges. Along with Gao and Rao other comrades were expelled from the Party for their alleged role in the "anti-Party affair." Especially hard hit was the northeastern Party branch where Gao used to be the leader of the Party but also of the army for several years:

Gao's fall was accompanied by the purge of virtually all the key Party leaders in the North-East Region.[2]

Altogether 12 leading cadres were also purged from the Party for having "colluded" with Gao and Rao. To quote one example: Pan Hannian, the deputy mayor of Shanghai, was also sent to prison where He died in 1977.

The Chinese media kept quiet about the Party purge as well as on the fate of the incarcerated Marxists.

8. The National Party Conference, March 1955

Exactly one year later a National Party Conference was convened to wrap up the Gao Gang affair for good. It was held on March 21-31. Gao and Rao were of course no longer present. Three main items were on the agenda:
(1) The Gao-Rao anti-Party alliance;
(2) The first five-year-plan;
(3) The establishment of a Party Control Commission.
Mao Zedong was present this time making the opening and final speech. Now it was time to reach a final verdict and to bring everything out into the open — the official version that is. The "masses of the people" were now given a chance to know "everything" about what had happened inside the Party.

The rising star in the Party, Deng Xiaoping, gave a long speech on the first day of the conference which remained unpublished though. After Mao Zedong's death in 1976 the speech was uncovered and found in a collection of documents. There all the accusations made against Rao a year before were repeated and even embellished. He also used Zhou Enlai's speech against Gao Gang and incorporated the main points in his own version. To quote one example to illustrate the perfidy with which Deng tried to crush Gao and Rao's reputation:

Gao Gang's anti-Party and anti-working class thoughts and actions have their historical roots. According to facts that have come to light, Gao Gang's role in revolutionary struggle in the Shanxi-Gansu-Ningxia area was exaggerated. During that period, his activities had already revealed

---

[1] Ibid., S. 252, source: *Zhonggong Dangshi Jiaoxue Cankao Ziliao*, 20:312, 314f.
[2] *New Encyclopaedia Britannica*, Vol. 5, Chicago, 1994, p. 113, quoted by W. B. Bland, ibid., p. 55.

tendencies of individualism and sectarianism. On several occasions when he had been confronted with hardships and dangers and when his personal desires had not been satisfied, Gao Gang had vacillated and become passive. He had a decadent life for a long time. After entering the cities from the countryside (that is when the Communist Party assumed power in 1949 — Frederick C. Teiwes), Gao Gang USED EVERY DESPICABLE MEANS TO MOLEST WOMEN AND HAD SEXUAL RELATIONS WITH A NUMBER OF WOMEN OF QUESTIONABLE POLITICAL BACKGROUND. GAO'S EXTREME MORAL DEGENERATION WAS A REFLECTION OF HIS COMPLETE POLITICAL DEGENERATION.

IT WAS NO COINCIDENCE THAT RAO SHUSHI SHOULD JOIN FORCES WITH GAO GANG IN 1953 TO FORM AN ANTI-PARTY ALLIANCE. EVIDENCE SHOWS THAT RAO SHUSHI HAD BEEN A CAREERIST AND POLITICAL SWINDLER FOR A LONG TIME. HIS SPECIALTY WAS HYPOCRISY. ALTHOUGH HIS MIND CONTAINED NOTHING BUT SORDID IDEAS OF PERSONAL GAIN, HE TRIED HIS BEST TO PRETEND TO BE A "MAN OF PRINCIPLE"...[1]

Deng — of course no careerist at all — should become Mao Zedong's successor in 1978 and rule China until 1997 as chairman of the Communist Party — for nearly 20 years. By using such questionable methods he climbed to the top of the Party. Apparently as a reward for his "bravery," Deng became Mao Zedong's new Finance Minister after the affair and was also co-opted into the restructured Politburo for his loyal services.

Did these self-righteous accusers know, by the way, how the new Soviet First Secretary, Nikita Khrushchev, settled scores with his own major adversary in the Soviet Party, Lavrenti P. Beria, the former deputy Minister President of the USSR at a plenum meeting in early July of 1953? Were they informed about Khrushchev's methods of purging his party from his chief rival? If we look at how the Soviet Gao Gang, Lavrenti Beria, was ousted from power by the Khrushchevites and their military backers, we find many parallels. Even the type of language used by the accusers are similar, sometimes almost identical. The methods of defamation and slander used were similar as well. Let's therefore have a brief look at what Beria, who was arrested at gun point by the Khrushchev people in the midst of a Politburo session on June 26 (1953) by a military unit led by Georgi Zhukov, was later accused of at a prolonged CC Plenum meeting lasting almost a week:

- Khrushchev (the upcoming First Secretary of the CPSU): "This is a devious man and a skilled careerist. With his dirty paws he had a tight grip on Stalin's soul..."[2]

---

[1] Frederick C. Teiwes, ibid., p. 264, Deng Xiaoping's speech before the 1955 National Party Conference, my emphasis.

[2] Viktor Knoll, Lothar Kölm, Ed., *Der Fall Berija. Protokoll einer Abrechnung,* Berlin 1999, p. 47; Beria's case – protocol of a reckoning.

- Molotov (Soviet Foreign Minister — GS): "Now we have become aware of the extent he has become a stranger to us and that he is a dirty and amoral type. Now we know that he has done a lot of mischief to the Soviet Union and that he is a big criminal and a dangerous adventurer."[1] "At times we obviously underestimated his anti-Party methods."[2]

- Schatalin quoting Zarkisov: "One year ago or one and a half years ago, I found out that he contracted syphilis as a result of his relations to prostitutes..."[3]

- Bakradse: "Beria was always guided by his careerist considerations."[4]

- Kaganovich: "He, Beria, wanted to seize power to liquidate the dictatorship of the proletariat and to restore capitalism in our country...He did not know Marxism-Leninism."[5]

- Tevosyan: "When trying to solve problems in the Council of Ministers he was not guided by the interests of the state but by those of his own career and his dirty plans."[6]

Mao himself once drew parallels between the Gao Gang affair in his country and that of Beria's in the Soviet Union. Beria was one of Stalin's closest collaborators and the main candidate for the top job in the USSR after Stalin's sudden and unexpected death in March 1953. Mao on 8 December 1956:

> We should not think that now, after the case of Gao Gang and that of Beria has happened and now that Stalin's mistakes and the Hungary affair have become something unheard of, that we can now take a rest and go to sleep.[7]

At the National Conference Mao mentioned Gao Gang's case twice: in his short introductory speech on 21 March 1955 and also in his closing speech ten days later.

Only in his first speech he briefly touched on the real topic at issue: the transition to socialism. According to him there was a peaceful transition in cooperation with the Chinese national bourgeoisie whose social status should not be touched. In this he claimed to have Lenin on his side:

> On the basis of Lenin's teachings on the transitional period, the Central Committee has summarized the experiences since the foundation of the People's Republic of China and, in 1952, when the period of the reconstruc-

---

[1] Ibid., p. 81.

[2] Ibid., p. 90.

[3] Ibid., p. 233.

[4] Ibid., p. 122

[5] Ibid., pp. 140, 154.

[6] Ibid., p. 298.

[7] Helmut Martin, *Mao intern. Unveröffentlichte Schriften, Reden und Gespräche Mao Tse-tungs, 1949-1971*, Munich, 1974; unpublished writings, speeches and talks by Mao Zedong, p. 28.

tion of the Chinese national economy had ended, it formulated the General Line of the Party about the transition period.[1]

However, Lenin rejected the idea that socialism could be built together with the Russian bourgeoisie and that the "dictatorship of the proletariat" was needed to enter into socialism. He never spoke about an "alliance of classes" or some sort of "New Democracy." Immediately after the October Revolution, on November 1917, the Russian Central Executive Committee of the Soviet Congress issued a decree on workers' control in factories. Apart from that, all abandoned enterprises were confiscated and placed under the administration of workers' committees. Lenin's first government soon adopted the decree giving green light. Stalin quoting Lenin:

> In order to win the majority of the population to its side," Lenin continues, "the proletariat must first of all overthrow the bourgeoisie and seize power and, secondly, it must introduce Soviet rule, smash to pieces the old state apparatus, and thus at one blow undermine the rule, authority and influence of the bourgeoisie ...
>
> The class which has seized political power has done so conscious of the fact that it has seized power alone. This is implicit in the concept of the dictatorship of the proletariat. This concept has meaning only when one class knows that it alone takes political power into its own hands, and does not deceive either itself or others by talk about popular, elected government, sanctified by the whole people." [2]

Mao, however, had different ideas. here is what the latter said in August of 1953 when the discussion on how to get to socialism was at its height in China:

> At present, there are two united fronts, two alliances: one is the alliance between the working class and the peasantry, this is the basis. The other one is the alliance of the working class with the national bourgeoisie.[3]

In another speech to Chinese traders and industrialists he was also talking about how the capitalist industry was to enter state capitalism. Those who would be ready to transfer their capital to the state, would get a profit share, a "dividend," amounting to 20.5% of the profits made by the respective enterprise.

Mao did not invoke "Lenin's teachings" to abide by them, but to make the delegates believe that he was a follower of Lenin and that his "general line" was Leninist. In fact it was not.

Apart from this fleeting remark, not a single word on the real issue in the Gao Gang affair was said by him — neither in his opening speech nor in his closing remarks.[4] Instead, he spoke at length about the many "sins" of the two dissidents,

---

[1] Mao Tse-tung, Vol. V, ibid., p. 171.
[2] Joseph Stalin, *Problems of Leninism*, New York, 1934, pp. 21f, Stalin quoting Lenin from: *Collective Works*, Vol. XXVI, p. 286, Russian edition.
[3] Mao Tse-tung, V, p. 117, speech on August 12, 1953.
[4] Ibid., pp. 171ff.

repeating the many accusations made by Zhou Enlai and Deng Xiaoping at the discussion meetings a year before (anti-Party alliance, conspiracy, schemers, plot, independent kingdoms, etc.). Only those remarks which his two lieutenants had not used against Gao and Rao are worth mentioning here, also showing his mode of thinking and the way he used to deal with his opponents and critics. Later, during the "Cultural Revolution," Deng Xiaoping himself became a victim of Mao Zedong's vindictiveness when he was called a "capitalist roader" and put under house arrest. His son died during this "Revolution".

Mao Zedong on the virus spread by the two dissidents:

> Comrades who did not fall victim to their influence, should not become arrogant but should beware of this disease. This is most important.[1]

So he was comparing the different opinions of his rivals with some sort of a disease, showing utter disregard of the two revolutionaries and even a fascist way of thinking. Such people needed to be liquidated to make sure that the "disease" does not spread further and infect others.

Then he continued, adding these remarks:

> You're immune against some diseases, once you've had them. The vaccination has a preventive effect. But it is not a sure guarantee, you can still get smallpox. Therefore it is better, to undergo a second vaccination after three or five years — in our case that means to hold another such meeting...If the case had been discovered one year later, most probably some more people would have been infected.[2]

The German Nazis called dissenters and critics of their inhumane rule "vermin" or "pest of the people." Mao called them "infectious".

Another tool: Moral disqualification:

In his speech to the delegates of the National Conference Mao Zedong often uses the adjective "evil" in connection with what dissenters did:

> Others knew something about some of their EVIL acts but were unable to see the plot behind it...So it took us a rather long time to realize that Gao Gang and Rao Shushi were EVIL elements.[3]

On the following page the term "evil elements" is repeated.

They are also labeled "class enemies":

> Such things have also happened in the past. During the Zhing-Gang-Shan period some people defected to the enemy from whom we would not have expected it. Probably you have had similar experiences.[4]

Mao had used this method before. Just a reminder:

---

[1] Ibid., p. 182.
[2] Ibid., pp. 182f.
[3] Ibid., p. 184, my emphasis.
[4] Ibid.

On 7 December 1934 he sent a military unit of his to the Provincial Executive Committee of the Communist Party in the Futien region, telling them that the committee was infected with counterrevolutionary AB people, that they were all traitors and "anti-Bolsheviks" and should be liquidated. The AB group was an organization of the landowners rightly considered to be the class enemy. By smearing his comrades as spies of the AB group, he then sent in his friend Liu Shao-qi and his punitive expedition there to take some of his own comrades prisoner, torture and massacre them.[1]

Gao Gang was a highly respected Communist revolutionary under whose leadership a local area west of Shanxi, where Yenan was located, was liberated from the Chiang Kai-shek nationalists and bravely defended against their blockade. Here lies one of the roots of his high reputation, reason enough to slander him and to belittle and even destroy his achievements during the Chinese liberation struggle. His actions qualified him for a leadership post in the Communist Party something that could not be tolerated by Mao Zedong.

Finally, Mao Zedong misuses science to serve his interests, pretending to be a man of science and philosopher:

> For each thing applies that appearance and essence are in contradiction to each other. Only by analysis and examination of a thing can human beings advance to the knowledge of the essence of a thing. Therefore the need for science. If this was not so and the essence could simply be discovered intuitively, why would science still be needed? What would be the use of examining things? This is necessary because a contradiction between appearance and essence does exist.[2]

Mao Zedong is posing as the great philosopher, as the wise man to impress the delegates. He is capable to look behind the curtain, he is able to expose the machinations of the deceivers, the false revolutionaries who, in essence, are counter-revolutionaries. He sees through them, exposes them — something of which the whole Party will benefit from. This time as well, he was able to see through them and to discover their true nature, their anti-Party nature! You can't fool the Chairman!!

These remarks borrowed from the German philosopher Friedrich Engels must have impressed the attentively listening audience greatly. In reality, he was misusing Marxist philosophy for his own ends, for his power play, for his aim to get rid of two of his main rivals and their many followers. How would a true scientist have acted? A genuine scientist would have been prepared to discuss the problem at stake in an open and fair debate — a debate on how to enter socialism and what needed to be done for the Party to achieve this goal. He would have

---

[1] Cp. Peter Vladimirow, *The Vladimirov Diaries, Yenan, China: 1942-1945*, New York, 1975, p. 171. Vladimirov, the Soviet correspondent stationed in Yenan in the early forties, quotes from CP party documents handed over to him in Yenan describing the incident.
[2] Mao Tse-tung, V., p. 184.

respected the views of his adversaries instead of intriguing behind their backs and purge them from this Party, leaving them utterly defenseless and bringing about great hardship upon them and their families.

Five or six years later, when Mao's Great Leap Forward proved to be a failure and he was again severely criticized for his policies, he acted in a similar way against his new opponent: Peng Dehuai, the Chinese Defense Minister, who had written him a private letter in which he voiced some moderate criticism because of his failed agricultural policy which had caused hunger and starvation in the countryside. And again: instead of entering into a fair and open debate, he copied the letter, had it distributed among the delegates of the conference (Lushan Conference, August 1959), called Peng a "right opportunist" and his followers an "anti-Party group," and made sure that he lost all his posts in the Party. Later, during his "Cultural Revolution," Peng was thrown into prison. During the Korean War (1950–1953) Peng Dehuai had commanded the Chinese contingent in Korea and contributed greatly to the near defeat of the US army. Before the crucial votes at the Lushan Conference, Mao Zedong had arranged that "reinforcements" from the provinces were transferred to the conference hall to support him against his many critics. Now having got more people on his side, he became more straightforward and "accused his critics of being "right opportunists" and described their criticism of his policies as the "frantic attack of right opponents on the Party."[1]

9. The 2nd Plenum of the Central Committee, November 1956

Following the 8th Party Congress of the CP of China in September 1956, two months later the 2nd Plenum took place at which Mao Zedong made a long speech. He also said something about the Gao Gang affair:

> At this point, I'd like to say something about the question of "illicit relations with foreign countries." Are there in China people who, behind the back of the Central Committee, pass on information to foreigners? I believe so, Gao Gang for instance was such a person. There are many facts proving that.[2]

Since Gao Gang had a close relationship with Stalin and the Soviet Union and also had good relations with Soviet experts working in China, by saying "illicit relations with foreign countries," Mao could only have had the Soviet Union got in mind. However, he himself had visited the country in late 1949 and stayed there for a full two months. He also had a meeting with Stalin in the Kremlin. So: he was a guest in the Soviet Union but Gao a Soviet spy!

---

[1] Parris H. Chang, *Power and Policy in China*, Pennsylvania State University and London, 1975, p. 118.

[2] Mao Tse-tung, V, ibid., p. 383.

Again, this shows the parallel with what had happened in the Soviet Union when, after Stalin's sudden death in March 1953, Khrushchev and his people settled scores with Stalin's most trusted collaborator, Lavrenti P. Beria. He was also called a "spy" to defame him. Khrushchev at the time:

> This shows that this person hasn't worked for the enemy only during the past few years. Obviously, he penetrated into our Party as an agent of international imperialism with far-reaching goals.[1]

Mao Zedong added this, later in his speech when he was talking about punishments for such "spies":

> At this point, I'd like to touch on another question, the question of how to deal with counter-revolutionaries. Do we have to execute the local tyrants (meaning Gao Gang — GS), the evil noblemen, the local despots and counter-revolutionaries who have committed the most serious crimes? Yes, that's necessary.[2]

Final Word:

The Gao Gang affair marks the turning point for China's course away from real socialism and toward state capitalism. With great fanfare, state capitalism was put forward as "socialism" by Mao Zedong and his entourage. Up to the present day, this is still being done by the Chinese leadership. China's state capitalism (now muted into corporate capitalism) is still being called socialism — "socialism with Chinese characteristics".

It does not come as a surprise that in recent times China has been lauded by Western corporate media. To quote just one example: the German *Westdeutscher Rundfunk*, a state media outlet, in a news item on China had this to say about Mao Zedong and contemporary China:

> Mao had real vision. Whereas Western companies plan only quarterly, China became the biggest economy of the world after decades of strategy.[3]

Sources:

Bland, Bill, *Class Struggles in China*, London, 1997

Chang, Parris H., *Power and Policy in China*, London, 1975

History of the Communist Party of the Soviet Union, German, Berlin, 1945

Guillermaz, Jacques, *Le Parti communiste chinois au* pouvoir: *de l'avènement du régime au mouvement d'éducation socialiste, 1949-1962*, Paris, 1979

Knoll, Victor and Kölm, Lothar, Eds., *Der Fall Berija, Protokoll einer Abrechnung*, Berlin, 1999

Mao Tse-tung, Vol. 5, *Ausgewählte Werke*, Peking, 1978

---

[1] Victor Knoll, Lothar Kölm, Eds., ibid., p. 162.
[2] Mao Tse-tung, V, ibid., p. 379.
[3] Found on *twitter* on May 27, 2021, "Mao had real vision".

Martin, Helmut, Ed., *Mao intern, Unveröffentlichte Schriften, Reden und Gespräche Mao Tse-tungs, 1949-1971*, Munich, 1974

Stalin, J. W., *Werke*, Vol. 11, Berlin, 1954

_____*Problems of Leninism*, New York, 1934

Teiwes, Frederick C., *Politics at Mao's Court. Gao Gang and Party Factionalism in the Early 1950s*, London and New York, 1990

Vladimirov, Peter, *The Vladimirov Diaries, Yenan, China: 1942-1945*, New York, 1975

13. Mao Zedong — Our Father. From Stories for Children about Mao Zedong[1]

Introduction (G. Schnehen)

The Russian Maoist Nikolai Bogdanov collected tales and stories about Mao which became very popular in China, especially in the 1960s during the so-called Great Proletarian Cultural Revolution, at the height of the personality cult around Mao Zedong.

> In 1972, a collection of tales was also published in Germany by Melzer publishers — a translation from Russian. In his introduction, Bogdanov, a Maoist, claims that the stories he found and translated into Russian would "relate some episodes from Mao's life and show some of his character traits." He claims that the "shoshudis," some popular storytellers, had allegedly told these stories on market places and other squares to make the folk tales popular among the masses. He also points out that the "stories would not contradict the truth."

We do not know whether this is true but we do know that the official Chinese media published special books for children to be read at schools or at home to make them believe in Mao Zedong and his many virtues, the father and liberator of the country, and to worship him like a hero or even like a god from a very early age on.

At school, children not only had to study the Little Red Book compiled and introduced by Defense Minister Lin Biao, but also these tales about Mao and his many deeds. Each little story is accompanied by some pertinent drawings to

---

[1] By Nikolai Bogdanov, English translation by G. Schnehen. Darmstadt/Germany, 1972.

support the content of the story. In his short introduction, Bogdanov also says that "having awakened to new life, the Chinese people cannot keep silent: they want to talk and to hear about one of their best sons succeeded in treading the glorious path from peasant child to the liberator of his people."

Young children waving the Little Red Book in the late 1960s

Here is the first tale.

Mao — the Son of a Peasant[1]

Mao, the son of a small peasant, was born in the little village of Shaoshan in Hunan province in Central China when Empress Tsy Si ruled the country. His father was a retired soldier, the strong Mao Shushen, his mother the kind and wise Wen-shi.

Hardly had the boy seen the light of day, when his mother carried him to the warm sun. She did not do that to brag about her dear first to heaven, but only because nobody was at home at the time to whom she could entrust him. All the peasants were in the fields digging them up after the heavy rainfalls. Wen Shi, too, rushed outside.

---

[1] Nikolai Bogdanow, *Erzählungen für Kinder über Mao Tse-tung*, Darmstadt/Germany, 1972, pp. 5-10; stories for kids about Mao Zedong. Mao Zedong was not the son of a small peasant. His father was a rich farmer who also employed servants.

She bound the child on her back with a broad towel, took the hoe in her hands, thus working for many days.

The sun was burning on the little Mao and he became dark-skinned like all the other peasant kids.

And when the little boy had learned to walk, he also had to bend his back to help his mother planting rice. He put rice husk by rice husk into the liquid mud under the water. And each little rootlet had to be pressed tightly by the thumb to prevent it from rising to the surface again. No husk was allowed to be damaged, so that it did not sink into the mud. And there were thousands and thousands of husks! And then Mao knelt down next to his mom and rubbed the clods of earth on the mountain fields to dust between his hands.

"Work, work, my son," Wen-shi told him, "we have a fairy godmother — our work, and she will reward us both."

Little Mao worked hard. He scattered small seeds in the ground, and through his care grew various vegetables and spices: yellow melons, fragrant like flowers, green cabbage, curly carrots and fiery pepper.

Happy days followed: the bringing in of the hay harvest. Father turned up on the field with the donkey team. The best, the ripest, and the most beautiful fruits were harvested and loaded onto the cart. At the top they put the little Mao and off they went. They went beyond the village and into the big world. And here Mao saw many people and many people saw him. But how come that no one recognized who he was?

"Hey, Mao Shu-shun, did you raise that three-cheese kid in the melon field, too?" some of them shouted.

"Look, on Mao Shu-shen's cart there's a live carrot sitting, with a mop of hair on the spine," the others said.

The boy opened his eyes wide and was amazed that the adults did not understand the simplest things. Dad only laughed happily.

(on the next page little Mao is picking something, carrying a basket in his hands)

They came to a big estate surrounded by a thick wall, equipped with towers and embrasures. At the gate there were armed guards. They drove on a paved courtyard. In the middle stood a tall house, its red tiled roof bent upward at the corners according to Chinese style. At the threshold lay a menacing stone lion. On the stairs stood a distinguished gentleman in brocade robe and next to him his wife with unusual white face, round like the moon, and his son dressed splendidly and fat like a holiday piglet.

At the sight of these people the strong and always proud Mao Shu-shen suddenly curtsied and bowed like a blade of grass in the wind, while spreading before him everything he had brought from the field. The little

Mao felt sorry for the best fruits of their good labor and plucked his dad at the sleeve. "Don't do that," whispered his father, "don't you see that they are our landlords? The best part of the harvest belongs to them!"

"And why?"

"That's the law of the land, my son. One half of the harvest belongs to the landowner, half of the rest to the Empress, half of the half belongs to the monastery, and still another half remaining from all these halves to the governor..."

Mao could not hear everything about the seventeen taxes levied by the rich from the peasants at that time.

(the following page contains another drawing, showing a peasant planting a tree)

The old man's speech was stifled by the rattle of wheels, the patter of hooves and the thud of footsteps. New carts and carriages, pulled by oxen, donkeys and even people, came to the yard. All of them led, carried and dragged the gifts of their labor to the landowner's grand staircase. Soon a whole mountain of vegetables, fruits, grain and spices was piled up. There was so much of everything that little Mao suddenly exclaimed:

"Enough, they'll burst!"

The peasants laughed out loud and the landowner's guards soon grabbed their clubs.

The father quickly turned the empty cart around and drove away from the landowner's yard to avoid catastrophe. At home, the peasants were talking for a long time about Mao Shen-shan's clever little boy.

The second tale: "*A human life*"[1]

In the past, a human life had little value in China. The people are numerous, almost 500 million, you could not even count them. The Chinese generals used to take neither doctors nor medics to war. If a soldier was wounded, they simply chased him away. Go wherever you like, but we do not need you anymore! Why should one care about a mutilated when someone with healthy arms and legs was available? Why bother taking care of a maimed man when you could take instead a man with healthy limbs?

---

[1] Ibid., pp. 116-118. When people were dying in the millions in China during the Great Leap Forward in the late 1950s and early 1960s and food had to be imported from capitalist countries to feed the people, Mao did not regret his decision to start the Leap, but was stubbornly defending it against his adversaries in the Politburo, among them Peng Dehui, who was then called an "anti-Party element." Peng was arrested in 1966 during the 'Cultural Revolution' and later died in prison.

It was different with the Communists. Now the commanders took care of each soldier as if he were his biological son. Mao, however, took care of all the people of China as if they were his dear relatives. Once, in the village of Sun Tsien-shan, which had just been liberated by the troops of the 8th Army, a big rally was held. Comrade Mao himself had come in a car to speak to the people. All the inhabitants had gathered to listen to him. Even the very oldest people got up from their warm stove seats. It was cold. A damp, penetrating wind blew from the mountains. But the people did not even notice. In the tense silence, they listened to Mao Zedong talking to them about the right of every peasant to his own field. Suddenly, in that silence, the indignant whispering of the women rang out:

"What are you doing here, fool?"

"You'll give your little son a cold here..."

"Look, he's burning with fever as if on fire!"

This whisper reached Mao Zedong's sharp ear. He interrupted his speech, looked at the poorly clad woman and asked her:

"What happened?"

The poor mother had no time to answer, her neighbors were faster:

"She's a bad mother. Two of her children have died already, and now she'll put to death the third. It has got a high temperature. It cannot drink a sip of water. Is it allowed that it is held into the cold wind?"

When Comrade Mao heard that, he touched the woman, who was standing there silently, on the shoulder:

"What's wrong with your little son, dear mother?"

"It is critically ill," whispered the woman, hastily knocking back the rags in which the little boy was wrapped.

"Why did you come here then?"

"Please look at him," answered the mother. "I've come to save him... Everyone says that the people are reborn by your looks, your gaze instills strength, gives life. Please be so kind and save my son...He is my last!"

Comrade Mao did not stop to take away the woman's belief that a gaze from him could help. He put his hand on the boy's forehead. He attentively listened to the heavy breathing and then he said:

"You're right, dear mother. The life of a son of China is a thousand times more precious to us than a thousand good words."

He interrupted the meeting, put mother and the child behind the windshield of the car, took his seat in the back and told the chauffeur to hurry to the nearest hospital.

The doctors treated the child as attentively as a wounded soldier. The terrible inflammation of the brain passed without a trace. Today the boy grows up fast and strong. His mother says when she strokes him tenderly:

"Grow, my happy child, grow my dear, good times have come for China. Every person is needed today. Everyone is dear to our father Mao Zedong."

14. Today's Maoists about the Great Leap Forward, the Personality Cult, and the Cultural Revolution

Introduction (G. Schnehen)

Today's Maoists still keep defending Mao's "Cultural Revolution," costing the lives of millions of people, and even the excessive personality cult around him. For them Mao was a full-blooded revolutionary, a Communist through and through, a fighter for "people's democracy," a "servant of the people" and a very principled man, who fought the revisionists tooth and nail, and has great merits for the communist movement.

His "Cultural Revolution" was a good thing, as it was a broad mass movement initiated by him against the attempts by "reactionaries" and "bourgeois-capitalist elements" within the Communist Party of China to restore capitalism, and even though it went out of control here and there (which was not his fault!), it was a no doubt a "socialist movement".

His "ideas" are still called "universal truths" by fundamentalist Maoists but less so by more moderate ones. Both keep quiet about his later foreign policy, when he even supported the fascist Chilean military junta of Augusto Pinochet. Whereas the more extreme Maoists (among them the German MLPD) call today's China "social-imperialist," the more moderate ones are defending contemporary China, calling it "anti-imperialist" or even "socialist" — worth support supporting.

As far as Mao Zedong's personality and his legacy is concerned, they all judge him positively and still call him a staunch Marxist-Leninist and also an "anti-revisionist," and they themselves want to be seen as defenders of Marx, Lenin, and even Stalin sometimes, although it is known that Stalin was no friend of Mao and once called him a false communist and a "second Tito" (1950).

If one dares to criticize Mao Zedong and his legacy, one is soon called an "anti-Communist," a "revisionist" or a "renegade".

There is also a third category of people: those who are of the opinion that Mao Zedong sometimes made mistakes but that he should be seen as being part of the Marxist-Leninist "family." his actions hostile to Marxism are euphemistically called "mistakes," some more and some less serious, but in all other respects he had been a loyal supporter of the revolutionary cause. These people are no Maoists in the strict sense of the word but sympathizers of Mao and Maoism.

Have they learned from the past, are they willing to learn from the past, are they prepared to analyze the past on the basis of facts? Let's take a closer look.

1. Richard Corell,

The Great Proletarian Cultural Revolution. China's Struggle for Socialism[1]

a. On the Great Leap Forward

Does the author tell us what happened in China between 1958 and 1961, when more than 30 million people died in China's towns and villages of hunger and starvation and do we get to know from him what caused this huge tragedy?

I found some passages where he mentions the Great Leap Forward:

pp 116ff, 10, *The Great Leap Forward*:

> The Great Leap Forward which began in 1958 was the bold attempt to increase the pace of transition from capitalism to socialism. China had to pay a high price for that, not least with measures of liberalization in the economy and also with a temporary victory of a revisionist line in politics. The September 1962 instruction called "San Tsu Y Pao" (Three Freedoms and One Arrangement) which was Liu Shao-qi's brainchild, was an expression of a post-leap policy to follow the capitalist path. The situation in the countryside developed as follows...(more details about what came after the Great Leap Forward, but nothing about the leap itself. So he doesn't want to go into it — GS).

> pp. 245ff (chronology of events):

> 1958: Foundation of the first people's communes in April. The Great Leap Forward begins. Lin Biao becomes Chairman of the Central Committee. At the 6th Plenum of the 8th Party Congress in Wuhan Mao Zedong's decision to resign as State President is adopted. Liu Shao-qi becomes his successor...

---

[1] *Die Große Proletarische Kulturrevolution. Chinas Kampf um den Sozialismus*, Frankfurt/Main, 2009

(more details about Peng Dehuai's criticism of Mao Zedong, author taking sides with Mao).

1959: At the conference (the Lushan Conference held in August 1958 — GS), Mao Zedong makes a convincing case that right-wing thought, right-wing ideology, right-wing activities have gripped the Party and points to the danger of an uprising of landowners, rich peasants and counter-revolutionaries. He concedes that some mistakes have been made during the Great Leap Forward and that for some of them he himself was responsible, but on the whole this overall social mobilization of all forces had been a good thing; the masses had taken the initiative and the cadres were willing to learn from mistakes...

1960: Withdrawal of Soviet technicians and advisors; they take spare parts and plans with them; more than 300 industrial projects and agreements reached with the People's Republic are breached. Due to massive natural disasters (drought, floods) a food crisis is brewing.

1961: In this severe economic situation, fundamental changes in the economic development strategy are introduced under the leadership of Liu Shaoqi, leading to liberalization. Steps back towards capitalism are taken, among them the policy of "Three Freedoms and one Arrangement" for the people's communes initiated by Deng Xiaoping.

1962: A period of economic recovery begins, the people's communes have consolidated; steady rise in agricultural production. The lack of Soviet support in industry is being compensated...

b. On Mao Zedong's personality cult

Do we get facts or statements?

I found one passage in his book dealing with the personality cult in somewhat greater detail:

pp. 163:

About the personality cult. Did the cult exist? Yes, it did — and even massively! Mao Zedong's portraits, posters, buttons, etc. etc. Up to a certain degree, this personality cult showed the high esteem and veneration for Mao Zedong in Chinese revolutionary history. A veneration for the man who taught the masses to liberate themselves and who mobilized them boldly, for the person who, as elected Chairman, had proved himself to be a wise, courageous and near-to-life helmsman. As Mao Zedong once told the American journalist Edgar Snow, the personality cult was consciously recognized only in 1965, when it seemed that some people wanted to get rid of him. He had a clear relationship with the cult. According to Edgar Snow, he said to him:

"What nonsense!" Mao exclaimed. Always the need to be venerated!... For example the "Big Four" (...). "What nonsense!" he kept saying...

On the other hand, this personality cult, however negative you may want to judge it, was a cult for a person who was eager to fight dogmas, cults, and authorities and to criticize them a person who was fighting against stagnation, against static thinking and who always listened to the power of the people. Everyone deserves respect who stands up and assumes responsibility, who takes on a position, who puts himself and his whole person in the "limelight" — not for the sake of the limelight, but for a real cause. Today in the Federal Republic of Germany, there are far too few of these people — in the struggle against imperialist wars and the danger of fascism! However, the veneration ends where the man, who deserves respect, is put on a pedestal, thus becoming unattainable and superhuman. Then the process starts where the masses and the individual become separated, as the cult separates them.

Well — the forms of the cult around Mao Zedong were sometimes funny, bizarre and ridiculous. Certainly, they sometimes were also an expression of lacking and backward consciousness, sometimes an expression of youthful over-zealousness. However, this cult was not manufactured, promoted or ordered from "above," it developed from "below," even against the official instructions which banned the naming of streets and statues after living persons.

But there was one person in the leading group for the Cultural Revolution who promoted the cult: Lin Biao...Today, in hindsight, one must say that Lin Biao probably only thought of himself by promoting the personality cult around Mao Zedong: the glamour he built up around Mao was meant to reflect back on himself...

c. On the Cultural Revolution

Just praise or objective analysis of facts? Do we get to know something about the many innocent victims?

p. 184:

It was not always about arguments (during the Cultural Revolution — GS). There were deaths. But the important thing is that it was not about wiping out people! The struggle was directed against ideas, revisionism was the target. This, of course, meant that the people, the carriers of these ideas were also attacked. The masses of workers, peasants, students, pupils, military personnel, Party members, and cadres were called upon to criticize extensively, to "fight, criticize, and transform" in the context of a Great Proletarian Cultural Revolution. The masses were mobilized and asked for assistance against the "Four Olds," against "the rulers in the Party and the state apparatus, who are going the capitalist way," against the "Chinese

Khrushchevs," against the counterrevolution in society and state. Mao Zedong and the whole CC of the Communist Party of China have never ordered to kill or to torture someone, and using force against dissenters was explicitly and repeatedly condemned — not just in the early stages (August 1966) but also during the height of the Cultural Revolution (1969).

"Heads do not grow back like chives," was a Mao Zedong slogan — a saying with which he came out against liquidating comrades with a different political line or with different opinions, in the context of "contradictions within the people." He stressed the necessity of an ideological struggle — increasingly so since 1956/57...

p. 232:

Against the background of this question, we consider the Great Proletarian Cultural Revolution to be a decisive contribution of the Chinese Communists under the leadership of Mao Zedong that gave a new impetus to the revolutionary and anti-imperialist movement worldwide. It made it more difficult for the predecessors of Gorbachev to liquidate socialism and the socialist camp. In China itself, it blocked the path towards capitalism and, at the same time, created the conditions on which today's China is building its economy. And even today, those rulers of the CP of China, who want to restore capitalism, get scared when thinking of the Cultural Revolution.

It was "great" because all spheres of life in China were affected, even the remotest corners of the country, and everyone's thoughts and actions; it was "proletarian" because it pushed forward the process of emancipation of the revolutionary class away from the culture of the bourgeoisie, and it was a "revolution" because it thoroughly overturned the hitherto prevailing forms of the exercise of rule under socialism...

2. Marxist-Leninist Party of Germany

(MLPD, — Maoists, founder Willi Dickhut)

a. The MLPD on the 'Great Leap Forward'
Unfortunately, I found no material, articles or books, either in their party organ *Rote Fahne* (Red Flag) or in their bookstore pertaining to the subject.
b. The MLPD on Mao Zedong's personality cult
Again: No articles or books found.
c. on the Cultural Revolution
On Thursday, May 26th, 2016, the organization issued a statement on *50 Years of the Great Proletarian Cultural Revolution in China:*
50 Years of Great Proletarian Cultural Revolution in China

August 8 marks the 50th anniversary of the beginning of the Great Proletarian Cultural Revolution in China. With the decision taken at the time by a narrow majority of the Central Committee of the Communist Party of China a hitherto unknown mass movement in the history of mankind to preempt the restoration of capitalism was launched under the leadership of Mao Zedong.

In 1949 the Revolution was victorious in China, which, however, does not mean that the building of socialism proceeds unimpeded. The class struggle, partly in new forms, went ahead. Using sabotage and even armed aggression, the old forces did everything in their power to regain power. Even greater dangers arose from the bureaucracy in the party, state, and economy: parts of these forces degenerated with privilege, careerism, and selfishness, and finally headed for the seizure of power as a new bureaucratic capitalist class. This is precisely what had happened in the Soviet Union, and this the Marxist-Leninists in China intended to prevent with the Great Proletarian Cultural Revolution.

On the anniversary of the establishment of a working group for the preparation of the Cultural Revolution at a CC Plenum of the CP of China in May 1966, bourgeois mass media unleashed a mudslide of anti-Communist diatribes about the Cultural Revolution. Where does this blind hatred come from after 50 years?

For the haters of the Cultural Revolution — even in today's social-imperialist Chinese leadership — "the years of the Cultural Revolution were ten lost years" or "ten years of chaos." The people of China were caught up in a frenzy of violence and chaos by Mao Zedong to satisfy his personal lust for power. Such allegations, often combined with freely invented numbers of victims in the millions, have no scientific basis whatsoever.[1]

3. Harpal Brar

Socialism with Chinese Characteristics. Marketisation of the Chinese Economy, London, 2020

a. On the 'Great Leap forward'

The Great Leap Forward (1958–1959)...

After an initial surge in production and construction, problems arose in quick succession. The communes lacked skilled personnel; rich peasants, who had been allowed to join the communes, resented leveling that came from the amalgamation with peasants from poorer collectives, and

---

[1] https://www.rf-news.de/rote-fahne/2016/nr11/die-kulturrevolution-schrecken-fur-reaktionaere-2013-vorbild-fur-revolutionaere.

indulged in sabotage; peasants resented arbitrary work assignments, inefficient management, and iniquities in remuneration; the breakdown of national economic planning led to inefficiencies in production and distribution of goods and materials; the lengthening of the working day to meet unrealistic production quotas led to physical exhaustion of the population. The realities of communization sat uneasily with the ideal of communal life envisaged when the campaign was launched.

On 28 November 1958, the Party leadership met at Wuhan...

...By the summer of 1959, most communes were a pale image of the original. The difficulties were further exacerbated by bad weather and by the abrogation by Khrushchev of the 1957 agreement under which the Soviet Union was to provide China with modern military technology, including, reportedly, nuclear technology...

...In the summer of 1960, Khrushchev abruptly recalled 1,400 Soviet scientists and industrial specialists working in 250 Chinese enterprises.

Thus, a combination of mistakes, extremely adverse weather conditions and the treacherous scrapping of agreements by Khrushchev led Mao Zedong to conclude that the communization movement could carry on no more, and this leads us to the next stage in the continuing struggle between the two sides at the top of the Party leadership.[1]

The author makes no mention of the more than 30 million Chinese who were starved to death in various regions due to Mao Zedong's policies in the late 1950s. Despite a record harvest, peasant workers were forced to take care of backyard steel production and to neglect farming and harvesting as a consequence. The blame is put on the Soviet leadership and their decision to end sending military advisers to China but also to bad weather and 'certain mistakes made' (sabotage of rich peasants who had joined the People's Commune and then committed sabotage there, lack of qualified personnel, etc.

On the whole, the Great Leap had been a good thing according to the Indian-born author which, as he alleges, contributed greatly to China's progress:

Although the Great Leap Forward has had more than its fair share of critics, both in the centers of imperialism as well as among the reformers, the fact remains that during this period the Chinese people, through their collective labor in massive projects, changed the very face of rural China, with the opening up of new lands, the construction of irrigation systems, and the construction of such communal facilities as school and health clinics...

The Great Leap Forward was undermined by a mix of mistakes, weather conditions of severe drought in some areas and major flooding in others, and the withdrawal of Soviet technicians. Nevertheless the Great Leap

---

[1] Harpal Brar, *Socialism with Chinese Charateristics*, ibid., pp. 16-19.

Forward transformed the rural economy and class relations in the countryside, leaving a legacy of accomplishments which can be gleaned from production statistics during these years...

This progress was reflected in increased longevity, much reduced infant mortality, a precipitous drop in illiteracy, and an improved health service for the masses. Through these measures, hundreds of millions of Chinese were to live longer and healthier lives, besides tens of millions of those who survived but could not have done so but for the social facilities in the field of health.[1]

Sadly, the author does not provide us with any statistical material or supplementary documentary evidence to make his case. One of the greatest tragedies in Chinese history is twisted into a blessing.

b. The personality cult around Mao Zedong

I found two pages where the personality cult is explicitly mentioned in the book. Page 15 says:

The 8th Congress (of the Communist Party of China in September 1956 — GS) stressed the need "to uphold democratic centralism and collective leadership, oppose the personality cult, promote democracy within the Party...and strengthen the Party's ties with the masses," a barely disguised attempt to accuse Mao of cultivating a cult of the personality...[2]

So the author does not agree with this assessment.

On page 63 he cites a Party resolution dated June 27, 1981, where the cult is mentioned again but this is not his own stance. He regrets that such a resolution was adopted by the leadership of the Communist Party of China.

There are no other references to the cult around Mao Zedong especially during the Cultural Revolution.

In his dedication to the book, the author writes:

To Comrade Mao Zedong

The greatest ever Chinese person, under whose leadership of the CPC the Chinese people achieved liberation, ended imperialist domination, unified China, abolished feudalism, expropriated the bourgeoisie, and laid the basis for socialist development through centrally-planned industrialization and collectivization of agriculture.

c. On the Cultural Revolution

---

[1] Ibid., pp. 76f.
[2] Ibid., p. 15.

Harpal Brar deals extensively with the Cultural Revolution on more than 50 pages (chapters 2 and 3). At the start of chapter two, he is setting the scene like this:

The Cultural Revolution

The Great Proletarian Revolution, to give it its proper name, was aimed at preventing capitalist restoration in China, its targets being capitalist roaders within the Party, the government, the army and cultural institutions. Mao Zedong and his supporters believed that Marxist-Leninists no longer exercised leadership in these organizations; instead the Party persons taking the capitalist road had entrenched themselves in the Central Committee which followed a revisionist political and organizational line, with its agents firmly established in all provinces, municipalities, and autonomous regions, in addition to all the departments at the center.

And further, as all other efforts and forms of struggle in the past had not yet produced a solution to this problem, the capitalist roaders could only be forced out of their entrenched positions by undertaking a great Cultural Revolution. This revolution would be tantamount to the overthrow of one class by another, a revolution that would have to be repeated periodically to settle the question of which class would win — the proletariat or the bourgeoisie...[1]

Food for thought (G. Schnehen):

The same Mao Zedong, who, in the mid -1950s, ousted the Marxist faction from his party and also their many followers and put them behind bars, at a time when he himself had opted for an alliance with the Chinese bourgeoisie[2], is now posing as a staunch socialist, fighting the "capitalist roaders," among them his former closest allies and comrades-in-arms he could always rely upon when it came to power struggles at the top of the party: Liu Shao-qi and Deng Xiaoping. Liu was a long-time deputy within the Party who, when Mao was absent, was told to chair important meetings and to rule in people like Gao Gang or Rao Shushi who were in favor of ousting the bourgeoisie from the state apparatus. Deng had belonged to those who had always defended Mao against his many rivals and adversaries, keeping Mao in power for decades.

Now (May 1966) he launches the so-called Cultural Revolution to "defend socialism" against his former closest allies, throwing the whole country into chaos. Liu is publicly humiliated (also his wife) and dies in prison just as Gao Gang died in prison in the mid-1950s; Deng is put under house arrest...

---

[1] Ibid., p. 25.

[2] Cp. Mao Zedong, *Ausgewählte Werke*, Vol. V., Beijing, 1978, p. 117, where it says: "At present there are two united fronts, two alliances. The first is the alliance between the working class with the peasantry, this being the basis. The second is the alliance between the working class and the national bourgeoisie."

Mrs. Jung Chang, a former "Red Guard," in her book on Mao [1] provides a completely different story as far as the "Cultural Revolution is concerned.

This is what Harpal Brar has to say about the book he seemingly does not like at all:

> Jung Chang and Jon Halliday's book *Mao: the unknown story* is intellectually scandalous, lacking in serious scholarship. They ignore the real story that gives primacy to the Chinese people and their part in the revolution led by the CPC under Mao's leadership...Chang and Halliday, despite their shoddy and selective research and scholarship, are popular in imperialist circles because they absurdly equate Mao with Hitler — an equation which is absurd as it is an insult to the intelligence of the reader, a lie which crosses all bounds of decency and common sense. [2]

Brar's final assessment of the Cultural Revolution:

> The Cultural Revolution, while at times very violent, was not a ten-year calamity for China, and the elite who say this cannot, and do not, speak on behalf of the vast masses of Chinese people. The elite discourse (speaking about the contemporary Chinese elite — GS) is guided by the 'Two Whatevers' (Whatever China does is wrong, and Whatever the US does is right). The elite discourse, ignoring inconvenient historical facts, portrays events and personalities in the style of a Peking opera, analogies to pure good confronting evil incarnate.

---

[1] Jung Chang, Jon Halliday, *Mao – the Unknown Story*, London, 2006.
[2] Harpal Brar, ibd., p. 84.

15. Mao Zedong and Zhou Enlai Drop the Mask

Their Conversations with US President Nixon and US Secretary of State Kissinger, 1972–1973

1. From The Memoirs of Richard Nixon[1]

Shortly before I left for China, I invited the great French writer and philosopher André Malraux to the White House.

Malraux met Mao Zedong and Chou En-lai in China in the thirties and, with some interruptions, had stayed in contact with them over the years. His description of the Chinese leaders in his *Anti-Memoirs* was the most fascinating and valuable reading material in preparation for my trip.

When talking to him in the Oval Office, I asked him if he thought they would have agreed to meet a few years ago.

"This meeting was inevitable," he answered.

"Even in the face of the Vietnam War?" I asked.

"Yes, in spite of it. China's behavior, as far as Vietnam is concerned, is imposture. There was a period when the friendship between China and Russia was still perfect, when they still allowed Russian weapons to reach Vietnam across their territory. But never ever has China helped anyone! Not Pakistan, not Vietnam. China's foreign policy is a brilliantly presented

---

[1] New York, 1978, pp. 557, 558, 562ff:

lie! The Chinese (the Chinese leaders — GS) themselves do not believe in it. They only believe in China. Only in China! For Mao China is a continent, it is an Australia in itself. Only China counts. If China wants to receive the Sultan of Zanzibar, then China will do that, or the President of the United States. The Chinese do not care...Once I asked Mao if he sees himself as the successor of the last great Chinese emperors of the 16th century."

Mao replied:

"Of course, I'm their successor!"

"I voted for you in the last elections [the last presidential elections in the U.S. in November 1972 that Nixon won by a landslide — GS]," Mao said with a broad smile.

"If the Chairman says that he would have voted for me," I answered him: "Then he probably wanted to vote for the lesser evil."

"I like right-wing people," Mao replied, who obviously was enjoying himself.

"People say that you are a right-winger, that the Republican Party is on the right, that Premier Heath [the then British Prime Minister — GS] is also a right-winger."

"..and General de Gaulle?" I added. Immediately Mao said: "De Gaulle is different." Then he went on:

"They also say that the Christian Democrats of West Germany are on the right. I'm quite happy when these people of the right come to power." ...

Mao pointed to Kissinger and said:

"Seize the opportunity! I think that people like myself sometimes sound like big cannons." Chou started to laugh, and it was obvious that now a new round of understatements would follow.

"For example, things like 'the whole world should unite and defeat imperialism, revisionism, all the reactionaries and build socialism...' "

"Like me and all those bastards," I said.

Mao leaned forward and smiled:

"But perhaps you, as an individual, do not belong to those who should be toppled," he said, and, turning to Kissinger, he went on:

"You also say that he doesn't belong to those who should be toppled, as in that case we would lose all our friends..."

2. From: Henry A. Kissinger, Memoirs, 1968–1973 [1]

p. 1,125:

Equally important was his statement given in passing and later repeated by Chou En-lai that China would not interfere in Indochina militarily, freeing us from a nightmare under which two American presidents had suffered. By ruling out a Chinese military intervention abroad and by explaining his views on Japan and South Korea to us, he told us that the vital interests of the United States would not be threatened by Beijing. Since we Westerners are generally slow to grasp, Mao returned to an issue which I had already discussed with Chou:

"I believe that people like me sometimes sound like big cannons when we say that 'the whole world should unite to destroy imperialism, revisionism and all reactionaries and to build socialism.'"

At the notion that anyone could take seriously a decades-old-phrase that was on every wall newspaper, he burst into peals of laughter and Chou joined in. In dealing with us, ideology played no role for the Chinese. The dangerous situation which they were in demanded the absolute priority of international politics. By reaching a tacit non-aggression pact with us, they practically relieved themselves from one of two fronts.

pp. 70-74

Thus, in the nineteen months since my first visit, Chou had made a complete about-turn concerning Japan. At that time he still considered Japan as a potentially aggressive nation that could team up with others to partition China and had accused us of consciously reviving Japanese militarism...But now China was in favor of a close partnership between the United States and Japan so as not to offend Japanese pride...

A united Communist Vietnam which would have won hegemony over Indochina was a nightmare for the Chinese, even though, for ideological reasons, it was not possible for them to say this openly...

It is interesting to note that, right from the start, Chou had proposed similar ceasefire conditions as they were stipulated in the agreements, the compliance of which would have allowed the government of South Vietnam to surely survive. Contrary to many of our domestic adversaries, he never pushed us to topple Thieu (the US puppet in South Vietnam — GS) and to install a puppet regime as suggested by Hanoi...

He spoke with great respect about the Laotian King Savang Vatthana as a "patriotic and honest man" and supported the legitimacy of the neutralist Premier Souvana Phouma...In other words: China supported our endeavors

---

[1] Page numbers refer to the German-language edition, *Memoiren*.

in Laos to establish a neutral, peace-loving non-Communist regime being independent of Hanoi...

It was astonishing to see that a political leader of a country, which posed as a shining light for all revolutionary forces, declared that its problems could increase if another country turned completely communist...

p. 82:

The father of the Communist Revolution in China, Mao Zedong, who had changed his country radically to preserve the purity of the teachings, took great pains to convince me that the phrases which could be seen on every wall in China were meaningless and that the national interest in foreign policy was above ideological differences. Ideological phrases were a facade behind which stood the taking into account of the balance of power.

p. 83:

We continued our talks on the international situation in this almost cheerfully jocular tone until 1:30 AM...

The United States and China should cooperate, requiring the institutionalization of our relationship. Setting up liaison offices in both capitals would be the right decision. He recommended to urgently increase our contacts and the extension of our trade and called the current state of affairs "regrettable".

Mao said that the United States would best serve our common interests by taking a lead in world politics, by which he meant creating an alliance against the Soviet Union. The times when Beijing used to denounce the American alliance system as a tool of imperialism, were long gone. Now their prevailing view was that it was the most important pillar of international security. American troops stationed abroad which had been denounced by the Chinese for decades on end, now served a useful task, if they were at the right spot...At the same time Mao and Chou pointed out the importance of a close cooperation between the United States with West Europe, Japan, Pakistan, Iran, and Turkey. He said that we should expand our system of defense and not lose sight of the fundamental threat posed by the Soviet Union. We should quarrel with our allies over short-term problems. Finally, he urgently insisted on strengthening the cohesion among the democratic industrial nations:

"As far as you, Europe, and Japan are concerned, we hope that you will cooperate. At times, it may be useful to quarrel and to criticize each other, but it is urgently necessary to cooperate on fundamental issues."

p. 84:

"You know — China is a very poor country," Mao said, "we don't have much, but what we have in abundance are women...If you want some of them, we can let you have them, maybe some ten thousand," he replied..."But if you take them, they will cause disaster with you, but for us it would be a relief." He burst into peals of laughter...

pp. 85f:

The goal of the Great Cultural Revolution which Mao launched in 1966 — and where else but in China could a bloody political regime change be called a "cultural" event? — precisely consisted in liquidating those elements of modernity not being rooted in China itself; the Cultural Revolution was an attack on Western influence and against bureaucratization which threatened to flatten China and to make it drown in a global culture...With a touch of melancholy he said, now China would have to go to school abroad. He had ended the Cultural Revolution and sadly he said that the Chinese people were "very stubborn and conservative." Now the time had come for the Chinese to learn foreign languages, thereby emphasizing of what he had said. The performance of the Beethoven Symphony was symbolizing this necessity. He said again that he would send a greater number of Chinese abroad for studying. He himself was now taking English lessons...

p. 87:

Mao and Chou are now pushing us to have a more aggressive American presence and expect us to make a stand against the Soviet plans in various fields; they want us to have closer relations with our allies and to preserve our defensive potential...

p. 813:

At the end Mao turned to Japan. He praised my decision to stop in Tokyo for a few days on my way home. Japan should not feel neglected by the U. S...

"For them good relations to the United States are most important," he said benevolently. "We only come in second place."

The apostle of World Revolution declared that he would do everything in his power to make Japan to set its priorities in such a way. Japan should not attempt to play off one country against the other in complete independence, as this could only arouse chauvinistic desires. We, too, should make our contribution and to keep close contact to Japan...

The paradox of this whole theory was palpable. When China was now supporting the alliance between the United States and Japan so enthusiastically, then it contradicted the distrust that I had still felt during my first visit in Beijing. Barely two years after my first contact; the graying revolutionary was lecturing the American Foreign Minister on how the United States should keep its alliances together. Starting from the opposite sides of the ideological spectrum, we had tacitly become partners in maintaining global equilibrium...

p. 814:

He was particularly worried about an American withdrawal from Europe...

A Short Comment and Final Assessment of Mao Zedong

(G. Schnehen)

According to Henry Kissinger, Mao Zedong gave his "enthusiastic approval" to the new American-Chinese relations. His long-time comrade-in-arms who had been following him for decades on end and had always carried out his instructions who, with some justification, can be called his tool and henchman, Zhou Enlai (same as "Chou En-lai" in the text!), was likewise now in favor of a close partnership between China and the US imperialists, even though he himself had favored an alliance with the Soviet Union years earlier. Now the same Soviet Union was considered to be the main adversary of both. However, the Soviets continued to support the anti-imperialist movements throughout Africa and Latin America and also continued to send weapons to the Vietnamese resistance fighters, the Vietcong. It had also taken sides with the fighting Chilean people, the Unidad Popular of Salvador Allende that had been elected into power in 1970 by the Chilean people but was overthrown on September 11, 1973.

While the talks with the American imperialists went on, the United States' carpet bombings over Cambodia and Vietnam went on unabated, killing hundreds of people on a daily basis.

During the Cultural Revolution (1966-1969) Mao Zedong pretended to fight those tooth and nail who, in his own words, "wanted to take the capitalist road" in the Communist Party of China, among them his long-time friend and close ally Liu Shao-qi, China's former president. But now he had become the best friend and accomplice of the United States and was eagerly recognizing its interests all over the globe, also in South-East Asia and Europe. Was this not reason enough to launch another such "Cultural Revolution," this time against himself and his best friend Zhou Enlai, as he and his chief diplomat were now obviously also "going the capitalist road" and could be classed as "capitalist roaders" or even as "imperialist roaders"?

Henry Kissinger also tells us in his reminiscences that he had a very high opinion of Mao that, in his view, he was a "titanic personality" — and so well read on top of it! How comes that someone like Kissinger, who has been working for the US empire for all his life and has helped organize countless coups and putsches all over the world hand in glove with the CIA to get rid of people not to the liking of the United States elites. These elites do not care one bit about democracy and the sovereignty of nations and states, and Kissinger has always been their frontman. And all of a sudden, this chief diplomat and organizer on behalf of the CIA became so friendly, even cozy, with the "champion of world revolution" and the chief opponent of all revisionists, opportunists, and counter-revolutionaries! Amazing!

But was really so amazing and did it come like a bolt out of the Chinese blue sky?

We have met Peter Vladimirov here on various occasions already, and this sharp observer came across Mao's predilection for the North-American imperialists very soon, having watched and studied the "Chairman" intensively in the liberated enclave of the CPC in North China. At the same time, the "Helmsman" had an aversion against the socialist Soviet Union and Stalin in particular whom he insulted on various occasion even in front of him. In his diary Vladimirov wrote:

> There is no doubt that the Americans will supply the Special Area with weapons.[1]

Three months later he had more concrete facts:

> Washington will establish independent relations with Yenan. These relations will include the supplying of the Special Area with arms, munition, equipment, etc.[2]

On April 21, 1945 he writes:

> I know every details of the talks (Mao's talks with the American secret service people in Yenan — GS). In exchange for American weapons and an alliance with the United States Mao Zedong promised to make a clean break with Moscow.[3]

---

[1] Peter Vladimirov, *The Vladimirov Diaries, Yenan, China: 1942-1945*, New York, 1975, p. 255, entry dated September 12, 1944.
[2] Ibid., p. 303, entry dated December 10, 1944.
[3] Ibid., p. 398, entry of April 21, 1945.

So even in these days the flirt with the American imperialists was already no secret. Officials of the American secret service, OSS, the Office for Strategic Services, the forerunner of the CIA, were often seen in Yenan (led by John Service) and enthusiastically welcomed by Mao Zedong and his entourage. Luscious banquets and dances were arranged to honor them in Yenan. Soon, the policy-makers in Washington thought that it might be wiser to support Mao Zedong's Communists instead of Chiang Kai-shek nationalists.

And Zhou Enlai who played a pivotal role in preparing the meetings between Mao Zedong and US President Nixon in the early seventies? What about him? In the early days in Yenan he had some differences of opinion here and there with Mao Zedong, Vladimirov writes in his diary. But soon he caved in and then became Mao's most trusted lieutenant, his chief diplomat and errand boy. Vladimirov:

> He thus grew from Mao's opponent into the most zealous supporter. At the end of 1943 he began carrying out Mao's most delicate missions, such as adjusting Mao's conflict with Wang Ming.

> All of Mao's important projects bear the mark of Chou's handiwork. He was the main initiator of contacts between the leaders of the Communist Party and the Americans. In general he is one of the Chinese who likes the West.

> Chou took a most active part in the talks with the Americans. It is he who stands behind all important actions of the CP's foreign policy. Chou supported Mao Zedong's stand on the question of the maximum isolation of the Soviet Union in solving the Far Eastern problem.[1]

But Mao Zedong was also very fond of the West in general, especially of the US. In his talks with Kissinger he said that now the time had come to learn English and he had already taken some private lessons. students should be sent to the United States for studying. Soon, a liaison office was set up to coordinate and institutionalize relations.

This at a time when the "Cultural Revolution" (1966–1969) had practically come to an end and Mao Zedong was firmly reestablished at the top of the Communist Party. Now, in the early seventies, he could have shown that he was a truly "proletarian revolutionary," conducting an anti-imperialist foreign policy, and now he could have supported the many national liberation movements and fronts in Africa, Latin America and elsewhere without having to show much consideration for this opponents in the Party many of whom had gone, perished in prison or sent into exile like Deng Xiaoping. However, the "Champion of World Revolution" did the exact opposite. After his talks with Kissinger in 1973 he was even prepared to supply the Chilean military junta, headed by the fascist general Augusto Pinochet, with weapons and finances. On Kissinger's behalf the

---

[1] Ibid., p. 409, entry of 28 April, 1945.

CIA had plotted a bloody putsch in the Latin American country on September 11, 1973, killing the acting President Salvador Allende and installing a brutal putsch regime. The "proletarian revolutionary" Mao Zedong also supported Jonas Savimbi's UNITÀ "movement" by sending Chinese pilots in support — a pseudo liberation movement created by the CIA to reign in the anti-imperialist liberation movements in Angola and Mozambique; he recognized NATO and also stopped supplying the Vietnamese liberation movement with arms. We have already talked about that in a previous chapter.

How, then, to assess Mao Zedong? He certainly was neither a Socialist nor a Communist, not even an anti-imperialist, but rather a power-hungry opportunist who, whenever people tried to depose him or to limit his machinations, purged his opponents brutally and by all means possible. He tried to poison Wang Ming, one of his main rivals in the Communist Party, which has been proven, to win the chairmanship in the CP of China in 1943. Shortly after the poisoning, a secret Politburo meeting was convened in which he was given the chairmanship over both the Politburo and the Standing Committee (20 March 1943). He made two attempts to liquidate Gao Gang, his Marxist rival: one in 1935 that failed and another in 1954 which succeeded; he persecuted Marxist intellectuals, among them Wang Shiwei in Yenan who was executed in 1947 probably by his secret police people (Kang Sheng). He was a hypocrite whose empty phrases were bogus and only empty "canons" as he himself admitted in his talks with Nixon and Kissinger in February 1972 — slogans which nobody should take too seriously. He was certainly no Chinese patriot either. How can a patriot tell another foreign leader, that he was not afraid of the A-bomb because, if 300 million Chinese died after the dropping of a nuclear bomb, then there would be another 300 million who would survive the incident, leaving China a great nation (Mao Zedong in his talks with the Indian Prime Minister Nehru in the 1960s).

Peter Vladimirov, the Communist Soviet TASS correspondent, had this to say about him:

> I feel I can be frank enough with my own diary. Years of life at Mao's side failed to make me respect him, to put it mildly.

> This man, who would not hesitate to destroy tens and even hundreds of thousands of lives, if the situation and his personal interests warranted it, is noted for his cowardice. I saw him "funk" many times when things took a serious turn. He puts his own health above everything else. Hardly a week goes by when Andrei Yakovlevich (the Soviet doctor — GS) is not called to him, although the complaints are minor...At the same time he is indifferent and cruel to the sickness and even death of others, even his relatives...[1]

Mao Zedong was no "revolutionary," he was a would-be Chinese emperor in the guise of a "Marxist-Leninist," a genuine megalomaniac and a Great-Han-

---

[1] Ibid., p. 396., entry dated 21 April, 1945.

Chauvinist. He himself once admitted that one could call him an "emperor." When his former friends tried to push him aside to prevent him from causing another catastrophe like the one during the "Great Leap forward" in the late 1950s and early 1960s, he reacted by launching the "Great Proletarian Cultural Revolution" — a bloody campaign to get rid of his many adversaries within the Communist Party under the pretext that "Chinese socialism" was at stake due to the intrigues of so many evil "capitalist roaders." Millions of people died, and China was plunged into chaos again for more than three years. Schools and universities were closed to allow fanatical students, his "Red Guards," to participate in mass rallies in Beijing to support his plea to get rid of the "bourgeois headquarters" in the Party. Books were burnt on his behalf because they were said to be "poisonous weed" which needed to be pulled out by their roots. Many of China's finest intellectuals and writers had to burn their own books, after a "visit" by his storm troopers after which many of them committed suicide or were even lynched by them.

Lenin once said Communists do respect and honor the cultural legacy of the past, they do not call it "reactionary" or even try to destroy it. Mao Zedong, however, tried to destroy China's cultural achievements leaving a trail of destruction behind him. Libraries were raised to the ground and books burned and thrown on piles the way the German Nazis did it in May of 1933 when they organized their own book burning, calling the books blacklisted "Schundliteratur" (trashy literature). A well-known German Communist writer (Bert Brecht) once said: "Where people burn books, then they will also burn people one day." This also happened in China during the "Cultural Revolution." Mao Zedong had launched the campaign, not the officials of his Party. He bears full responsibility for what happened. No one can absolve him of that.

No genuine Socialist or Communist leader deserving this name would act like that, only fascists and tyrants do such things. By posing as a Communist and as a "Marxist-Leninist" he has done great harm to the Communist cause — he contributed largely to destroying it once and for all.

Epilogue

The selected texts presented in this book are meant as a contribution to gaining a better understanding of the essence of Maoism and Mao Zedong Thought (Mao Zedong's "ideas") which has hijacked Marxism and also Leninism, turning them into something that are not for the benefit of the working people but essentially for the benefit of international elites — stark anti-communists. In order to do so, it is important to have a broader selection of texts and documents available. It is not enough to be content with sayings or some selected writings by Mao Zedong and his speechwriters. It would be wrong to neglect and ignore other texts or books only because they are allegedly "bourgeois," "revisionist," or "reactionary" (as they are often called by supporters of Mao Zedong even to this day). Research should not be spurned just because it was conducted by non-Marxists; such work may be of considerable value, even if it comes from strong opponents of Communism or Marxism, or people who are against any ideology whatsoever. Important contributions may come from all directions. This phenomenon of Maoism has, up to the present day, not been dealt with very profoundly. We must look to contemporary witnesses, independent and critical writers, who do not belong to one political camp or another, who have no political affiliations at all but an independent, open and incorruptible mind. These are the true researchers — people who simply have the intention to contribute to our enlightenment.

I have included some here, some of which have been defamed by Maoists to the utmost. The task is this: to solve the riddle of Mao Zedong by applying scientific means and being objective, by leaving one's prejudices behind and by studying primary sources. Secondary sources must be looked upon with great distrust and skepticism, especially Wikipedia, which is famously unreliable and biased when it comes to political topics and historical, social, and political events.

One day we are going to find out what really happened in China and who really benefited from it. Was Mao Zedong maybe a tool of the international elites or did he use them for his own advantage? This question has never been addressed, to my knowledge. I do not believe that it is necessary to be a Marxist (a term rejected by Marx) to understand what really went on in China in the days of Mao Zedong and why events took that specific course. Marxism is a social science among others, it is neither a dogma nor an ideology consisting of certain untouchable tenets. Marxism is a scientific method, a useful and efficient tool for analysis, not a religion — one tool among many.

But Maoism has undermined Marxism to such a degree that hardly anything of its original content has been left of it. And that is also one of the reasons why the "left" that calls itself "Marxist" is so utterly confused and unable to understand what is going on in the world these days. They have learned conclusions by heart but have lost the Marxist methodology, the way to analyze things objectively, reasonably and unbiased.

Today Maoists and other leftists support color revolutions organized by George Soros in Belarus, they support the Corona and the climate hype, are in favor of wearing masks, harsh lock-downs and risky vaccinations hyped by Pfizer and Moderna. One gets the impression they are being pulled through the ring on a nose ring by today's global elites without even realizing it.

My motto is Karl Marx's favorite one: question everything, ask the right questions and always think again. Everything in history makes sense. It is a matter of dragging to the surface the essence of a thing, the logic of things, which lies hidden under a thick layer of debris and undergrowth. Maybe we should act like archaeologists when making excavations and, when having found something interesting, to reconstruct the old building or the ancient column of bygone days. This is tiresome and sometimes also frustrating, but it is certainly worthwhile.

If you are a fan of Marx or simply someone who has studied Karl Marx' works, among them the magnificent *Das Kapital*, you have an advantage: You learn to see things in context, not in a static state but in permanent motion. This helps to comprehend historical phenomena as history is an ongoing process. Dialectical thinking is needed. It can help to comprehend historical phenomena better and to reach more profound conclusions.

Having analyzed these questions for decades, I still find this conclusion valid to a large extent: Mao Zedong was no Marxist and no Communist either. I go along with Peter Vladimirov who wrote:

> On behalf of socialism Mao betrays socialism, on behalf of the Communist Party he destroys the Communist Party, on behalf of democracy he imposes terror.[1]

---

[1] Peter Vladimirov, ibid., p. 202, diary entry dated February 12, 1942 (Yenan).

BIBLIOGRAPHY

Books

Andert, Reinhold und Herzberg, Wolfgang, *Der Sturz. Erich Honecker im Kreuz-verhör*, Berlin/Weimar, 1991

Apel, Erich, *Neue Fragen der Planung*, Berlin, 1963

Apel, Erich und Mittag, Günter, *Planmäßige Wirtschaftsführung und ökonomische Hebel*, Berlin, 1964

Badstübner, Rolf und Loth, Wilfried, eds., *Wilhelm Pieck—Aufzeichnungen zur Deutschlandpolitik, 1945–1953*, Berlin, 1994

Bahrmann, Hannes und Links, Christoph, *Finale. Das letzte Jahre der DDR*, Berlin, 2019

Banac, Ivo, *The Diaries of Georgi Dimitrov, 1933-1949*, New Haven and London, 2003

Baring, Arnulf., *Der Aufstand in Ostdeutschland vom 17. Juni 1953*, Berlin, 1972

Beria, Sergo, *Beria — My Father. Inside Stalin's Kremlin*, London, 1999

Bethkenhagen, Jochen et al, *DDR und Osteuropa. Ein Handbuch*, Opladen, 1981

Bland, William B., *The Restoration of Capitalism in the Soviet Union*, @www.oneparty.co.uk/html/book/ussrindex.html, second edition, London, 1995

Borsdorf, Ulrich und Niethammer, Lutz, *Zwischen Befreiung und Besatzung*, Wuppertal, 1976

Creuzberger, Stefan, *Die sowjetische Militäradministration in Deutschland (SMAD), 1945–1949*, Melle, 1991

____*Die sowjetische Besatzungspolitik und das politische System der SBZ*, Weimar, 1996

Dennis, Mike, *Politics, Economics and Society of the German Democratic Republic*, London/New York, 1988

Deriabin, Pjotr, *Wachhunde des Terrors*, USA, no location, 1984

Deutsches Institut für Wirtschaftsforschung, *Handbuch DDR-Wirtschaft*, Berlin, 1984

Dodd, Martha, *Meine Jahre in Deutschland, 1933-1937. Nice to see you, Mr. Hitler!* Frankfurt/M, 2005

Eisenberg, Carolyn, *Drawing the Line. The American Decision to Divide Germany, 1944–1949*, Cambridge, 1997

Furr, Grover, *Khrushchev Lied*, Kettering/Ohio/USA, 2011

Görldt, Andrea, *Rudolf Herrnstadt und Wilhelm Zaisser*, Frankfurt/Main, 2002

Gossweiler, Kurt, *Die Taubenfußchronik oder Die Chruschtschowiade, 1953–1964*, Munich, 2002

Götz, Hans-Herbert, *Manager zwischen Marx und Macht. Generaldirektoren in der DDR*, Freiburg/Breisgau, 1988

Grimm, Thomas, *Das Politbüro privat. Ulbricht, Honecker & Co, aus der Sicht ihrer Angestellten*, Berlin, 2005

Haase, Herwig E., *Das Wirtschaftssystem der DDR*, Berlin, 1983

Hartmann, Ralph, *Die Liquidatoren*, Berlin, 2008

Hoxha, Enver, *With Stalin. Memoirs*, Tirana, 1979

Hübner, Peter, Tenfelde, Klaus, eds., *Arbeiter in der SBZ/DDR*, Essen, 1999

Janson, Carl-Heinz, *Totengräber der DDR. Wie Günter Mittag den DDR-Staat ruinierte*, Düsseldorf/Wien/New York, 1991

Kantorowicz, Alfred, *Deutsches Tagebuch, Zweiter Teil*, Berlin, 1980

Kappelt, Olaf, *Braunbuch DDR. Nazis in der DDR*, Berlin, 1981

Keiderling, Gerhard, ed., *Gruppe Ulbricht in Berlin, April–Juni 1945. Eine Dokumentation*, Berlin, 1993

Koch, Egmont R., *Das Schalck-Imperium lebt. Deutschland wird gekauft*, Munich, 1992

Kraushaar, Wolfgang, *Die Protest-Chronik, 1949–1959*, Bd. II, 1953–1956, Hamburg, 1998

Krebs, Wolfgang, *Der deutsche Film von 1929–1945 — Heinz Rühmann, ein Berater?!* *Zeitgeschichte 2001*, @http://www.kinosessel.de/ruehmann1.htm

Krenz, Egon, *Wenn Mauern fallen*, Vienna, 1990

Krenz, Egon, ed., *Walter Ulbricht. Zeitzeugen erinnern sich*, Berlin, 2016

Krol, Gerd-Jan, *Die Wirtschaftsreform in der DDR und ihre Ursachen*, Tübingen, 1972

Kuczynski, Jürgen, *Ein linientreuer Dissident. Memoiren 1945–1989*, Berlin, 1994

Lenin, W. I., *Gesammelte Werke*, Bd. 33, Moscow, 1973

_____, *Ausgewählte Werke*, Bd. 3, Berlin, 1970

Leonhard, Wolfgang, *Die Revolution entlässt ihre Kinder*, Cologne, 1955

Loth, Wilfried, *Stalins ungeliebtes Kind*, Munich, 1996

Marx, Karl, *Das Kapital*, Bd. 1, Berlin, 1971

____*Das Kapital*, Bd. 3, Berlin, 1969

Meissner, Boris, *Russland unter Chruschtschow*, Munich, 1960

Mewis, Karl, *Im Auftrag der Partei*, Berlin, 1972

Milev, Yana, *Das Treuhandtrauma*, Berlin, 2020

Mittag, Günter, *Um jeden Preis. Im Spannungsfeld zweier Systeme*, Berlin/Weimar, 1991

____*Fragen des neuen ökonomischen Systems der Planung und Leitung der Volkswirtschaft*, Berlin, 1963

Müller-Enbergs, Helmut, *Der Fall Rudolf Herrnstadt. Tauwetterpolitik vor dem 17. Juni*, Berlin, 1991

Nattland, Karl-Heinz, *Der Außenhandel in der Wirtschaftsreform der DDR*, Berlin, 1972

Neubert, Ehrhardt, *Geschichte der Opposition in der DDR, 1949–1989*, Bonn, 1997

Neumann, Philipp, *Zurück zum Profit. Zur Entwicklung des Revisionismus in der DDR*, Berlin, 1974

Nitzsche, Gerhard, *Die Saefkow-Jacob-Bästlein-Gruppe*, Berlin, 1957

Oelßner, Fred, *Rosa Luxemburg. Eine kritische biografische Skizze*, Berlin, 1951

Ostermann, Christian, *The United States, the East German Uprising of 1953 and the Limits of Roll Back*, Working Paper No. 11, http://cwihp.si.edu (Wilson Center)

Pano, Aristobal und Kapetani, Kico, *Der kapitalistische Charakter der Produktionsbeziehungen in der Sowjetunion*, http://www.revolutionarydemocracy.org, in: *Socialist Albania*, No. 4, July 1980

Pirker, Theo et al, *Der Plan als Befehl und Fiktion*, Wirtschaftsführung in der DDR, Opladen, 1995

Podewin, Norbert, *Walter Ulbricht. Eine neue Biografie*, Berlin, 1995

_____*Ulbrichts Weg an die Spitze der Macht*, Hefte zur DDR-Geschichte, Nr. 49, Berlin, 1998

Pollok, Ethan, *Conversations with Stalin on Questions of Political Economy*, Working Paper No. 33, Washington D. C., July 2001, http://cwihp.si.edu (Wilson Center)

Przybylski, Peter, *Tatort Politbüro. Die Akte Honecker*, Berlin, 1991

Roesler, Jörg, *Zwischen Plan und Markt. Die Wirtschaftsreform in der DDR zwischen 1963 und 1970*, Berlin, 1990

_____*Das neue ökonomische System. Dekorations- oder Paradigmenwechsel?*, Hefte zur DDR-Geschichte, Nr. 3, Berlin, 1993

Sabrow, Martin, *Erich Honecker. Das Leben davor, 1912–1945*, Munich, 2016

Schabowski, Günter, *Das Politbüro. Ende eines Mythos*, Hamburg, 1990

_____, *Der Absturz*, Berlin, 1991

Schirdewan, Karl, *Aufstand gegen Ulbricht*, Berlin, 1995

Schumann, Frank und Wuschech, Heinz, *Schalck-Golodkowski. Der Mann, der die DDR retten wollte*, Berlin, 2012

Schürer, Gerhard, *Gewagt und verloren. Eine deutsche Biografie*, Berlin, 1998

Siegler, Heinrich von, *Wiedervereinigung und Sicherheit Deutschlands, 1944–1963*, Bd. 1, Bad Godesberg, 1967

Stalin, J. W., *Ökonomische Probleme des Sozialismus in der UdSSR*, Berlin, 1953

_____, *Werke*, Bd. 10, Berlin, 1953

_____, *Über die Grundlagen des Leninismus. Fragen des Leninismus*, Berlin, 194

Steiner, André, *Die DDR-Wirtschaftsreform der sechziger Jahre*, Berlin, 1999

Stern, Carola, *Ulbricht-eine politische Biographie*, Cologne, 1964

Stulz-Herrnstadt, ed., *Das Herrnstadt-Dokument*, Reinbek/Hamburg, 1990

Suckut, Siegfried, *Die Betriebsrätebewegung in der Sowjetisch-Besetzten Zone Deutschlands, 1945–1948*, Frankfurt/Main, 1982

Ulbricht, Walter, *Antworten auf aktuelle politische und ökonomische Fragen*, Berlin, 1964

Voigt, Dieter, *Montagearbeiter in der DDR*, Darmstadt/Neuwied, 1973

_____, *Sozialstruktur der DDR*, Darmstadt, 1987

Voslensky, Michael S., *Nomenklatura. Die herrschende Klasse der Sowjetunion*, Vienna, Munich, Zurich, Innsbruck, 1980

Weber, Hermann, *Grundriss der Geschichte der DDR, 1945–1990*, Hamburg, 1991

____*Der deutsche Kommunismus. Dokumente*, Cologne and Berlin, 1964

Weber, Hermann, Mählert, Ulrich, eds., *Terror. Stalinistische Säuberungen 1936–1953*, Paderborn, 1998

Journals

Allgemeine Zeitung Berlin, Nr. 29, Oktober 1945

Alliance! A Revolutionary Monthly, No. 6, August 2003

Beiträge zur Geschichte der Arbeiterbewegung, 41. Jahrgang, März 1999

De Waarheit. Volksdagblad voor Nederlande, 1945

Der Spiegel, 1994, Nr. 19, 9. Mai

Deutsche Volkszeitung, 1. Jahr, 1945, Nr. 20, Nr. 39

Einheit. Zeitschrift für Theorie und Praxis des wissenschaftlichen Sozialismus, 7. Jahrgang, August 1952, Dezember 1952

Internationales Leben, Nr. 42, 1995

Neue Welt, Heft 13, Berlin, 1948; Heft 20, Berlin, 1951

Roter Morgen Nr. 15, Dezember 1971

Vierteljahreshefte für Zeitgeschichte, 41. Jahrgang, Nr. 2, 1993; 39. Jahrgang, 1991

Yale University Press, New Haven, 1997

Textbooks

Politische Ökonomie, Lehrbuch, Berlin, 1955

Politische Ökonomie und ihre Anwendung in der DDR, Berlin, 1969

Politische Ökonomie des Kapitalismus und Sozialismus, Berlin, 1975 und 1982

Reports

Protokoll der Zweiten Parteikonferenz der SED, Berlin, 1952

Protokoll des VIII. Parteitags der SED, Bd. 1, Berlin, 1971

Gerichtsprotokoll des Slánsky-Prozesses, Prag, 1953 (Hrsg.: Prager Justizministerium)

Other Sources

Archiv der Gegenwart, *Deutschland 1949 bis 1999*, Berlin, 2004

Cold War International History Project

Keesing's Record of World Events

Wilson Center, Virtual Archive, cwihp.si.edu; digitalarchive.wilsoncenter.org

Statistisches Jahrbuch 1976

www.dokumentArchiv.de

www.revolutionarydemocracy.org